Beyond Female Masochism

QUESTIONS FOR FEMINISM

Edited by Michèle Barrett, Annette Kuhn, Anne Phillips and Ann Rosalind Jones, this socialist feminist series aims to address, in a lively way and on an international basis, the wide range of political and theoretical questions facing contemporary feminism.

Beyond Female Masochism

Memory-Work and Politics

FRIGGA HAUG

Translated by Rodney Livingstone

VERSO

London · New York

First published by Verso 1992
© Frigga Haug 1992
Translation © Verso 1992
All rights reserved

Verso
UK: 6 Meard Street, London W1V 3HR
USA: 29 West 35th Street, New York, NY 10001-2291

Verso is the imprint of New Left Books

ISBN 978-0-86091-562-1

British Library Cataloguing in Publication Data
A catalogue record for this book is available from the British Library

Library of Congress Cataloging-in-Publication Data
A catalogue record for this book is available from the Library of Congress

Typeset by Leaper & Gard Ltd, Bristol
Printed in Great Britain by Biddles Ltd

Contents

Sources

Eight of the chapters in this volume are revised and expanded versions of essays translated from German for this collection; the remaining four have been previously published in English and are reprinted here with permission. Chapter 1, a talk given at the 1st People's University, West Berlin, 1980, was first published under the title, 'Opfer oder Täter? Über das Verhalten von Frauen', *Das Argument* 123, 1980; Chapter 2, a lecture delivered at the People's University in West Berlin and Stockholm in 1983, first appeared as 'Erfahrung und Theorie: Die Langweile in der Ökonomie und die Farbwerke Hoechst', *Das Argument* 136, 1982; Chapters 3 and 4 were first published in *New Left Review* nos 143 and 162, 1984 and 1987; Chapter 5, a lecture given to the German Association for Behavioural Therapy, Berlin, 1988, appeared in Frigga Haug and Kornelia Hauser, eds, *Küche und Staat*, Argument-Verlag, West Berlin 1988; Chapter 6, originally a talk given at the 8th West Berlin People's University, 1987, was first published under the title 'Arbeitsverhältnisse', in Maiers and Markart, eds, *Festschrift für Klaus Holzkamp zum 60. Geburtstag*, Campus Frankfurt am Main 1987, and in revised form as 'In der Arbeit zu Hause sein?' in Kornelia Hauser, ed., *Viele Orte überall? Feminismus in Bewegung*, Argument-Verlag, Berlin 1987; Chapter 7 was first published as 'Zeit der Privatisierungen? Verarbeitungen gesellschaftlicher Umbruche in

Arbeit und Lebensweise', *Das Argument* 156, 1986; Chapter 8 first appeared as 'Arbeitsforschung im Zeitalter der Mikroelektronik', *Forum Kritische Psychologie* 20, 1987; Chapter 9, originally a talk given at the 2nd West Berlin People's University, 1981, was published under the title 'Männergeschichte, Frauenbefreiung, Sozialismus', *Das Argument* 129, 1981; Chapter 10 originally appeared in *New Left Review* 155, 1986; Chapter 11 was first published as 'Rosa Luxemburg und die Politik der Frauen', in Frigga Haug and Kornelia Hauser, eds, *Küche und Staat*, Argument-Verlag, West Berlin 1988; and Chapter 12, a paper presented at the conference 'Crisis in Europe', Sydney, Australia, 1990, appeared in *Feminist Review* 39, 1991.

Preface

The choice between the women's movement and the workers' movement sounds strangely old-fashioned nowadays, even though no solution to the dilemma has been forthcoming. Nevertheless the earliest feminist critiques of the theory and traditions of the workers' movement had a great effect on me. My thinking, like that of many women, was given new impetus by Sheila Rowbotham's, Lynne Segal's and Hilary Wainwright's *Beyond the Fragments* (1979); by Rosanna Rossanda's *Einmischung*, or 'Interventions' (1983); and by Heidi Hartmann's *Women and Revolution*. More recently, Donna Haraway's penetrating studies (*Primate Visions*, 1989, and *Simians, Cyborgs, and Women*, 1991) have opened my eyes not just to the fact that feminist scholarship can be disrespectful, subversive and imaginative, but to the real pleasure to be derived from the emancipation from ossified ways of thinking.

My approach to research is simultaneously individual and collective. Commuting between two cities, I am involved in a project in Berlin to keep Marxist thought alive, while in Hamburg I am engaged in teaching and research into feminism both in and with women's collectives. Memory-work, a concept which informs many of the essays in this collection, is an attempt to organize work contexts so as to make it possible to work on memory and experience in both a constructive and a destructive way. To convert Marxist theory into a theory of emancipation for women means, among other things, diverting a powerful and long-standing anger into detective work. In this spirit I have taken up a whole set of Marxist ideas: the notion of human beings as producers of their own circumstances, histories and personalities; the conceptualization of things as caught up in a process full of contradictions and a methodology which, recognizing this complexity, situates human actions in the context of both production and gender relations; the political and praxis-orientated approach which consists of taking as a starting point people's actual experience; and concrete theories of work, ideology, learning and social action.

But to make such ideas a reality involves bringing to the surface knowledge that has suffered from a twofold process of burial and obfuscation. It turns out on closer examination that almost all the features of Marxism which are crucial to the theory and practice of women's liberation have been forgotten and repressed in the established tradition of Marxism-Leninism. Furthermore, the specific deformations of women's conditions tended for the most part to elude the masculine gaze (including Marx's own). The necessary excavation work calls for the experiences and memories of all the women who can be involved in the process of research. Since this research potentially affects, and is addressed to, all women, it is neither possible nor meaningful in the absence of a women's movement. In that sense my book is testimony to an epoch of women's movements; it works for emancipation and is made possible by it.

Berlin and Hamburg,
August 1991

PART ONE

Socialization

PART ONE

Socialization

ONE

Victims or Culprits?
Reflections on Women's Behaviour

My title, 'Victims or Culprits?', with its interrogatory inflection, may appear somewhat inane. It is an impertinence to suggest that women might be the 'culprits', and the alternative is such a truism that the answer can be given in a single word and we can all go home and forget the whole matter. Of course, we all know that women are primarily victims. There are abundant proofs of this: women's refuges, the vast numbers of rapes and assaults. Furthermore, women may not practise certain professions. They are denied full access to public life. They are not allowed to enter the high temples of power. They spend their lives in subordinate auxiliary professions. They are barely represented in influential organizations. They are doubly burdened by the chaos of screaming children and housework, while their husbands slump in front of the television, relax with beer and skittles, flirt with their secretaries, have exciting adventures and endlessly clamber up the ladder of success. It cannot be denied that women are the victims. They are mainly the victims of their husbands, but at all events of social relations. Their public standing is low. Then there is advertising. Parts of women's bodies are used extensively to stimulate the purchase of consumer goods. They are also used to excite feelings, for example when you are shown a girl in shorts or just a girl's backside on a motorbike in order to encourage you to buy a particular brand of cigarette.

Or again, you see beer sold with the aid of a woman's breasts. The process reaches the point where you find products such as an ashtray shaped like a woman's belly, or nutcrackers modelled on a woman's thighs, and so on.

Women are no better respected at work. Their work and the esteem in which it is held can be summed up in the words of a personnel manager who in other respects was quite amiable and humane. Speaking about working with computers, he remarked, 'Once the possible sources of error have been grasped and the test program is functioning automatically, this is just plain prison work and can be carried out by women.' And another observed, 'Our women must be able to stand for long periods, be accustomed to hard work and be under forty. They must not be overweight, not like an Italian Mamma.' In short, women's work is synonymous with unskilled work. This catalogue, which indicates that women are the victims of men and of social relations, reflects the perspective of most feminist writers as well. Thus far we are all in agreement: women are oppressed. What's to be done? How can they rescue themselves?

To simplify grossly: any such rescue has to overcome two obstacles. First, the oppressed bear the marks of their oppression. As we can see from the remark of the personnel manager, the women in this company had not had the same training as the men working there; they have been denied the same work experience, so their expertise is less. Women today cannot do everything.

Second, women have problems in their struggle for their own emancipation because they do not always really want what they want. This makes extra difficulties for women who want things to change and who want to liberate themselves. They do not only have to fight against obstacles in the world outside, they also experience difficulties with themselves. I have in mind here what is often thought of as problems with relationships, problems which act as a brake on the revolutionary impulse. The expression 'problems with relationships' is really a euphemism for the breakdowns in private relationships which thwart their attempts at liberation. The question that arises in my mind in the first instance is this: What is the origin of the structures, the social relations in which women are oppressed and whose marks they bear?

There is no need to dwell on the answer to this, since it is universally known. Women exist primarily for the family. The family is the basic unit of society and women have the task of ensuring the safety and well-being of the next generation. Women's lives, their existence as wives and mothers, looking after the needs of their husbands, the children's upbringing, and in exchange the need to give up all other goals or aims in life – all this can be summed up as the social function of women. This function is commonly identified with women's nature. We have to admit that this is not wholly unjustified. After all it is women who bear the children. But we are then confronted by the question of whether women's nature is really so intractable. Are women so unable to control their lives that this nature should fill their lives to the exclusion of all else? So the question I must now put to myself is: What is the relationship between the 'domination of nature' which is so highly regarded in our society, and which has reached such an advanced stage, and the nature of women? Or, to put the question of the extent to which women's social role is based on their nature in a brutally over-simplified way: Is it necessary for women to have such a large number of children that it fills and dominates their entire lives?

The question seems absurd, but a glance at history shows that this has in fact been the position up to a time which seems frighteningly close to the present. I need refer to only two facts which are amply documented in recent research (see Sullerot, for example). Accurate knowledge about birth control is an acquisition of the present century. The possibility of not breast-feeding – an exhausting activity which tied mothers down for two or three years or more – and the development of sterilized baby food did not take place until the end of the nineteenth century. Up to the beginning of the present century, that is, a woman who lived with a man might give birth to as many as nineteen children, of whom barely half would survive. (We may note in passing that there has been much discussion in the women's movement about the capable, independent women working in crafts and trades, such as butchers and other craft-orientated groups. These women, too, had a large number of children and in practice were pregnant for most of the time.) The dramatic increases in population in consequence of such behaviour and in spite of the high rate of infant mortality were modified by the fact that not all women were able to marry and, since some were segregated from society (for example in convents), not all bore children. But if women spend a quarter part of their adult life either pregnant or breast-feeding, it is self-evident that they will scarcely have the time or opportunity to undertake anything else (and we may add that before this century the likelihood of dying in labour was high). In these circumstances it is not unreasonable to assert that such women are at the mercy of their own nature. This subjection of women to their own nature became unnecessary and superfluous with the development of birth control and the possibility of feeding the baby with food other than its mother's milk. Despite this women are still kept in the home as if nothing had changed. The point here is not to campaign against breast-feeding; but if we are to fight for liberation, it is vital to understand the preconditions of that struggle, and a grasp of the ways in which nature acts as a stumbling-block for women is an essential part of this. Only now, when it has become possible to appropriate our own nature, can breast-feeding become a pleasure, since it does not have to be done year in, year out.

Women's function in the family acts as a brake on their development and leads to their exclusion from the core activities of society. It makes them dependent and is a source of oppression. Beaten down in this fashion, excluded and degraded into instruments for stimulating consumption, women are exiled to hearth and home and, even worse, they are made the objects of public ridicule. Those who laugh at misogynist jokes are all able to agree that women are bad, stupid, vain and useless. Their activities are consistently defined negatively. Whole books could be filled with jokes in which women appear only as viewed through masculine spectacles. Here is a typical one. Fred is asked, 'Are you married?' 'No, I only look like this because someone has just stolen my car.' Jokes of this sort make me turn my back in a fury. But since women are often exposed to such misogynist jokes, they mainly shrug them off without thinking about them further. These, however, are not the only kind of misogynist jokes.

In search for jokes which would reveal the low esteem in which women are generally held, I came to perceive another, rather different layer of meaning. Here, for example, are two jokes which could be interpreted as the usual anti-women jokes. The learner driver says to her driving instructor, 'I always go when the lights are red. Green doesn't suit me' − which implies that women have nothing in their heads but their appearance. In another, a Jewish joke, a husband tells his friends, 'My wife is really very clean. She is the only person in New York who washes the rubbish before she throws it away.'

For all that these jokes are based on an agreement to enjoy a laugh at women's expense, they also have another dimension, one which implies and encourages a more critical stance. For they show that women are damaged by the environment in which they exist and even by their own activities. This applies to the stupid joke with the driving instructor in which the woman drives through red lights; and even holds good for the joke which highlights the absurdity of too much cleaning. My claim is that malicious though these jokes are, they contain a consciousness-raising element. They tell us something about the threats to women implicit in these spheres, which are after all women's own realm. By exaggerating they make the self-evident problematic, and by this means they point to the need to liberate women from their own sphere of activity.

How should we conceive of such liberation and change? Do they not call for a transformation in women, and is this not what the jokes implicitly require? We should remember that motherhood, marriage and the family represent an extraordinary constraint, dependence and blocking of women's potential. If this is generally accepted, how can women possibly still desire these things? Other options are available; women are not forced into this way of life. To overstate the point I would say that by desiring marriage and motherhood, or at least by secretly longing for them or striving towards them, women become willing accomplices in their own oppression.

Jokes clearly reveal both the wasted lives and also the fact that women are starting to defend themselves – but in the wrong way. This is conveyed, for example, by this very nasty anti-women joke: 'Many women are like cigarettes. The poison gradually accumulates in their mouths.' Jokes like this show that women are beginning to defend themselves, albeit in a distorted rather than a liberating manner. We must therefore inquire into the source of the oppression which women are so ready to accept. How does it gain possession of women?

To advance the argument I would propose the following hypothesis. All oppression not based on the use of extreme force functions with the connivance of the oppressed.

As we have shown, the assumption that women are pure victims is self-defeating, if we are to consider the possibility of their changing, of their actively bringing about their own emancipation. For it would be quite unclear why liberation should be either possible or desirable and, above all, who would actually carry it out. In short, we would be unable to explain how women, who are victims and objects, could ever become subjects. In other words, the belief that women are merely victims remains silent about how women could ever be transformed from people who are the subject of the actions of others into people who act on their own behalf. Tied hand and foot, they would be forced to remain silent, they would have to stay as they were and would be unable to raise themselves from their degraded situation, as long as we retain the conception of women as victims. If, on the other hand, we proceed from the assumption that people, and therefore women, create themselves, it will follow that individual women will, of course, find themselves surrounded by ready-made oppressive structures to which they are expected to respond in a subservient way. But these structures only survive as long as they are continually reproduced by those who live within them. This implies in its turn that these structures can be altered by those who reproduce them. This is in fact the only way that we can conceive of changing them. That is to say, the idea that women can change the conditions in which they live is predicated on the assumption that they assist in creating them in the first place. It implies, as we have already observed, that as long as oppression does not rely on external force, it requires the connivance of the oppressed. Every action, therefore, contains an element of acquiescence. Being a victim is also an action, not a destiny.

How does this acquiescence operate? I propose the following thesis. The process of socialization does not imply, as current socialization theories claim, a straightforward process of moulding, the imposition of certain qualities of character from above. The process of socialization is itself an activity which requires acquiescence at every stage. How does it work? According to critical psychology the development of individuals, that is to say, the growth of children into adults and every other kind of development, is a process involving a constant disruption of people's security of mind. You learn something, acquire a certain level of knowledge and the ability to act. In order to progress further you have to abandon the position you have just reached. This makes you feel insecure or, to put it a different way, you experience conflict. The following stage is an attempt to resolve that conflict and achieve security on a higher plane. In this process, in which development means permanent insecurity and permanent conflict, there are normative social structures or authorities such as the family, parents, and so on, which provide emotional support and help you to advance from one stage to the next.

The fact that development entails conflict implies also that it contains the possibility of non-development. As long as societies are characterized by oppression and exploitation, the all-round development of individuals in society will be prevented by social relations and by the dominant authorities. In our society the efforts of women to develop advanced skills are particularly affected by their exclusion, self-imposed or not, from the social process of production. By such means as bribery, diversion, repression or compensation they are persuaded to accept more restricted spheres of activity. Before illustrating this, I should like to formulate a provisional starting point for empirical research. In every study of oppression it is necessary to make a precise analysis of people's activities and attitudes. It is important to pay heed to the hidden compensations, rewards and soft options which they may contain as a sort of temptation deflecting us from alternative possibilities of action. This applies as much to the past as to the analysis of individual socialization processes in our own day.

Let us illustrate these ideas with reference to the family and wage labour. We shall proceed from the assumption that to be a wife and mother and nothing more than that in modern society is itself oppressive, for reasons that are very well known: women are excluded from participation in social decisions and, in addition, are unable to support and nurture themselves; their earnings are not considered their own; they cannot feed and clothe themselves; cannot rent a room of their own without their husbands' consent; and so on, and so on. This leads us to the question of why women 'voluntarily' choose such a condition, even though they are often conscious of that oppression and still do not prefer a career. This question can easily be answered.

The disadvantages of being a wife and mother are obvious, but so too are the rewards. These can be quite trivial. For example, the housewife may not immediately perceive her dependence on wage labour. If she has no children as yet, she does not have to get up so early in the morning. She does not need to sell herself; she can dispose of her time as she wishes, or at least it may seem that she can. In many ways, then, she may be choosing a life that has more to offer in the short term over one which is more demanding but more socially integrated and which would bring greater satisfaction in the long term. The difficulty of opting for the more challenging life is increased by the fact that the emotional security of staying at home functions as a kind of temptation, and this is socially supported as the dream of eternal love. Learning has risks, and self-development implies risks as well. The questioning of traditional roles requires emotional support; but at the same time, alternative roles for women are scarcely available and so that emotional support is not forthcoming. Up to now, there has been no opportunity for women to assume positions of power, and therefore no social provision for that assumption of power. Even their participation in wage labour, at least in such a way that they are afforded an opportunity to develop their skills, is something that society has not planned for. There is therefore virtually no social and emotional support, no opportunity to build up their confidence, no chance of being anything but outsiders. It is hard to be optimistic about women's social development, hard to see how they might lift their heads and stand upright and erect.

If women are to improve their position, then, they need the support of a collective, a culture of their own. For this reason the women's movement assumes an outstanding significance; it becomes a necessity for every step women take away from what is socially expected of them.

Better control of her own nature – through birth control and alternatives to breast-feeding – and the existence of the women's movement are therefore the prerequisites of real emancipation. This also implies that if women are to change themselves, they need individually to dissolve structures of thought and feeling within themselves.

The question I should like to ask is this: What is the point of analysing women's actions from this angle? Or, in other words, what is gained by an analysis which maintains that the oppression of women can only be understood if we accept that women have acquiesced in their oppression at every stage? Of what use is it? My preliminary reply is that if women wish to change matters, and if the women's movement wishes to achieve anything, we must acknowledge that existing personality structures are obstructing the process of change.

Think, for example, of the enormous amount of energy which most women expend on private relationships, energies which they direct against themselves in every – inevitable – crisis. These relationships are, therefore, primarily self-destructive. Furthermore, the need for change is inevitably opposed by an inertia which is already a fixed part of the personality. This inertia reflects the claims of immediate pleasure, of enjoying one's life here and now, instead of the arduous efforts required for change. The private relationships just mentioned are not only self-destructive; they also pose excessive demands on women's feelings. If women desire to bring about change, they must find ways of enabling themselves to act autonomously. This means that they must change their attitudes and this in turn calls on them to change their own personality structure. Why should this be so?

If we proceed from the assumption that women lead oppressed lives and that they have to experience their own oppression day by day, it will follow that their personalities will bear the traces of their lives. If they are thought to be incapable of action, they will only succeed in reversing this judgement by questioning parts of their own personality. This is true of learning processes in general. As women increase their competence and independence, and as they extend their control to other facets of their lives, they will also encounter areas of experience which they are unable to master. These will include all the areas which protect the dominant structures of society. For women it also includes all sorts of social activities which have been inhibited in the course of individual socialization. The prohibition on women's developing, on 'growing up', would drive individual women mad, or make them ill and incapable of action, if they were to become aware at every step that they are prevented from becoming competent. Of course, many people do fall sick or go mad and this applies particularly to women. But those who do not go mad and who continue to function within a restricted sphere of activity are compelled to *reinterpret, repress or ignore* those activities where their competence is not recognized and not made possible. These reinterpretations then become an integral part of their personality. This may mean that these repressed areas appear not to exist or, if recognized, are regarded as boring. Emotionally they may appear to have no place in a woman's consciousness. But if women wish to change the conditions from which they are suffering, they will have to come to grips with these aspects in their own personality which acquiesce in their own incompetence. In short they will have to change their own feelings. This will result in feelings of insecurity and even crisis, a crisis which women cannot face up to without help. Women will only be able to live through such a crisis if they obtain emotional support.

This brings me to my conclusion. It may be objected that if that social support is not forthcoming – and it certainly isn't – political groups and organizations, a political collective in short, can fill the breach. It is my contention that this is not enough for women because in all attempts to reorganize their feelings or to abandon old structures for new, usually as the result of a crisis, there is a further as yet unmentioned source of tension which prevents this reorientation. This source of tension is in the men with whom they share these collectives and organizations. After all, men are in part the beneficiaries of the already existing personality structures. They will therefore be unable to provide unprejudiced assistance if, for example, women decide to dispense with the idea that a 'personal relationship' should take priority over all other social activities, if they attach less importance to the family, if they want to take decisions and ensure their voices are heard. It is the women's movement's historical right – and need – to make these changes possible and to carry them out.

References

Haug, F., ed., *Frauenformen*, Argument-Sonderband 45, West Berlin 1980. (Revised and updated edition under the title *Erziehung zur Weiblichkeit*, West Berlin 1991.)

Holzkamp, K., 'Zur kritisch-psychologischen Theorie der Subjektivität I & II', *Forum Kritische Psychologie* 4 and 5 (Argument-Sonderband 34 and 41), West Berlin 1979.

Holzkamp-Osterkamp, U., 'Erkenntnis, Emotionalität und Handlungsfähigkeit', *Forum Kritische Psychologie* 3 (Argument-Sonderband 28) West Berlin 1978.

—— 'Grundlagen der psychologischen Motivationsforschung II. Die Besonderheit menschlicher Bedürfnisse – Problematik und Erkenntnisgehalt der Psychoanalyse', Frankfurt am Main 1976/1978.

Sullerot, E., *Die Wirklichkeit der Frau*, Munich 1979 (Paris 1978).

TWO

The Hoechst Chemical Company
and Boredom with the Economy

I have to force myself to read the financial pages of my daily paper. The laws governing what I find there are generally familiar to me; at the same time I have absolutely no power to intervene in their workings, and they seem utterly removed from my immediate experience. The financial pages bore me. As a Marxist I know I must take an interest in the economy. So every day I force myself and read: *No increase in activity at Volkswagen. Klöckner expects to be in balance. Hoechst announces an unchanged dividend for 1982.* Somehow it is simultaneously soothing and worrying. Crisis in stagnation. The laws of profit, class issues, exploitation and, behind it all, increasing unemployment. The sheer magnitude of the phenomenon I am confronted with gives me a bad conscience for not devoting more time to studying the financial pages, and so I switch instead to the local news. *A woman leaps into the back yard from the fourth floor.* I can understand her despair. *An oil sheik has the interior of his private plane fitted out in gold, even the bathroom fittings are in twenty-four-carat gold.* This too can count on my interest. I too have a bathroom. I can assess and condemn this superfluous luxury in gold, in a plane too, and at the same time I am aware that such practices are counter-productive exceptions to the system. Production for its own sake, not for the sake of the consumption of luxury goods, is what determines the laws of capital.

I make myself return to the financial section and once again I read about capitalist normality, not its excesses. *Worldwide turnover at Hoechst rises by 15 per cent to 34.4 thousand million.* That too is beyond the grasp of my imagination. I notice that I compulsively translate events in the economy into the terms of my own little household. To appropriate the laws of society as a whole, means reinterpreting them in terms of the rules governing my own private life. And the other way round too. This works up to a point. Money is needed to acquire goods; use-values are created; goods are consumed; there is a division of labour. But the way in which people produce their lives, divided up into classes and for the sake of surplus-value, is not what determines the laws of the household and hence daily life. Conversely, looking after children, the form of the family and women's subordination to men are not issues that can be described in the language of exploitation, capitalist domination and class struggle. Thus we find ourselves in the paradoxical situation that from the standpoint of everyday life the crucial questions of the laws governing society are incomprehensible and therefore boring, while the vital problems of everyday life are irrelevant from the standpoint of class struggle and therefore of radical left politics.

And yet there must be a connection between large-scale processes and the way in which the mass of the people live their ordinary lives. I laboriously force my way through the jungle of figures in the financial pages. The incomprehensible rate of growth at Hoechst, I read, is due to an above-average performance in the pharmaceutical division which grew by 20.9 per cent. The fibre division showed even stronger growth with an increase of 31.6 per cent. My interest is aroused by references to particular products, which may be a matter of indifference to the manufacturers. Why did pharmaceutical production rise so dramatically? And who needs the increased quantities of fibre? How do people experience these articles? And how do they experience the system as a whole? The concepts I have derived from my study of political economy provide little guidance. *Class; class struggle; work, indifferent; forces of production; relations of production; exploitation and surplus-value* — they do not really enable me to work out *how* to grasp these structures. Daily life cannot simply be inferred from the laws of capital, anymore than the laws of profit can be said to have a direct impact on domestic life in the family. And what can be said of everyone's daily life, namely that it cannot be explained by the laws which govern large-scale production, is even more valid when applied to women's issues. The oppression of women is older than capitalism. The home, which tends to determine women's lives, is not directly explicable by the laws of capital. The responsibility for husband and children, the physical and emotional labour involved in looking after relatives – these are tasks that conflict with the logic of wage labour and profit-making (see this volume, pp. 161–84). Love and caring are incompatible with competition and a business mentality.

This brings us to a second paradox which I should like to characterize in the following – simplified – way. Women's oppression is clearly related to the spheres of activity to which women are tied and which are by definition antagonistic to the laws of capital. That means not only that Marxism and the theory of the emancipation of the workers fail to explain this oppression, but that those aspects of a woman's life that constitute her oppression are represented by Marxism as features of liberation. Thus maternal love, the gratification of needs independently of achievement, love, care domesticity – all these are socialist and even communist aims and yet at the same time they are the fetters in which women live today. In the labour movement socialism was for a long time depicted as a woman. And even today women at home are given the task of redeeming men from the alien domination they encounter outside the home. (Without devoting even a fleeting thought to the oppression of women, André Gorz and Alain Touraine, among others, celebrate the women's movement as a liberation movement for men because it could bring domestic values into the world of men. 'The task will not be to liberate women from household chores, but to achieve recognition outside the home for their non-economic rationality ...' [Gorz, 1980, p. 78]. 'Thanks to the women's movement we men have rediscovered our right to feelings and relationships with children' [Touraine, quoted by Gorz, 1980, p. 79].)

By way of summary I would claim that boredom with the economy stems from our failure to take the trouble to study the ways in which people experience the structures described in the critique of political economy in their daily lives. And that is a question of the way in which individuals are socialized to internalize those structures and how they subjectively appropriate and transform them.

We perceive the various dimensions of life – love and work, the private and the public, the home and the economy as separate spheres.

We have our ideas and feelings about each of these spheres in isolation, in accordance with the division of labour, and yet we live out these different divisions within a coherent life. As far as women are concerned, this means that we live in almost total ignorance of the connections between capitalism and women's oppression. At most we wax indignant about unequal wages and the loss of welfare benefits, and even more indignant about the abortion laws and divorce costs. A further consequence is that we are unable to say how the entire system reproduces itself, thanks in part to the oppression of women, what action women could take to bring about their own emancipation or even what future to predict for a labour movement which ignores women's issues.

Collective Empiricism as Memory-Work

We observe, therefore, not only that women are under-represented in science and culture, in the government and the economy, but also that women's experience has made scarcely any inroads into theory – into the founding concepts of Marxism, for example. And difficult as it is to understand that a system which is based on competition, imperialism, exploitation and war can rely on the support of its citizens, it is no easier to comprehend why women do not take up arms against a structure in which they are constantly placed in an inferior position to men, second-class beings (see Mouffe, 1982 on this point). This leads me to pose two questions. First, how are these deficiencies at the level of theory to be made good, that is to say, how can Marxism be expanded to include feminism? And second, how can women learn to intervene in their own socialization? In other words, I am asking about a practical theory which seeks to understand women's experience from the point of view of changing it.

The absence of women from all relevant social spheres of activity and the premonition that the situation in the realm of theory was not significantly different, led the women's movement to resolve to go in for a politics of consciousness-raising. The personal is political – this slogan was for many women a challenge to discuss their day-to-day problems with each other in small groups. To do this would lead them out of their isolation into the sense of a collective experience. Of course, the mere exchange of personal experiences does not necessarily lead to greater understanding. Initially the recital of stories of oppression or violence does boost your self-confidence, but in the long run it saps your courage instead of making action easier. Consciousness-raising groups tend to break up after a relatively short life, or else they simply run out of steam. This is a common experience. As Brecht has said, experience does not necessarily lead to understanding, even though it is perfectly true that there is no understanding without experience (see Haug, 1981).

The dilemma I have just sketched between a theory poor in experience and an experience bereft of theory leads me to propose a collective empirical project: memory-work (see the *Projekt Frauengrundstudium* [Project on the basic study of women's issues], 1980 and 1982). To discover how the lives of the majority are actually lived, we have to inspect them. One way is to write down stories – sketches of everyday life, experiences that could happen to anybody (see Haug, 1980). To prevent a simple duplication of the everyday with all its prejudices and lack of theoretical insight our task would be to *analyse these stories collectively*. In order to uncover the social construction, the mechanisms, the interconnections and significance of our actions and feelings, we must *proceed historically*. Our proposal, therefore, is to retain the strengths of the consciousness-raising groups, to make connections between the everyday and the large context, while avoiding the vices of ignoring the totality and losing ourselves in untheorized details. Our project is one of *collective memory-work*, with the emphasis on collective and memory and work. Its product would be a great and essential empirical undertaking that would be both new and enjoyable.

In this formulation the project is new, but its components have been discussed for some time. This makes it both easier and harder to implement. Precedents seem to be everywhere; at the same time, we shall be accused of crossing the borders between the various disciplines. These include the methodology of the social sciences, literature, the controversy about experience, about language and its importance, and about culture and ideology.

I shall attempt to clarify my own procedures, taking account of these controversial issues, but I do not confront them at length.

Subject and Object

In the empirical social sciences controversy has long raged about whether research into human beings does not rob them of their human specificity, the fact that they are acting subjects and not merely objects. Is it right to examine human beings as if they were insects? (See especially Adorno, 1969 and Haug, 1978). Is it right to treat movements, qualities and modes of behaviour as if they were fixed things? At one end of the spectrum this has led to instructing interviewers to behave as unobtrusively as possible lest their own humanity obscure the object of investigation. At the other extreme the interview is used for educational purposes to ensure that the object under study is transformed in the process. At the heart of this disagreement about the right approach to the study of people and the right relationship between subject and object, stands our view of human beings and what to do about them. Should we study their modes of behaviour so that governments will be able to influence their actions better, or should we regard them as social beings who become conscious of their own actions and the obstacles that stand in their path in order to bring about change and to reconstruct the world for more human goals?

My formulation reveals my own preference for upright people who stand erect and who are not merely the victims of class and gender relations. This partisanship clearly affected my choice of empirical method. An approach which treats people as objects was unacceptable for us. It is obvious that the collective writing of stories as a method of finding out about life is an unambiguous invitation to conceive of research as a mode of self-activity. The researcher is identical with the object of research. This solution of the subject–object problem is almost too easy.

But making everyone a researcher is not so simple. The problems begin with the choice of theme. After all, 'everyday' experience is a chaos, initially at least. Who should decide – above all in a collective – what should be discussed? Questions about who has the monopoly on choosing topics for discussion raise further questions about the interests of the many. The problem is familiar to anyone who has ever taken part in a consciousness-raising group or even been forced to listen to long perorations at family reunions or on a train journey. Basically no one wants to hear what others have to say. We have heard it all before, and anyway it is not told in an interesting way. The speakers inflate their own importance and play down that of others. This universal gossip is unbearable. Even in consciousness-raising groups everyone sits waiting for her turn and would far rather talk than listen. Such justifiable complaints contain a number of practical hints about how to deal with such narratives – I shall return to them later. At issue here are the question of interest and the choice of topic.

My view of the matter is that the lack of interest in other people's stories is not just, or even principally, the result of a poor story-telling technique. It springs rather from the belief that what everyone does, experiences or feels is basically of no importance for anyone else or, above all, for society as a whole. But since this everyday life is where society reproduces itself, an understanding of it would, or so I argue, modify each individual's attitude towards herself and to others. One would take oneself and others seriously. Questions about how social structures – such as the nature of wages, money, the growth of the textile industry, and so forth – are perceived, modified and endured by me in my everyday life, and how others deal with the same structures, would transform us all, without our fully realizing it, into experts on our everyday life. We would cease to appear to each other as time-wasters or competitors eager to steal the show. We would become investigators with a common purpose, knowledgeable people who can supply the fragments which have been used to create the social totality and which now can be rebuilt by us. The fact that our individual experiences can come together into something shared changes our relationships with each other. The learning stance makes us impatient and eager to acquire further information and at the same time we become more tolerant towards the deficiencies of the story-teller's narrative. This holds good, I would maintain, for every topic which establishes a link between our daily experience and the larger social structures we find ourselves surrounded by. The question of which topic to single out for discussion can best be decided by the pressures which individuals feel. They probably have most to say, and hence to contribute, where the pressure of suffering is greatest. And anyway, in the course of discussion the issues tend to shift, to lead on to others, open up new perspectives, and so forth. More on this point later.

If we decide collectively what is important to us, the group will be the guarantor from the outset that we shall not slide into sectarianism.

The very consensus demonstrates that we are all concerned, that compromise is possible, that conflicting interests can be harmonized and that a process of investigation can be launched (for a detailed discussion see Haug, 1983).

The Social Construction of Subjective Experience

It will be objected that it is an illusion to imagine that experiences can serve as the basis of knowledge. To rely on experience is to suppose, mistakenly, that individuals are in a position to make 'objective' judgements about themselves. Whereas in reality they give a subjective interpretation of what has happened to them! So here the subject/object problem, which we have resolved so satisfactorily in the context of scientific research, reappears with renewed force. Objective validity must be denied to what has been experienced subjectively. The reason is that individuals twist and turn, reinterpret and falsify, repress and forget their experiences in pursuit of a construction of their personality to which the past has to be subordinated. Hence what they say about themselves and their manner of dealing with experience is of no account; it is coloured subjectively.

Let us convert this criticism of 'subjectivity' into the object of our research. How do people alter, falsify and distort their everyday world, and why? The why is connected with identity. That is to say, people build the data of their lives in such a way that they can live with them in a more or less non-contradictory way. And where they cannot do so in fact, they do so in their minds or their memories. So what we can investigate is not 'how it really was', but how individuals construct their identities, change themselves, reinterpret themselves and see what benefits they derive from so doing. In short, we can explore how they inscribe themselves in the existing structures.

The criticism of subjectivity gives wings to our efforts. After all, our aim had been not to identify the existing structures, but to see how they became what they are, to observe the way in which everyday life is analysed in such a way that individuals reproduce society as a whole over and over again. The criticism has really turned into its opposite. It is actually essential to examine subjective memories if we wish to discover anything about the appropriation of objective structures. This is not to assume that these memories are wholly at the disposal of the individual, as the connotations of 'subjective' might imply. On the contrary. How individuals perceive things, and whether they judge them to be well and good, beautiful or desirable, despicable and reprehensible – all that is the meat of the class struggle, as it is fought out from day to day in people's hearts and minds. Once we realize this we can look to the theory of ideology and culture for some theoretical assistance in our collective empirical enterprise. The individual's analyses of reality, which we have decoded as her or his way of appropriating the world and which we wish to track down in our everyday stories, move on the terrain of dominant cultural values and counter-cultural, subversive efforts to extract meaning and pleasure from life. Such analyses will end in compromises (on this point see Willis, 1979 and *Projekt Ideologie-Theorie [Project on Ideology and Theory]*, 1979). In order to provide a sort of theoretical framework, it is worthwhile taking account of habits, customs, rules and norms, of what is expected and generally believed, of the moral expectations and semi-theorized attitudes which we entertain in our minds, and to treat them as seriously as the hopes which attach to a process of self-socialization, as opposed to moulding by forces external to us. It will then turn out that our own actions, in so far as we can recall them, tend to lie to one side of social expectations and our own desires, that is to say, the problems are displaced. Investigating our own compromises also means discovering the unexplored possibilities of a different life and the areas where changes are necessary and possible.

Our collective research, then, has the ambitious goal of discovering how individuals insert themselves into existing structures. We must investigate how they construct themselves and partly modify the structures in the process; we shall see how they reproduce society, where the possibilities of change lie, where the fetters are most oppressive, and so forth.

Literature or Writing – First Steps: Language

Simply to write up experiences and memories changes a good deal. It is necessary to make a selection, to set priorities, choose a suitable vocabulary, distance oneself appropriately, uncover similarities, posit a reader and hence fill in necessary details and make connections between events, and so on. Above all, it is vital to make conscious what has been experienced, just as if it had already been made conscious before. That doesn't just require effort, it also calls for a quite different view of things, and, conversely, you suddenly discover in the course of writing all sorts of things that you hadn't realized that you wanted to say and which now press in on you. In short, writing is a form of production, an activity which creates a new consciousness. Writing is also a source of pleasure, as can be seen when, after a long struggle, you suddenly find the right word, the one which expresses precisely what you wanted to say. Writing is a craft, a specialized skill which is part of the division of labour. Men of letters pursue it as an art.

Hence the third front on which the debate about telling stories is fought out, is the front between writing and literature. When we call on women to write down their stories, are we not just following the fashion for 'authentic' literature? I do not wish to intervene here in the debate about high and low art, about genius and everyday language (on this point see Manthey, 1979). But I do find it necessary to draw attention to some of the undesirable side effects of such a division of labour in life and in writing.

This brings us to the problems of analysing stories. In the first place, there is the problem of inarticulateness. It appears in such stories as a verbal poverty, as the inability to express oneself. Questions about what exactly happened, how someone felt, what had triggered off an emotion – all come up against the same brick walls, the inability to communicate one's desires and inhibitions and hence to find a way through. I regard such inarticulateness as a real obstacle to emancipation and not just as a sign that a person is not a creative writer. If women are to emerge from the obscurity of pre-history and to take their place in political life, this act requires them to be conscious about life, and that in turn means that their experiences have to be understood at the level of theory. They must therefore be conveyed in language. In this sense to delegate the power over language to the chosen few is an obstacle in the path of emancipation. One task of the collective, therefore, is to act as a 'language school', but one which, unlike a real school, attempts to find words which will both describe experiences and also make action possible.

This holds good for the most common method of articulating

memories: the cliché. The cliché can be described as a mode of heteronomous socialization in language. Unlike inarticulateness it is
loquacious; it can reckon on a sympathetic hearing, while it effectively
puts a stop to thought and understanding. 'He gazed into her eyes';
'her heart gave a leap'; 'the colour drained from her cheeks'; 'a sob
rose to her throat' – it is significant that women's emotional world
seems to have been colonized by clichés which, like corsets, produce
the impression of the appropriate feeling and desire. The writer E.A.
Rauter (1978) said of cliché that 'it is like putting a plumstone in your
mouth after someone else has spat it out, instead of a plum.' In a sense
clichés also condemn you to remain on the well-worn path of societal
expectation. At all events they are an impediment to understanding.
For example, during our research into the insertion of bodies into the
scheme of dominant expectations a woman wrote: 'I realized that my
long, curly hair was fashionable and was attracting attention.' In
contrast, Doris Lessing gives this description of a woman's *hair*, an
issue of almost mystical importance for women:

> The hairdresser sent her out with a very dark red haircut so that it felt
> like a weight of heavy silk swinging against her cheeks as she turned her
> head. As she remembered very well it had once done always.
>
> Lessing, 1990, p. 39

My intention is not to compare the account of an ordinary woman with
a successful writer, but to show the practical, political implications of
the difference between the two descriptions. Lessing shows the erotic,
sensual dimension of touching your own hair – something that no one
would understand if it weren't so palpably obvious to everyone. In our
ordinary woman's description, on the other hand, you feel that her
relationship to her own hair is determined exclusively by fashion and
the notice taken of it by other people. I think of it as a piece of vulgar
sociology that is created by prefabricated phrases which just happen to
be lying around and which are inevitably used if we fail to reflect, feel
or remember. These phrases are all too quick to take the place of our
own formulations and yet they can still claim to express our very own
experience. In this instance they lead us away from sensuous pleasure
and physicality and promise freedom only as the independence from
fashion, and so on.

Quite in contrast to its reputation, our ordinary language is also fairly abstract. When feelings, thoughts and experiences are ignored in their concrete reality, and are only spoken of, as it were, from a great height, it becomes difficult to speak of women's experiences in a narrative form without a special effort. For example, a woman trade unionist wrote as follows: 'In the course of his union activities he was able to make numerous contacts which will be of use to him in his application for a better position.' There is no word here about what is involved in 'making contacts', no word about the cost of forming such a network of relationships. Whose boots does he have to lick? Does he take care to remain in someone's good books by refraining from speaking his mind? Does he have to flatter? (Could she, a woman, make such contacts without finding herself in a highly ambiguous situation?) Why does he 'need' and what is a 'better position'? Such questions can be put in a collective discussion. After a time it even becomes a source of entertainment in which people compete to unmask the true meanings of events lying behind such phrases (see Morisse *et al.*, 1982 on this point). One method of giving such conformist abstractions the slip is to concentrate on a specific situation. This makes it possible to take pleasure in describing the details involved and thereby to recognize other things than those normally allowed on to the agenda by abstraction and prejudice. In short, it makes it possible to escape from the norms of behaviour and to discover the sensuous dimension of experience.

Contradiction, Absences and Interest

Contradiction is a particular problem that arises in the process of analysing people's stories. The collective provides a favourable context in which to criticize things which are tolerated without question in individuals. In particular, it means we can criticize the incompatible opinions, judgements and events which normally thrive in a system of peaceful coexistence in which non-intervention is the rule. The aim in doing so is not to eliminate the real contradictions of life through one's choice of words. On the contrary, the task is to break up that peaceful coexistence which is mainly the product of non-recognition, denial and repression. For example, we have no difficulty at all in producing endless horror stories about how our mothers prevented us from doing this or that and turned us into the stunted people we are. Equally, since most of us are now mothers in our turn, we can also write stories about the obstacles placed in our path by our daughters, or about the baneful influence of schools on an idyllic mother–daughter relationship, and so on. In my view, these perceptions, too, are based on vulgar sociological theories of the kind purveyed in glossy magazines, but also in 'scholarly' works. These theories serve to displace structural problems into disagreements between two individuals, or, to put it another way, to make general social problems appear as the product of individual guilt or failure. Such theories have no difficulty in surviving, unless we confront them with experiences which conflict with them. This, too, is a task of the collective.

Silence is another way of coming to terms with the unacceptable. In people's memories it appears as an absence or a rupture. The recognition that these silences must be investigated and that the attempt must be made to propose theories to explain them, was of great importance for the women's movement (see especially Irigaray, 1980). After all, we have been accustomed for so long to being absent from history that in our thoughts and speech we tend to collude in ignoring the sheer existence of women. To hear what has not been said, to see things that have not been displayed, requires a special kind of detective training (on this point see Sölle, 1981). But the very thought that such a thing exists and is important, that is structures the field of perception and provides a guide to action, gives a significant boost to such training in detection. Collective discussion about the role of silence in our stories is particularly enjoyable because it combines a creative expansion of the stories with the discovery that different vantage points bring different ways of seeing, and that each person possesses her own vantage point which comes into conflict with the traditional way of seeing things, even if that view has been accepted hitherto.

For that matter the whole question of vantage point and interest is an education in the possibilities of action. Normally we experience and write in such a way as to suggest that something has happened to us, that our lives are organized for us by impersonal forces personified in wicked characters. Other people's actions can be explained by their qualities of character, but we are simply at the mercy of these forces. I would maintain that such a view of other people must lead to a paralysis as far as action is concerned. At best it will lead to a habit of complaint. The theoretical insight that – like myself – other people act in pursuit of various interests, means that when we analyse our stories emphasis must be placed on explaining people in terms of comprehensible interests. It is this step that calls for the greatest revision in our analysis of our stories. The labour of showing other people in terms of their conditioning and their interests changes our ideas about ourselves and our own actions. Instead of seeing ourselves as the victims of people and circumstances, we must see ourselves as people who work with those people and circumstances. That this insight is important not just for writing but also for political activity in general becomes clear when women report on their defeats in political battles, for example, when they talk about the problems of creating alliances.

Conclusion

I shall break off my discussion of the various ways of analysing these stories at this point and restate my practical proposal in the context of my original observations. In order to make it discussible, I shall re-affirm what it is supposed to achieve. I began with my sense of boredom with macro-economic problems and linked this up with the failure to understand daily practices at the micro-level – female practices in particular, with their preoccupation with looking after the family, caring, the household, and so on. In order to discover how society as a whole re-creates itself through the lives of the majority in their day-to-day activities. I decided to make the experience of individuals productive for the formation of theory. This is essential if women's oppression and incorporation into the reproductive processes of society as a whole are to be understood and changed.

My proposal is not intended as a substitute for politics, but as a part of cultural politics. It is aimed above all at women in the women's movement in the broader sense. It combines grassroots activities with research as it takes place in the various disciplines on the principle of the division of labour. In general it is intended to place a question mark against all divisions of labour and therefore of special claims to competence. The fact that we know so little about how people actually experience social structures seems also to be a question arising from the division of labour. There is a way of analysing structures – this is the critique of political economy – and there are views about people. Thus the fact that women are absent from thinking about economic problems explains why they are bored by economics and regard such matters as irrelevant to themselves. There was the question of Hoechst and its growth rates, for example. There was the question of pharmaceutical products and artificial fibres. If we ask ourselves how you actually go about increasing the production of artificial fibres, we at once see the answer. We can say that one factor is that mass consumption can be increased because women fall for every change in fashion. We then lean back with a satisfied smile, exclude ourselves from this analysis and think we have found the answer at the very point where the real questions begin. How is all this really experienced? Why do women act in this way, if indeed they do? What things matter to them? What hopes do they have? Or desires? How do they wish to live? What plans do they have? Where are they going? How can they live? How do they insert themselves into the existing structures so that 'fashion', for example, can become a powerful subject that makes them the object of trade?

In conclusion I should like to present a little story which arose in the course of a project which was concerned with the question of how women actively turn themselves into objects, how they disappear as subjects in consequence of their own subjective activity, and how they become objects to gaze at and touch – the objects of male desire. What triggered off our investigation was an encounter with a woman at the university who wore a transparent dress and, underneath it, tiny purple bikini panties. Dressed thus and wearing very high-heeled shoes, she moved through the landscape waggling her bottom and issuing a generalized invitation. We wondered what she really intended to achieve and could not imagine that her unambiguous appearance really represented an unambiguous intention, although we had no idea what else it could mean. We realized that without going as far as her, we, too, were constantly monitoring our own appearance and somehow displaying ourselves and as it were judging ourselves with the eyes of others according to unknown criteria. In short, like her we failed to live in a straightforward manner, in tune with ourselves, and instead made more or less successful efforts to influence the impression we made. Our aim then was to research our public selves, the images we had made of ourselves, the sense in which we were living as objects (see Haug, 1983). This is the story:

THE KNICKERS

At long last spring came round again and it became warmer. Soon she began to pester her mother to allow her to wear knee-socks once again. One morning, when the thermometer climbed to 13° the much longed-for knee-socks were laid out with her other clothes. It was still absolute madness to wear them and her mother warned her that she would not fail to come down with the flu. So she would also have to wear pale-blue woollen knickers over her pants. She found this dreadful, because the wool was scratchy and the knickers were so babyish. But for the moment she acquiesced, because it meant that her heavy tights would come that much closer to being stored away in the attic. How wonderful to feel the air around her legs again at long last, she thought on her way to school. Most of the other girls were not yet wearing knee-socks and she was the object of envy, since it showed what fantastic parents she had and that she was able to get her own way with them. During break they played french skipping for the first time that year and they all tried to outdo each other with high jumps and complicated manoeuvres. From about knee-high she began to hold her skirt down at the back so that no one, and the cheeky boys least of all, should be able to catch a glimpse of the blue knickers. That was difficult; it spared her their teasing, but made her make mistakes, which annoyed her. In the afternoon she went into town with her grandmother. In the underwear department she complained that the knickers were stupid and that she would take them off on the stairs before going into school and that she would not put them on again until just before she was back home again. Her grandmother asked the salesgirl about woollen knickers for her. In addition to the familiar blue ones, only in a slightly stronger blue, they had the very latest thing, just in: white knickers made of very soft material and with three rows of ruching at the back. They were made of an easycare fabric – much more convenient than wool as well. She thought they were brilliant. The same material as her mother's underwear. She begged and begged until her grandmother gave in and agreed she could have them for Sundays. Sure thing, she thought and the very next morning she stuffed the woollen knickers back into the wardrobe and put the frilly knickers on in barely contained excitement. She could hardly wait until break, or rather until the jumping at french skipping had reached knee-high. Using her arms to help her she jumped as high as she could go. The girls all asked her where she had bought them. That's what they would like too. The boys all shouted, 'Bum-wiggler, bum-wiggler!' Let them shout, that's what grown-ups wear. Boys just don't understand.

I can scarcely offer a detailed interpretation of this story, or even describe the process of interpretation which was followed by further versions of the story. But I should like to point to a number of features of the story which in my view have a general significance. The story is written from experience, with empathy. None of us would find it difficult to recall similar incidents and feelings. We can all identify with it and at the same time we can observe some peculiarities.

In the first place there is a contradiction. In the beginning it was the boys who were to be prevented at all costs from seeing the pale-blue knickers; at the end, their views are insignificant, because they are stupid. We find both points of view comprehensible – in other words, the importance of people's opinions changes according to the context. The fear of being ridiculed by the boys pales into significance before the prospect of being grown up. Moreover, there is the complex situation that she is doing something for other people, but accepts the fact that they have misinterpreted it and despite this she is able to construct her identity in terms of the way she appears to others.

No less clear, in my view, is the compromise she makes. Linguistically, the writer incorporates other points of view by an act of legerdemain in which alien phrases are imported into her own speech. For example, 'It was absolute madness' – here you can hear her mother's voice. Or again, 'They had the very latest thing, an easycare fabric' – that is the salesgirl talking. These standards will be taken over later on; their origins will be forgotten.

The story is silent about certain relationships, relationships which seem to have fossilized: the knickers *are* babyish. The story of this effort to become grown up still has to be decoded. Why is it important to show that we can get our own way with our parents? Since we like to represent ourselves in later years as victims, we should look for the break in continuity and examine the true strength of those situations in which we appeared as the victors.

But we also learn something about the triumphal progress of the Hoechst Chemical Company. Its products encounter a manifold complex, for the most part unconscious, of feelings, bodily sensations, smells, tastes, personal relationships, memories of victories and defeats, of friendships and voices, hopes and plans. A white frill in a shop window releases a violent feeling of freedom and excitement, triumph and energy, sun and friendship. The connection is then broken off. It is with such things that the advertising industry works as it prepares the way for high sales. We too must work at it in our efforts to increase our consciousness of life.

References

Adorno, Theodor, et al., Der Positivismusstreit in der deutschen Soziologie, Darmstadt 1969.

Brecht, Bertolt, Kleines Organon für das Theater. Schriften zum Theater vol. 7, 1948–56, Frankfurt am Main 1964.

Gorz, André, Abschied vom Proletariat. Jenseits des Sozialismus, Frankfurt am Main 1980.

Haug, Frigga, 'Dialektische theorie und empirische Methodik', Das Argument 111, 9/10, 1978.

——— 'Erfahrungen in die Krise führen', Die Wertfrage in der Erziehung, Argument-Sonderband 58, West Berlin 1981.

——— 'Erinnerungsarbeit', in Sexualisierung der Körper, Argument-Sonderband 90, West Berlin 1983. ('Memory-Work', in Female Sexualization, Verso 1987, Chapter 1.)

———, ed., Frauenformen. Alltagsgeschichten und Entwurf einer Theorie weiblicher Sozialisation, Argument-Sonderband 45, West Berlin 1980. (Revised and updated edition under the title Erziehung zur Weiblichkeit, 1991.)

——— 'Frauen und Theorie', Das Argument 132, 3/4, 1982.

——— 'Männergeschichte, Frauenbefreiung, Sozialismus', Das Argument 129, 9/10, 1981 (this volume, pp. 161–84).

Irigaray, Luce, Speculum. Spiegel des anderen Geschlechts, Frankfurt am Main 1980. (Speculum of the Other Woman, transl. Gillian G. Gill, Ithaca, NY 1985.)

Lessing, Doris, The Summer before the Dark, Paladin 1990.

Manthey, Jürgen, ed., Literaturmagazin 11, Schreiben oder Literatur, Reinbek bei Hamburg 1979.

Morisse, Inge, et al., 'Unsicherheit in der Politik – Gewerkschafterinnentagebuch', Das Argument 135, 9/10, 1982.

Mouffe, Chantal, 'The Sex/Gender System and the Discursive Construction of Women's Subordination', Internationale Ideologie-Diskussion, Argument-Sonderband 84, West Berlin 1982.

Projekt Frauengrundstudium: Frauengrundstudium, Argument-Studienheft 44, West Berlin 1982.

Projekt-Ideologie-Theorie: Theorien über Ideologie, Argument-Sonderband 40, West Berlin 1979.

Rauter, E. A. Vom Umgang mit Wörtern, Munich 1978.

Sölle, Dorothee, 'Feministische Theologie', Das Argument 129, 9/10, 1981.

Willis, Paul, Spass am Widerstand, Frankfurt am Main 1979.

THREE

Morals Also Have Two Genders

In a talk entitled 'Women – Victims or Culprits?', at the first West Berlin People's University in 1980, I attempted to construct a theory of the process of women's socialization. My chief concerns were to show the role played by women themselves in reproducing their own oppression, and to argue that self-sacrifice is a form of activity. From the outset the opinions outlined in this brief lecture, and subsequently developed in my book *Frauenformen*,[1] became the subject of heated political debate, because of their implicit postulate that women too would have to change themselves. One point of conflict was the question of guilt. Doesn't simply raising the possibility of the complicity of women in their own subjugation mean holding them responsible for the social conditions which oppress them? Such a stricture is moral in nature and so I stood accused of being moralistic. Of course, the words 'victim' and 'culprit' themselves shift uneasily between the realms of ethics and law.

But as the controversy over them showed, any attempt to discuss the role of morality in the socialization of women is always likely to raise the temperature of the debate. It was the realization of this that induced me to take a closer look at the relationship of women to morality.

31

Preliminary Thoughts

What actually are women as moral beings? The question at once turns out to be too complex. I must therefore go back a stage and pose a simpler one: What are women?

A glance at a dictionary, or even better at several dictionaries, is always salutary when tackling very general or fundamental problems. You not only learn what you already knew or suspected, but you also discover extra pieces of information. These not uncommonly document prevailing opinion without making any bones about it, but to see in cold print opinions which we normally accept tacitly as if they were self-evident facts, often serves to call their truth-value into question.

Of all the dictionaries I consulted I was most struck by this entry from an older encyclopaedia (published in 1818): 'Women are the representatives of love, just as men are the representatives of law in its most general sense. Love is reflected in the form and nature of women and any profanation means their disgrace. The public and domestic position of women has always been, and still is, the true mark of genuine culture in the state, the family and the individual.'[2] This quotation is a blend of the predictable and the remarkable. The association of women with love is familiar and harmonizes with their social status: a woman presides over the household, she is a wife and a mother, her task, we would say today, is concerned with relating to others. But of what concern is that to the state, why is it seen as a parallel to the law and how is the law embodied in men?

Information of this kind speaks at once in riddles and in certainties. Does it have any bearing on morality?

What Actually Is Morality?

I automatically relate this question to myself as a woman and, no less instinctively, I immediately conceive of morality, and particularly the absence of morality, as connected with sexuality. *For example, if I were immoral, or strayed from the path of virtue, or left the straight and narrow, fell into bad company or offended against decency; even worse, if I lost my innocence too soon, if I became a fallen woman; if my way of life were tarnished; or if I were deceitful, if I fell into disgrace, became a worthless person because I gave myself to the first comer and so was dishonoured; if I yielded to temptation and hence was ruined* ...

Viewed from my female vantage point the field of morality seems to bristle with loaded words which oscillate between love and economics, law and love. *Worth, giving, gift, guilt or debt* ['*Schuld*' means both], the right *path, taint, honour*. When uttered 'neutrally' these words mobilize in my head whole bookshelves on the theory of value, the significance of gifts in anthropology, imprisonment for debt and punishment, and so on. But their meanings are subtly altered and acquire sexual over-tones if I associate them with the noun *woman* or the adjective *female*, as in *the worthless girl*, or conversely *the untainted, innocent, virtuous girl*; *the dishonoured woman, a woman's honour.*

A glance at our collections of proverbial sayings, as well as quotations from the classics of literature, provides further evidence of the nature of our unexamined beliefs. The seat of female morality is to be found in women's nature, in their bodies or in their relationship to them. A moral woman can be recognized by the way she experiences her body.

Here, by way of illustration, is a sample from our cultural heritage:[3]

Firstly, the Bible: 'As a jewel of gold in a swine's snout, so is a fair woman which is without discretion' (Proverbs 11, 22).

Gottfried von Strassburg (1210): 'Of all things in the world on which the sun has ever cast its rays, none is as blessed as the woman who always observes moderation in her life, with her body and her behaviour, who honours and loves her self.'

Walther von der Vogelweide (1170–1230): 'A woman who loves virtue must be greatly desired. A woman becomes of value to herself when she is desired by one of the best.'

Abraham a Sancta Clara (17th century): 'A beautiful woman without virtue is like a golden goblet full of bad country wine.'

Friedrich von Schiller: 'To strive for virtue is a great matter. Woman devotes herself to this away from the world and in the gentle bosom of love.'

Johann Gottfried von Herder: 'A beautiful woman lacking in virtue and innocence is a poisoned tree to which one vainly looks for blossom and fruit.'

Johann Wolfgang von Goethe: 'Once a woman leaves the straight and narrow path, she cannot be stopped from going blindly to the bad ... she becomes the mere tool of natural impulse.'

Friedrich Ludwig Jahn (*Deutsches Volkstum*, 1810): 'It is seldom possible to save a fallen, degraded and dishonoured woman.'[4]

These literary fragments and proverbs provided unwelcome confirmation of my spontaneous feelings about women's morality. But I still found it hard to understand why the fundamental categories in the field of morality should possess these peculiar overtones of law, economics and sex all at the same time. These discordant notes suggested to me that if I wished to decode the secrets of women's morality, I needed to know more about morality in general. All these unresolved questions induced me to explore the problem of morality from a different angle. I decided to adopt a historical approach to the moral socialization of women and to the evolution of morality in general. This enterprise forced me to emigrate completely from my own body and brought me to the astonishing discovery that the history of morality and ethical judgements, handed down in the philosophical tradition, had absolutely no connection with my previous assumptions and arguments about female morality.

Theses on Moral Philosophy

To indicate this complete disconnection, let me outline a few opinions from the history of ethics. The comic, even absurd, effect given by juxtaposing a list of these is a fortuitous by-product of the procedure. If particular statements seem so arbitrary, this is because the social conditions and practices out of which they arise will be ignored. For our purposes, it is enough simply to mention their connections with morality.

It becomes evident from a historical survey that 'morality' has something to do with 'theory', with 'perfection', 'sympathy', 'progress' and 'human dignity'. With some effort we may discern that all attempts to define the nature of morality are concerned with establishing connections between individuals, the law and the state, between economics and politics. Morality should guarantee the social order, and should regulate behaviour, particularly in those areas which the law does not reach.

For Michael Scotus morality (*scientia moralis*) had four departments: how the state should be governed, how people should conduct themselves with their fellows and their family, and how they should order their own lives. Which values are held to be moral at any one point in history depends on the view of human beings adopted at different times. (I am not here concerned with the way in which these views are determined by the balance of social forces at any given moment.) If people are inordinately ambitious, avaricious or domineering (as they are in Kant, for example), then they are not ethical by nature, but only become such by freely accepting the moral law. In that event they follow their own will, and not the dictates of nature.

Such a philosophy of freedom becomes a philosophy of the state since without it mere force would prevail. People must be educated to morality. In 1789 Fichte wrote a theory of moral education and some years later Hegel adapted Kant by formally installing subjectivity as the morality of the state: 'To the extent to which the ethical is reflected in the individual character determined by nature, it is virtue which constitutes moral uprightness in as much as it exhibits nothing but the simple adequacy of the individual to the obligations imposed by society.'[5] Finally, Spencer was to assert: 'Hence every action is joyful, if it is socially necessary.' Morality refers the good to the social, because (as in Durkheim, for example) people cannot live alone. An ethical sentiment is a feeling of respect for the moral law, or so we are told in Metzke's Dictionary of Philosophy.

My head reverberates with the metallic sounds of law and state, politics and economics, freedom and will, discipline and order, respect and the Good – how did I ever come to associate morality with sex and the body? How could I have linked virtue with chastity, propriety with questions of sexuality? Whatever induced me to introduce woman's relationship to her body, and hence her relationships with men, into the semantic field of morality? After all, you can see from any history of morality that it is concerned above all with knowledge and reason, with freedom and law, and with the war of all against all. Even we women suspected something of the sort. Still in search of guidance, I turned once more to the large Brockhaus Encyclopaedia, and looked up *propriety* [*Anstand*], with the idea that I would at least discover a general statement about what constitutes propriety in a woman.

Propriety ... the behaviour called for by a society, whose performance elicits its approval, where failure to observe it (impropriety) leads to mockery, laughter or stronger forms of disapproval (such as ostracism). A society normally makes more or less explicit demands that a certain general standard of behaviour be maintained. At the same time, particular codes of conduct may prevail in different classes, sectors or professional circles. As a rule definitions of proper behaviour are derived from the codes prevailing in the educated classes, which provide criteria of decorum that can be summarized in compendia (such as Knigge).[6] However, there are enormous variations and contrasts in these from country to country. Propriety can be distinguished from tact, as its exercise by the individual, while etiquette can be regarded as its outward forms.[7]

Thus I have learned that, with its variants tact and etiquette, propriety is determined by custom. This is a circular explanation, since it leaves us with the question: what determines custom? However, at least we have been told that propriety is determined by prevailing custom and – somewhat reluctantly – that it is the dominant classes which determine proper behaviour, while representing it as normative for society as a whole. We discover in short a highly simplified, one-dimensional, even vulgarized version of the account we derived from our readings in moral philosophy. Once again, we find no support for our spontaneous intuition that morality is somehow connected with female chastity, and proper behaviour with female propriety.

But individual words are never wholly unambiguous, and perhaps I had been barking up the wrong tree. Perhaps I should have looked up *decency* [*Anständigkeit*]. I went on to do so:

> *Decency* ... A subdivision of common 'morality' which has only recently acquired currency as one of the virtues. It has no philosophical pedigree and has its origins instead in 'human' impulses. It is related to 'chivalrous behaviour', 'fair play' and the French 'honnêteté', and is to be found in a person's treatment of comrades, but also of subordinates, for example in willingness to forgo advantages for their sake without making any fuss, or even in taking action on their behalf at a risk to oneself.

The Brockhaus is quoting here from O. F. Bollnow's book *Einfache*

Sittlichkeit. Once more we find ourselves baulked and referred else-where, as in a treasure hunt where successive clues are hidden and whenever you find one, you discover that it points you in another direction. The semantic field in the text on decency – chivalrousness, comrades, at risk to oneself, taking action [*Einsatz*] – reminds us that the first publication of Bollnow's work was in the period of fascism: this conception of decency can only be applicable to men. But not because such discourse directly addresses the body, as we found to be the case with women; on the contrary, its allusions to the body are wholly abstract, as to an unnamed entity that must be sacrificed to loftier ideals.

Theories of Moral Development

Standard accounts of the general principles of morality and ethics fail to confirm my intuitions about the nature of female morality. But in the last analysis morality is not just the object of philosophical debate; it also forms part of education discourse. Here then, if nowhere else, it should be possible to discover the guidelines of the moral education of women. So I made another attempt to get to grips with the problem by studying the theories of Durkheim, Piaget and Kohlberg – the fathers and their sons.

In Durkheim matters are quite straightforward: the assumption of control over education by the state generated a need for values that would serve as a guide to conduct. The transmission of moral values thus became a task for schools. The school was now the competent authority responsible for 'the spirit of discipline', the 'autonomy of the will', and 'integration into social groups', and from there to everything else down to and including patriotism.[8] It is not hard to recognize in such ideas categories and concepts derived from the history of moral philosophy. But once again, there is no mention here of the body, let alone of sexuality.

But surely Piaget has some answers? After all it is he who writes about the formation of moral judgement in children.[9] He investigates their games and studies how they rationalize their decisions in cases of conflict among themselves. He proceeds empirically and does not simply deduce what ought to happen from first principles or supreme norms. He discovers two sources of morality: first, heteronomy or determination by others. In such cases rules are set in authoritarian fashion from outside and simply taken over and followed to the letter, rather than in the spirit. The power of such rules is not normally very great. In practice children commonly play according to rules which are quite different from those they nominally believe to be right. The second source of morality is autonomy or self-determination. Here the rules arise out of the collaboration of a peer group. The children involve themselves as little legislators and develop a real taste for making and changing rules. We can regard this process as the birth of democracy. The development from heteronomy to autonomy characterizes the history of peoples, as well as children, and moulds their sense of justice, which progresses from the concept of retribution to that of reparation.

But why does Piaget's study of children's games only lead him on to rules and principles that will eventually govern production and the state, instead of to the body-ethics of women? The answer is as simple as it is illuminating: he only investigated the games played by little boys. A perfunctory glance at the games of little girls discouraged him because they displayed no enthusiasm for rules, laws in all their varieties, or for the encoding and changing of rules. They just hopped around on the same pattern of squares marked out in chalk, quite without imagination, with the same simple rules that persisted for centuries, and their enthusiasm never seemed to get beyond the point of balancing a small stone on their foot.

The Morality of the Sexes

Women are the representatives of love, just as men are the representatives of law. We began by attempting to decode the meaning of this sentence and now have more than a hint that it is to be taken literally. There really is a connection between law, justice and male morality. I thought I would make the experiment of applying to men the values ascribed earlier on to women. *A man who leaves the straight and narrow is perhaps someone who has forged a cheque; his virtues – and he has more than one – are a matter of honesty, competence, a sense of justice, truthfulness or courage; and if he has turned to vice, he probably drinks or gambles so that he can no longer carry out his work. If he is worthless, as like as not he will squander his money; he may commit fraud or theft, or some other offence against property. Should he be ruined, this means he is in debt or bankrupt. If he is dishonoured this is also likely to refer to money or property. In short, as Heine says, morality is the ability to pay one's way.*

Thus men's morality refers in the main to their business ability. I find it astonishing that it should come so naturally to me to interpret moral values in a sex-specific way and yet have no conscious knowledge of doing so. No less surprising is the final result of my researches, which is that there are not, as we might easily have assumed, two different moral systems, one for women and one for men, but that like human beings morality is bisexual.

It is with a new attention that I now reread lines which used to move me deeply, such as Schiller's; 'Life is not the greatest good of all, but of the ills the greatest must be guilt.'[10] I observe that even sentences like this were and still are read and understood in a gender-specific way. At first we probably just apprehend it in a general sense and feel that great issues are at stake, sublime sentiments, tragedies and emotional torments. But as soon as we women find ourselves practically involved or try to think of a situation where our lives seem – or ought to seem – a thing of little worth, we think of such stories as that of Hebbel's Maria Magdalena: a tragedy that arises because of something that happened between a man and a woman and now a child is on the way. On the other hand, when men think of guilt, what comes to mind is something that affects their work, or their bank, or nothing less than their country or the entire legal system. For example:

Partingaux, the expert in disposing of poisonous chemical waste, has stubbornly refused, ever since his arrest at the end of March 1983, to disclose the whereabouts of the poison containers on the grounds that he was an honourable man who could not break his vow of silence. For this vow he is said to have received over £80,000.

So it is not true that each sex is assigned different values from the outset – women are caring, men are brave – but that the same values have different meanings for each sex, they imply different practices and demand different responses. Morality calls both sexes to order, but each sex obeys after its own fashion.

Hence morality becomes a powerful force separating the sexes. For men it centres on property, for women on the body. Even an apparently innocent turn of phrase such as 'to initiate a person' typically means that men are inducted into the mysteries of business, whereas women are introduced to the praxis of sex. What are the implications of this bisexuality of morals?

Morality and Society

Let us retrace our steps a little and take another look at the shape of morality in general. We might ask: What need have we of morality? From our sketch of ethical philosophy we recall that morality is a hinge linking the individual to society. Its function is to facilitate the cohesion of society – which can only be the product of conscious efforts by individuals whose natural wills are in conflict with one another.

If we think of human nature as itself a social product, a consequence of the particular relations within which human beings produce their lives, then in a very abbreviated and programmatic way we can venture the following formulations. In societies dominated by competing interests morality looks after the common weal, as the inner adaptation of the individual to the social totality. Since the interests of individuals are mutually opposed, they have to be made to take second place to the pursuit of social ends. The state functions as the guarantor of such behaviour, formally overriding class interests through the ideological powers of its educational and legal systems. In the course of their various social practices the members of society come to reproduce the kind of ideological behaviour that assures acceptance of the whole. Of course, mere renunciation of individual interests does not suffice to create a firm foundation for morality. Morals can only thrive if ideological values also proclaim an aspiration to the common good, or their memory of one. To want to be good, to have faith in the good, are not just scenarios for a few people who have not yet noticed how tough the competition is, or failed to see that the individual pursuit of the good life is a strategy only for the naïve and foolish. It is a universal yearning. The result is to reproduce a society where moral education helps to generate consent to a social order in which any collective regulation of the production of life has been transported into a remote empyrean of abstract values – from which its shadow returns to earth as the virtue of individuals, an inner bearing that transforms and transfigures the general inability to achieve genuine collective control of their lives. Such a bearing can be called ideological subjection – subjectivity as subjugation.

Yet insights like these are still concerned essentially with masculine ideological subjection and, more specifically, with that space beyond the reach of law in which the behaviour of economic agents in class societies is regulated. But when social norms return from the ideal world to ours, they are not only value-forming, they are also bisexual. What strikes us at once is that the subjection of women assumes guises different from that of men. This can easily be seen from a glance at the other values that constitute subsystems in the moral universe: values like maternal feeling, care, warmth, gentleness, friendliness, and so on. Within the women's movement this has sometimes led to the conclusion that women live more humane lives than men.[11] The argument has been extended to the claim that such values should come to prevail throughout the whole of society. The feminization of society would mean the peaceful abolition of war, armaments, ecological problems and many others besides. Instead of investigating what disabilities were made bearable by the existence of such 'feminine values', it is somewhat surprisingly suggested that these are not social demands, but rather essential traits of women.

A book by Carol Gilligan, *In a Different Voice* (1982), has caused something of a sensation. Working in the tradition of Piaget and Kohlberg (and as a colleague of the latter) she discovered in her seminars on moral education that girls showed less interest than boys in discussions of the principles of justice and that they tended to resolve their conflicts in a different way. She inferred from this that women have a quite distinct ethical system, one to be preferred to the masculine sense of justice and individual competition, because even in our society it is already orientated towards different needs. The book became a bestseller in the United States.

The assumption here is that there exists a different code of ethics, capable of application to society as a whole – thus, by implication, that there are two entirely separate moral systems. I fear that this approach may lead to a mistaken politics. For the endorsement of one particular value system does not just remain on the terrain of morality itself.

What is being suggested to us is that the problem of morals – and their consequences – can be resolved by a simple change of values themselves, instead of by transforming the practices which determine the meaning of what is or is not ethical itself.

This appears to me to be a fatal error, when we confront the problem of the oppression of women. How could we even conceive of this oppression if we so unconditionally ratified feminine values? We would regress to fairy tales, in which society is the theatre of a struggle between good and evil and evil triumphs because it is the stronger. How could we even begin to understand the relationship between masculine and feminine morality? Or explain the relationship between the sexes themselves?

Moral Socialization

Let us consider these questions by looking once again at the process through which the dominant value system is assimilated. We may assume that moral education has an effect of ideological regimentation. This implies that morality has different meanings and spheres of applicability for boys and girls, and results in different practices. Each of us starts off with quite general distinctions of good and bad. Our ideas of good and bad conduct then determine our relationship to society and our integration in it.

In a seminar on moral socialization at the College for Economics and Politics in Hamburg we carried out the experiment of trying to recall memories of our own integration. In view of the extensive literature on moral education, concerned with the education of boys, I shall omit here everything that emerged about the role of fear, guilt, disgust, mutual reinforcement of moral values, and so on. Instead I shall confine myself to some typical features of the process of moral socialization of women. I should like to present two accounts of life in a children's home. Both were written by girls/women. The reason for their selection is that the only account of a childhood we received from a male participant in the seminar (which was attended by both men and women) also dealt with a children's home. It provides a tacit backcloth to the stories of the two girls presented here and makes it possible to give a gender-specific analysis of them.

MORALS ALSO HAVE TWO GENDERS

IN THE CHILDREN'S HOME

She was nine years old and had left home for the first time without her parents, to spend four weeks in a children's home in Spiekeroog. There were about forty children there and she didn't know anyone apart from the baker's son, and he had to sleep in a different room anyway. She had been very agitated while the rooms were being allocated. She was somehow afraid that she would end up on her own. But she managed to find three other girls whom she quite liked the look of and who wanted to share with her.

Unfortunately it emerged on the second day that one of them was a bedwetter and had to be sent home. So that left the three of them. All the children were split up into small groups according to whether they were swimmers or non-swimmers. They could only go into the water twice a day for ten minutes and had to be accompanied by their teacher ...

To start with there was a dried-up piece of cake and some rosehip tea, which she hated. She asked one of the women whether she might not have some raspberry syrup, but the woman just grumbled at her and muttered something about 'spoilt brats'. She then wrote to her parents that it was horrible in the home and that the food was terrible and asked whether they couldn't send her a parcel with raspberry syrup. She told them to write a letter, because the teachers always read the postcards and scolded them if they had written anything bad about the home. After a long interval her parents wrote back, saying that she should buy the drink with her pocket money. But she wasn't allowed to buy anything to eat and drink, because some children were there to lose weight and the home couldn't make any exceptions. She did slip out of the house once and bought her drink in the dairy, together with a bar of the chocolate marzipan she loved. But the syrup did not taste as nice as usual, because she had to drink it in the lavatory, so as not to get caught. If she had been found out, she would have been forbidden to go on the next excursion – a boat ride around the island – and have had to help out in the kitchen instead. Two girls had already been forced to stay at home and she did not want this to happen.

THE HEALTH CURE

I was five years old. So there was just enough time before the beginning of school for me to be sent on a six-weeks' slimming cure. No one explained to me why I was being sent away. There were lots of children in the home. All of them were supposed to put on weight. At mealtimes they were stuffed full of sweets and desserts. All except me, of course. I would have rather liked a pudding or an ice cream occasionally. When they served up thick semolina soup, it was easier to go without and the other children envied me my privileged situation. After lunch all the thin children had to have a rest for two hours. But not me. At first I was quite happy not to have a rest, but the two hours passed very slowly without anyone to play with. Sometimes I would go along to see the cook and was given a chocolate – 'but only one'. I used to crumble it up on my toy grater, so that it lasted longer. After a time I realized that I was 'fat' and that was why I was different from the others. The other children realized it too. When I cried because I was lonely or homesick, they would cry out, 'Auntie Trudel, Fatty is crying again'. She used to take me on her lap and console me. When we went on walks on the heath, we used to walk in twos, but no one wanted to walk with fatty. So I used to walk hand-in-hand with the teacher. The grown-ups were all very kind to me. On a number of occasions I was allowed to play in the cottage belonging to the Principal or she would read all sorts of lovely stories just to me. So after a while I gradually stopped crying. When I went back home, I was greeted with a bar of chocolate and my mother gave me back my cloth comforter, which the women in the home had taken away from me on the first night.

In the story of the boy which we have not included, the essential features of Piaget's observations were confirmed. Chief among them were resistance to rules, experienced as a conflict with authority; horizontal socialization within the peer group, in opposition to the adult world; a wish to make rules for oneself; status gained in the peer group as a result of oppositional behaviour. In the girls' stories, on the other hand, there are typically different features.

1. Identity appears to be strongly focused on one's own body. Pleasure, well-being, play a decisive role. The function and appearance of one's own body, and its normality, are crucial reference points.

2. The standard of normality is at once an individual measure and a determinant of social integration. Deviations are grounds for isolation. The function and appearance of the body determine inclusion in or exclusion from the group. There are the swimmers and the non-swimmers, the thin children and the fat, the healthy and the sick, those who have to eat and those who aren't given any sweets. Because they

are related exclusively to one's own sense of well-being, independent and oppositional alterations to the rules lead to nothing but further segregation and isolation, as for example, when the child devours marzipan and a raspberry drink in the lavatory.

3. The rules appear as more than just external and they are not entirely without rational foundation. In their corporeal mediation they appear to be as natural to the individual as the body itself, from which the process of socialization or regimentation ensues. The fact that the rules appear to be so closely knitted together with the body makes them seem peculiarly 'fated', something to be obeyed implicitly, something endowed with the quality of a social duty for which one can be held responsible, or which can be a source of guilt. 'I realized that I was fat', and therefore lonely, we might add. In this context suffering is also experienced as something which can be alleviated by the rules.

Adults seem, on the one hand, to be in complicity with the judges. On the other, they appear as comforters, as beings who act as a force for both reconciliation and regimentation. They can help a child achieve social integration or they may represent that integration by organizing groups of children, providing them with standards or offering friendship. Rules are broken, but this does not lead to a horizontal social stratification. Instead it leads to greater solitude.

This arrangement creates a peculiar polarization. On one side there is the social group, integration into which depends on good behaviour centred on the body and its normality. On the other, we have well-being, the enjoyment of one's own body. Both extremes are directly mediated by the same physical constitution. In these conditions, how can we become active? What changes should we introduce? The whole arrangement functions like a trap. Why should we strive to change the rules when, by obeying them, we can achieve our inclusion in a social group? Conversely, why should we conform to rules which are somehow directed against the well-being of our own bodies? Caught in this dilemma, it can be assumed that strategies for change will typically remain within the bounds of what is understood as normality and its rules. Individuals will usually attempt to expand the scope of the pleasure available to them within the prescribed limits.

Such a structuring of the available space will then result in a simpler, more flexible adaptation to the rules. The sense of belonging to a social group is not an achievement arising from resistance, but a product of compliance and its visible signs, the approved standards, the appropriate pleasure and the happy mean. In contradistinction to Piaget's findings, self-motivated activity in girls is unlikely to consist in laying down rules independently, or in the codification and refinement of existing rule-systems. What would be the point of inventing such rules – for example, what would be the good of proclaiming one's own short or fat shape the norm, as long as one still experienced deviation as guilt? It is only logical, therefore, that what we find in the stories of little girls is that they tend to stretch their pleasures to the limit of what is allowed – the chocolate is grated, one indulges oneself a bit. Moreover, and again in contrast to Piaget, the adult world is not really perceived as an external constraint which provokes resistance. Indeed adults are subject to the same constraints. Their own relations with society involve a sort of complicity. Whilst generally abiding by the rules, they nevertheless reward deviations with affectionate gestures. They secretly hand over a piece of chocolate, or even a whole bar; stories are told in cosy intimacy; it is possible for the teacher to take you by the hand while out walking. Thus deviation creates a kind of network of solidarity which exists as a subsystem of the rules, whose dominance is never challenged and which can unleash their power at any moment and destroy that solidarity. The outcome of this situation is that those who are capable of bestowing such affection, such pleasure without loneliness, are the possessors of an incalculable power. Whereas one's own power, the socialization possible in the corporeal order, is confined to breeding the 'right body'.

Class and War

In conclusion, I should like to advance some provisional ideas about the benefits of a functioning bisexual morality for the ruling powers. We began by inquiring into the meaning of a statement which associated love with women and law with men. I should now like to pose a more specific question about the significance of these linkages for the reproduction of the social system.

It is not difficult for women to associate themselves in their own minds with love and also with the body, and men with business and law – on the contrary, it enhances our sense of our own value and confirms our feminine aversion to juridical ways of thinking and business ways of acting. Moreover, we become quickly accustomed to thinking of ideological subjection as essentially associated with men and fondly imagine that women are not ideologically enslaved. We may be oppressed and denied entry to many areas of social life, but for that very reason we are more intact, less implicated in the dirty work of society, such as class struggle or war. Women, so we imagine, are subject to men, and men are subject to the state. The relations with the ruling powers are indirect. Men stand between women and the state. There is no call for us to be astonished, then, if the encyclopaedias and the histories of philosophy are full of formulations concerning male propriety and ethics, and contain nothing but gaps where there ought to be something about women. To confirm this once more I opened the large Brockhaus again and looked up *morality*. Morality, I read, is concerned with

the totality or minimum stock of norms of conduct (and outlook) deemed binding in a given society over a considerable span of time. These norms arise under the influence of a culture and are part of its ethos. In the course of socialization they are internalized.

Thus far there is no cause for unease; we see the same distanced style as before. But without warning Brockhaus then goes on to say:

In the Western democracies morality is increasingly in the process of being privatized; the state is progressively reducing the area of its involvement (e.g., the legalization of deviant behaviour, consumption of drugs, abortion, pornography).

We might also add: prostitution. To our amazement the state discovers us women and our bodies where we, starting from our bodies, failed to discover it. Within juridical structures, which claim a universal relevance, but into which it is chiefly boys that are socialized, we suddenly encounter a link between law and the body – and, centrally, women's bodies – and once again moral norms make their appearance in this legal form as if they were universal ethical laws. This little discovery could easily be augmented and ought by rights to serve as the starting point for a larger piece of research. For the present, however, I should like to do no more than offer the following tentative propositions.

Our bisexual morality seems on the one hand to be specific to each sex, while, on the other, it gains in power and authority from the fact that it can constantly change sex. Thus each sex can claim that its morality is general and so both sexes, although separate, can ostensibly live in a universal moral system. The effect is to enable individuals to regard their own values, and the practices relating to them, as universally valid, even though they may be in the process of submitting to other, perhaps diametrically opposed values.

This jumble may bring relief – a woman may have a strong character even though she thinks of her body as ugly – but it may also be explosively reactionary. Thus demagogic political speeches often play on the ambivalences in this system of values. The result is typically a structure full of inconsistencies and illogicalities, which yet often go unnoticed because they appeal to ideals that are sexually specific. In consequence the men and women listening to them each feel addressed in turn, while those passages not addressed to them nevertheless encourage a relaxed acquiescence. Thus when our Federal Chancellor, Helmut Kohl, gave his recent speech on the state of the nation, he contrived to express the desirability of freedom and self-determination, peace and treaties with the GDR, together with the need for German reunification and an end to class conflict. These incompatible goals were put forward all at once and represented as the passionate desire of the citizens of both West and East Germany. His choice of words was both familiar and comprehensible: we might say that all men were called on to agree. He spoke of *culture and dignity, work and freedom, ideas and interests*:

> We want a nation of free citizens, which overcomes class antagonisms, reconciles conflicting interests and establishes a community that affirms its historical heritage and the virtues and values common to and binding upon all Germans. The Germans, all Germans, recognize themselves in the freedom-loving image of man enshrined in the constitution.

But when he came to address the tasks awaiting us and to complain about an absent normality, his language changed. Not that he spoke directly of bodies, let alone sexuality. Nevertheless, his vocabulary here pertained unmistakably to the realm of corporeal practices and hence to that of women. We now heard of *the most private places, neighbourly relations; we are opposed to violence, in favour of affinities and bonds, of unimpeded travel; we are against the Wall and barbed wire, against placing life and health in jeopardy; we should not remain silent, but heed our feeling that we all form one people. The division of Germany should be made more bearable and less dangerous; there should be mutual responsibility, a 'condition of common life in Germany in which the natural weft of our relationships becomes ever denser and closer'.*

In his concrete proposals to the GDR Kohl's language once again bristles with power and strength, *weapons and willpower, rights and interests*. It is plain that the moral division of labour functions as a kind of female legitimation of a foreign policy articulated in masculine terms.

My earlier discussion suggested that morality means one thing in business and another in love. The relationship between the two meanings was not, however, one of mutual exclusiveness or mutual oppression – as if, for example (as women have tended to believe), men suppress the caring instinct in themselves – but rather one of an interlocking division of labour and reciprocal buttressing of the system as a whole. As with the general division of labour within society, so here too there is a division into upper and lower orders, each with its own practices and codes. But these are not two sets of people, one with a good set of values and the other with a bad, so much as interconnected structures which sustain each other. I have attempted here to show how they interact in the spheres of politics and class consciousness.

In this context I think it would be useful to rethink the problems of militarism and war, and the training for them. A *proper* [*anständig*] soldier, after all, is by no means the same as a *proper worker*, or a *proper businessman*. Camaraderie is connected with bodies, and war is at the very least compatible with love of one's country. In military training the body obviously plays a major role. The drills – chest out, stomach in! – are plainly not sexy, but nevertheless resemble the type of instruction that women issue to themselves daily. Here too we encounter male virtues, such as bravery and fortitude, which are not incorporated into the legal code in any direct way. These virtues, which overcome the body, and hence display it in a state of subjection, are legalized in war: cowardice and lack of courage can be treated as desertion and punished with death. It would appear, therefore, as though what happens in a war is not that the ordinary business virtues of men are summoned and deployed, but that the morality of war is composed of both sets of virtues: *to sacrifice oneself as a hero* – that is the ultimate combination.

Thus we come to the conclusion that the power of the state is not the expression of a masculine morality which has been erected into a universal ethical code. That power derives instead from the iridescent tones, the shifting meanings and combinations of values, in short the bisexual nature of morality, which makes it possible to appeal to everyone, each in his or her own way. One effect of this is that we become used to thinking of contradictory stances as being as normal as the fact that there are men and women. The exchange of love for money, for example, is something we regard as possible and impossible in the same breath, wanting love both to be the free expression of feeling and to be secured by contract. Or again, we believe that men are prepared to die for the sake of glory, and that women should be willing to sacrifice themselves for them. Or, finally, we accept that they should commit murder in obedience to higher principles while believing that we are the defenders of life – this idea, too, is an effect of a bisexual morality.

If we are ever to escape from our self-imposed bondage, one urgent task must be to investigate the interconnections between the bisexuality of morality, with its distinctions and conflations, and the problems of class, politics and war.

First Steps

A conviction that the system of domination in which we are imprisoned is so firmly constructed that there is little we can do about it, is so widespread at present that I would like to formulate some of my conclusions as proposals of a practical character.

1. The general history of morality, moral philosophy and moral education manages to get by without women. However, morality itself does have a meaning for women and finds expression in our everyday practices. We should seek to raise our understanding of morality from the level of spontaneous experience to that of a conceptual or scientific

knowledge. We must learn how to appropriate it for ourselves; the present lacuna in the moral education of girls needs to be filled.

2. Whereas the masculine meaning of morality focuses largely on business, property and money, women are socialized via their body. Their corporeality is the foundation of their identity as well as of their subordination to men and their isolation. Collectives are necessary to resist this isolation, if women are to develop other goals and strategies and to make their own way in the world.

3. Since the ruling morality derives its strength from the divisions and arbitrary reconjugations of its sex-specific meanings, we should turn our energies to creating a coherent structure of benefit to all. We need to create that unified code which is essential for a common existence, one capable of bringing together production and pleasure, love and social transformation.

4. Since the ruling morality thrives on guilt, we should struggle against this fertile soil for its domination. At present the real debt that individuals owe to the community, namely the obligation to participate in conscious planning of social production, is distorted into guilty service of sectional interests. To overcome this we need to enquire what our true debt is, both to ourselves as a human community and to future generations. That would mean transforming and humanizing the structures of society and preventing the destruction of the earth.

Notes

1. *Frauenformen. Alltagsgeschichten und Entwurf einer Theorie weiblicher Sozialisation,* Argument-Sonderband 45, Berlin 1981, revised and updated 1991; see also this volume, pp. 3–12.

2. See U. Gerhard, *Verhältnisse und Verhinderungen. Frauenarbeit, Familie und Rechte der Frauen im 19. Jahrhundert,* Frankfurt am Main 1981, p. 138.

3. Taken from F.F. von Lipperheide, *Spruchwörterbuch,* Berlin 1976, and L. Röhrich, *Lexikon der sprichwörtlichen Redensarten* (4 vols), Freiburg/Basle/Vienna 1973.

4. Walther and Gottfried were mediaeval poets; Abraham a Sancta Clara was a famous Viennese Jesuit preacher and satirist; Jahn was a Romantic reformer remembered for his chauvinism and foundation of the student (duelling) corps – *translator's note.*

5. *Grundlinien der Philosophie des Rechts,* Frankfurt am Main 1970, p. 298.

6. Adolf, Freiherr von Knigge (1752–96), was the author of a standard guide to etiquette which has made him the German equivalent of Emily Post – *translator's note.*

7. *Enzyklopädie* (20 vols), Wiesbaden 1960, vol. 1, p. 559.

8. See Emile Durkheim, *L'Education morale*, Paris 1925.
9. See J. Piaget, *The Moral Judgement of the Child*, London 1932.
10. *The Bridge of Messina, IV – translator's note.*
11. A note also struck in André Gorz's *Farewell to the Working Class*, London 1982.

FOUR

Daydreams

Fantastic ideas, memories of one kind or another, fleeting impressions, daydreams, castles in the air, unconnected images, that float past us in moments of passivity.... We sacrifice much more time than we like to admit, to their idle play.

John Dewey, *How We Think* (1910)

In a valuable book on the social history of resistance, Honegger and Heintz[1] argue that the absence of women in movements of social resistance cannot call into question their ability to resist as such, but rather raises the problem of defining resistance. If one recognizes as resistance only *collective* lawbreaking, then women do not appear in the accounts. Women's resistance is *individual.* The editors of the book go on to suggest an expansion of the concept to include spontaneous refusals to act. This suggestion confused me. I had thought of resistance as being both individual and collective and had quite naturally understood collective action as political, and had placed individual action in the domain of psychology – psychoanalysis above all – and the theory of education. These disciplines are full of studies of individual cases of resistance. Indeed, their boundaries have marked out the areas which allow the various kinds of resistance a valid meaning. For example, in *psychoanalysis* resistance means a defence against making unpleasant psychic elements conscious, perhaps through repression. Problems of conscience play a large part in this context. In *law*, resistance is defined as actions directed against the authority of the state and the exercise of state office. But even *electricity* involves resistance. It can be observed when voltage is applied to an electrical circuit; it prevents the flow of current and can itself be used as a component. In *mechanics*, resistance is a force which prevents the movement of a body. And in the field of *politics*, finally, we talk about resistance when movements are fighting for self-determination against tyranny and outside control. The disciplines are drawn closer together, because even in politics *legal* resistance has to be defined. New disciplines are added: legitimacy can be considered in terms of ethics or of philosophy of the state. Here the principal debates are either based on Germanic feudal law – where political resistance is related to the sovereignty of the state; or they are placed in the tradition of religious resistance – in which case resistance is a duty of conscience for each individual.

The definitions specific to each field are an interesting encouragement to more comprehensive considerations, and are also related to one another in an odd way. Having started with individual conscience in psychoanalysis, I end up with individual conscience, but defined as political resistance. The spontaneous order of my own mind has been quite muddled up. The distinctions between the various areas are clearly not upheld by the individual disciplines. However, they canalize the individual's thinking and, as a result, allow quite uncontrolled inroads of the so-called public spheres into supposedly private ones by producing and maintaining them as separate. Resistance clearly always seems to be an individual and a collective question, both personal and political. It would seem to be a matter of importance to investigate the relationship between the various resistances and their separation: that is, the separation of the individual and the collective, the private and the political, the individual and society.

I suggest, therefore, that the question of who resists and in what form should not be solved by altering the definitions. The question arises in an area – or several areas – occupied by a number of disciplines and authorities. But that makes the observation of discipline boundaries just as interesting as their transgression. The point is not to decide when individual resistance is political or political resistance is individual but rather, *which politics pursues which resistance?* And how does the position of the individual woman in society determine the form of her acquiescence or resistance?

If I am researching resistance and possibilities for resistance, I must pay attention to individual power relations (an aspect of psychology), which are themselves the result of the possibilities and realities of action for the individual in social conditions (an aspect of political economy). Such an approach conflicts with the attempt to think of resistance either as a simple problem of personal development or – as soon as social conditions are also taken into account – as a standing firm against forces conceived as quite external. To set individual relations of domination against those that surround them does not avoid the problem of almost automatically conceiving resistance as a question of character, of thinking in terms of 'personal courage', 'incorruptibility', 'nonconformism', 'inner security'.[2]

The field of 'women and resistance' may therefore be defined in the following way. Irrespective of whether women are to be found in movements of social resistance or not, everyday private forms and practices are an important area for the investigation of feminine resistance. Since the personal and the private are also the site of the reproduction of the social relations of domination, this sphere and the way in which privacy is produced and maintained will tell us something about women's social being, about their resistance and acquiescence. The fact signalled by Honegger and Heintz[3] – that women are less often to be found in movements of social resistance – means that we must look at women's everyday practices to discover the specific shape of their forms of resistance.

The Realm of Utopia

As the oppression of women takes place every day and everywhere, we can expect a great diversity of resistance: from quarrelling, deceit and resentment to ways of coping, such as illness, flight from reality and many more. Without in any way dismissing these forms, I should like to limit myself to one dimension which seems particularly suitable and illuminating for understanding feminine resistance behaviour: the utopian dimension of the daydream. It was a film that gave me the idea. Barbara Streisand, in the main role, imagines that she is whisked away from the sandpit where she is watching her children and taken secretly in a mysterious car to the headquarters of a revolutionary committee in which she is a sort of leader, and a skilled public speaker. In the end she works in collusion with Fidel Castro who turns out to be a lesbian in male disguise. Remembering my own experience, I thought that if we analysed our consciously constructed daydreams we might learn something about the forms that are felt as especially oppressive, and about the kind of liberation that is actually desired. I thought daydreaming might be a sort of isolated resistance. As a preliminary hypothesis, I assumed that these dreamed wishes were in any case an indication of energy, a sort of experiment. It might be important to transfer all these isolated energies into some form of collective action which would allow us to realize our wishes.

Let us start by trying to define daydreams. They should be determined not as dreams in which the unconscious is in control, but as deliberate and conscious constructions of the imaginary. I do not, however, want to include simple wishes – for a house or a car, for a holiday abroad, and so on – though these could be elements of a daydream. I want *daydreams* to refer to the widespread practice of arranging people and activities in specific constellations, situations and combinations, of imagining scenes where the dreamer takes the main role, and replays it again and again. The dreaming thinkers or the thinking dreamers are thus consciously removed from reality. They know they are dreaming, and they want to. Dreaming brings them pleasure and satisfaction. Another distinctive feature of daydreams is that they are not surreal. Like nightdreams, they displace pieces of reality (which can include books, films, people, and so on) but they try to use these to construct coherent and plausible scenes. By analysing daydreams and the particular shifts of everyday life occurring in them, I am trying to learn something about the life, suffering, resistance and oppression of women. Daydreams fill daytime hours, they use up energy, they are *life* time. They are one way women have of spending their lives in an imaginary space, intentionally, actively and repeatedly.

At first I thought that daydreams were a specifically female form; presumably all women use their imagination in some such way during the course of their lives. Then again, that seemed fairly unlikely. So I started with small-range surveys in different age groups, social strata and regions. The result? There was hardly a single woman who did not spend some time daydreaming, for several hours, at least a couple of times a week, and sometimes daily. From my own experience, I knew that this dreaming was not only satisfying; it was also painful, a compulsive repetition ('like an addiction you can't give up', as one woman said). So in my analysis I tried to find out how to stop people daydreaming, how to get them to spend their time in better ways. At the same time I had an optimistic feeling that perhaps daydreams were in their own way already acts of resistance – as in the film I mentioned earlier – not quite a conscious intervention in actual relations of domination, but perhaps representing a potential for resistance which could be set free. One discovers many such 'disorderly' assumptions in one's mind before undertaking closer research into a subject. Drawn from information that had been stored up, was not needed at the time, and was only later incorporated without examination in a kind of sedimentation of knowledge, these assumptions were mobilized at the beginning of the investigation as a series of prejudices. During the student movement, for example, a number of articles were published about the daydreams of women assembly-line workers, arguing that their work was so unbearable and so crushing that they had to flee reality and construct a better world inside their head – usually based on films. The relationship between bad working conditions and flight into fantasy seemed plausible. But the women I talked to prepared these dreams for themselves irrespective of working conditions, stratum or situation. Were the lives of all women comparable to those of women assembly-line workers?

The topic of daydreams, with its themes of 'flight', 'fantasy', 'imagination', 'withdrawal', takes us into a twilight zone. While its daylight aspect still leaves it open to analysis and rational discussion, its dreamside reflects a dark inner life, a sliding into hysteria, disease, psychic disturbance. (In fact most of the women I spoke to feared they were mentally sick.) But although I consulted classic authors on the interpretation of dreams, my aim here is not to give a kind of psychoanalysis of daydreams but to bring the dream into the daylight of our social relations. Before looking at some of the daydreams themselves, we should consider some of the classic authors who have dealt with the imagination. For dreams, we turn to Freud; for daytime fantasies and longings, we turn to Ernst Bloch.

Freud

The first surprise is that although Freud dealt so extensively with night-dreams, he had hardly any interest in daydreams. He mentions them only occasionally, as 'the essence and the model of nightdreams' (vol. xi, p. 387).[4] 'We know,' he stated, 'that this is the case.' Given this assumption, it is even more astonishing that he did not pay greater attention to daydreams – because they could have given him a great deal of information on the relation of the conscious to the unconscious.

Freud tells us that daydreams are products of the imagination, that they are very common among healthy as well as sick people, and that they 'are more accessible to study if you take yourself as the object of study' (vol. xi, p. 95). They last from pre-puberty to mature age, and their motivation is transparent. In the various volumes of his work, he indicates on five separate occasions that the imagined scenes of daydreams satisfy either erotic desires or aspirations to power and ambition, and that the division is according to gender. Men satisfy their ambitions, while women, 'who have devoted their ambition to success in love', satisfy erotic desires (vol. xi, p. 95). Freud is not inter-ested in whether it is possible to devote your ambition to success in love without sanction. This is not due to a lack of interest in women, but because he thinks that men also hide behind their ambitions nothing more than the erotic need to attract certain women. In volume vii he mentions that adults are ashamed of their daydreams and protect them as intimate secrets, and that they would rather admit to a crime than unveil a fantasy (p. 215). Finally, he maintains that daydreams have three temporal elements: they are connected to a recent impression and to an infantile experience where there was wish-fulfilment, and a dreamed future is constructed around this material. For Freud, then, daydreams as fantasies are subject only to the pleasure principle (vol. viii p. 234); women have erotic dreams or, in other words, the 'origin of their dreams is sexual' (vol. vii, p. 217); and they follow a linear development as child wishes are prolonged unbroken into the future. 'The essence of imaginary happiness is the independence of desire from the approval of reality – this is obviously visible in daydreams' (vol. xi, p. 387).

Bloch

Bloch is quite different. Turning passionately against Freud's idea that nightdreams and daydreams are similar, he sees the latter as 'anticipations of imaginary forces', 'hurrying on ahead', 'anticipations of a better world' (p. 100).[5] Daydreams are not overwhelming or constricting, not bits left over from the day, but are inspired by the 'will to a better life' (p. 103); they are a utopian model of what people would like to be. The action of the dreams takes place in a utopian setting (p. 105). Because people live in social relations of domination, they dream of 'freedom from wage labour', 'of victory in class struggle', of 'peace', 'solidarity and friendliness' (p. 101). Daydreams contain visions which are of general interest; they are 'the raw material of poetry' (p. 107). They 'design a more beautiful world', 'perfect visions', they are 'luminous preliminary stages of art'. They are social utopias, 'beauty' and 'radiance' and, based on 'knowledge of the wickedness of the world', they move in the direction 'of its improvement'. They are not 'renunciations' – instead 'wishes are radically fulfilled' with the 'intention of perfection'. Daydream fantasies 'open the windows on to realizable possibilities.' Their motive is a 'longing which is the only honest quality of all men' (p. 113). 'Altogether daydreams move towards the field of anticipatory consciousness' (p. 117).

Three Daydreams

Now we will consider the daydreams of three women fairly arbitrarily chosen, keeping the thoughts of Freud and Bloch in mind. The dreamers are: a thirty-five-year-old housewife with two children, divorced, remarried, with an unfinished university career; a twenty-five-year-old woman, unmarried and without children, who worked in a kindergarten; and a forty-one-year-old clerical worker, divorced, with one child, Catholic and a foreigner. All three women are or were politically active in social movements.

FIRST DAYDREAM

I am on holiday. I want to switch off and forget about everyday life. I don't want to talk, I don't want to discuss things, I want to be involved only with myself. Nobody's going to distract me from myself. I want to crawl into myself. I am living in a hotel. Because other people don't interest me I see them only as vague shadows, they remain in the background.

During the day I lie on the balcony and read. At mealtimes, I sit alone at a table for two. The food is exquisite, exclusive. I present myself as a cool beauty, disinterested. No one speaks to me. I am left in peace – but I notice that men find my aloofness and disdain fascinating. They look at me admiringly, they whisper about me. After dinner I go for a walk on the beach. First, I get changed – now I am not wearing the elegant dress, but a loose white shirt and shorts. I go to the beach. It is empty, the air is fresh, there is a light breeze. I have long hair that blows in the wind. I see myself without glasses, an all-over tan, long legs. I walk along the beach in the water, dreaming, thinking how wonderful life is. I like myself.

Suddenly I see a dot in the far distance, moving, getting bigger, and I recognize it as a man. I feel disturbed, then I think – he is as lonely as I am – because he is walking alone. I look him over. He is tall with short black hair dishevelled by the wind. He has bright blue eyes, a strong face, firm features, wrinkles around his mouth, a wonderful tanned body, a loose open shirt, hair on his chest, small tight shorts, terrific legs. He strolls casually past me. As he passes I quickly look away. The same thing happens three or four times.

Then it happens again. But this time I don't go so far along the beach. Instead, shortly after the encounter, I sit down on a sand-dune nearby. He also seems to have changed his mind this evening, and after a little while he returns to the beach. Although I am aware of this, I don't show it and I don't look at him. I remain sitting with my head on my knees, looking out to sea. He comes up to where I am sitting and although I still don't react, I am on edge to know what will happen next. He is there, he crouches down and says hello. Only now do I look up: he is smiling, I can see his beautiful teeth and his eyes. I too say hello and smile – he looks at me admiringly. He tells me that he has seen me several times, and always alone. And he has been wondering why I am so alone. I laugh a little, I cross my arms and lean back and tell him that I love being alone, that other people get on my nerves. He lies down on his side, and he turns and looks at me, and says he can understand that very easily. I lie on my back and look at the sky, looking at him only occasionally. We talk about other people, about how stupid and irritating they are, we talk about God, space–time, Kant.

Night falls and it becomes cooler but we want to go on talking. He suggests that we go to his hut, close behind the dunes, to go on chatting and drink wine. I say OK. We go. The hut is a timber cottage with a small verandah. The interior is all timbered, with furniture from Habitat, warmly lit by a kerosene lamp. There is only one room with a separate alcove for the kitchen. I don't see a bed. I sit down on the sofa, he gets the wine, I feel cared for: he is doing something and I can sit back. While he is busy with the wine bottle and glasses, I think, now you are really going to turn him on. He comes and sits beside me on the sofa, I slide a bit closer and look into his eyes. (*Casablanca*). When he says something, I stop taking him seriously, I laugh at him, he feels insecure, he says so and then I kiss him – and passion breaks out. The rest is shadowy and uninteresting. I spend the holidays with him, he looks after me, does the cooking, goes shopping. I do nothing but read and we talk about the books I read. Then it all becomes boring in my imagination.

I now think this dream is trashy and infantile, but when I am dreaming it, I think it is wonderful, especially when this guy comes up – there's the same thrill every time.

SECOND DAYDREAM

It is noon. The whole family is at the table. I eat quickly and little, say that I have a headache, apologize and withdraw. I am twenty years old and don't know what headaches are. But I am unhappy and want to be alone with my thoughts. I hear the others laugh and talk. However, I don't want to be with them. I am not happy. I am afraid that they will notice *it*. Nobody must find out my secret. Otherwise I am lost. Mother would almost certainly send me away from home for a long time in the hope that I forget and 'get back to normal'. Forget you? Never. I love you. You love me. Did you know what love was when you chose the long black soutane. You didn't know. At the age of twelve your family sent you to the seminary and at thirty you came home. Finished with your studies but knowing nothing about life. In Rome, you almost forgot your mother-tongue and now you are too often with us to practise it.

We are in love and console each other only by telephone. In the presence of others we hardly dare exchange looks. I think, I can control my facial expressions better than you do, but my hands shake, my mouth is dry, a fire is inside me. You must show greater indifference.

Please. If your feelings are discovered, you will disappear from here very quickly. They would send you to a very remote village, to Sardinia or Sicily. You are beautiful as never before. You wear a jumper. How strange – you seem tall and free to me. Our eyes melt into one another, our hands touch. You sit on my bed. Nothing separates us, nothing disturbs us, it is fulfilment. Thoughts don't need to be translated into words. We tell each other so much *without needing to speak.* The others don't disturb us. They are scattered over the meadow. Nobody cares about us, we don't need to hide. You kiss me in such a way that *I no longer know myself.* I don't watch you as you leave. I have your taste on my lips. I wait for you ... then I don't know any more. I see you coming over the meadow towards me again, until finally I can touch your face, feel your closeness and the happiness of being with you.

THIRD DAYDREAM

Through the devastated fields, past the forests whose half-dried trees stretch their bare branches against the cold grey rainy sky, moves the endless chain of half-starving, beaten, exhausted figures. More dead than alive, they drag themselves without hope towards the gates of the concentration camp, driven by the truncheon blows of the overseers. The figures are all men and the order to throw off their clothes, which consist only of rags in any case, degrades the half-dead men only a little more. They are now standing naked in long rows, their tired, almost burnt-out faces lowered, while one of the brutal guards beats up one person or another for some small misdemeanour. Or doesn't he, after all? Because now, *I* come into it. If I am to be the camp commandant, it can't be all that brutal under my direction, because I am the saviour or – yes, that's better – there is a higher commander who is cruel, arbitrary and inspires fear, and I have sneaked in, disguised as a sub-overseer – my liberating intervention will be a liberation for one person only, for him. Because he too is among this naked, grey herd, without hope like them, until he – I am just striding past – raises his eyes and *recognizes me in a fraction of a second.* We look at each other, and at once I walk on indifferently, but he knows that his suffering is now over, that hope, even certainty, is there. The story of the rescue is getting lost in the dark, the climax is over.

Once again from the start. Should I be the camp commandant after all? I could still postpone the moment when he recognizes me. I could increase the suffering. No, I would actually have to minimize it, but this would destroy the grandeur of the moment in which he *recognizes* me for the first time – so, a sudden rescue after all – perhaps I am coming to save the entire camp? That's not really so important, the only important thing is the moment when he becomes aware of me from the depth of his misery – I must experience this once again. He lifts his tired eyes: despair – which through the long period of suffering has been rendered incapable of showing even fear any more. His gaze meets mine as I unexpectedly walk past him in totally unrecognizable disguise. *Like a hot sun we are both struck by this gaze,* which on his part is mixed with passionate gratitude and a plea to carry out the rescue *soon* since he cannot survive much longer ...

If I saved others along with him, they could increase the gratitude and could share in the knowledge that I belong only to him, that I will nurse him alone among the many. I lose interest in elaborating this any further. Try once again: the lead-up to the recognition? How much torture and humiliation should the men suffer in this scene?

A look at the clock. She sighs, found out, relieved, startled. Once again two hours have passed since she sat down in the chair just as they have done every day since she granted herself this experience, taking this pleasure for herself, enjoying the shock. He will come home soon now, and in fact, where are the children? Should she clean up a little? Or iron? There is still no milk – she will quickly have to do some shopping. She is tired, listless – she doesn't want to shop or clean up or do any of the other things that might need doing. He'll be in later, as usual. But the children must be called, they should go to bed soon.

Surface and Structure

To work through these and similar daydreams, you need to break through the paralysis and shock which you experience on hearing or reading such fantasies. After some weeks of doubt and despondency I began to formulate some preliminary suggestions for ways of looking at such fantasies. Right from the start, I want to give up all claim to any in-depth interpretation of the underlying truth, of the essence. Instead, I try to decode what is obvious, what lies on the immediate surface, and I ask you to be amazed at these, quite obvious, findings.

We can't ignore the fact that all three fantasies deal with gender relations. Situations of power/powerlessness are elaborately constructed so that the dreaming women are powerful, they manage the situations, they are protectors and saviours, experienced and superior, while men are insecure, helpless, inexperienced, defenceless, lost and dependent.

The imagined scenes are – with different material and with varying degrees of ingenuity – all constructed to reach a single climax. The pleasure of the fantasy consists partly in postponing this climax in order to heighten it. This is done by adding elements which increase the dreamer's self-esteem in various ways, usually, again, by emphasizing the man's humiliation. To be great oneself is an important part of the drama. It is underlined by loneliness and by the isolation of the struggle. Loneliness is desirable, a sign of independence. It is achieved by presenting all other people (with the exception of one) as mere props in the scene. Language as communication becomes superfluous. Social forces come into the picture as raw material for constructing this meeting of the two sexes as a scene. They are also used as material for constructing the final climax of personal power. We find material elements drawn from fascism (a concentration camp and violence), church and state (seminary and family), and finally places and objects from the commodity sphere (hotel, weekend house, furniture from Habitat). The locations are ones of enclosure, separation, seclusion. The interest in constructing the climax is as overstated and excessive as the lack of imagination in its portrayal. The climax is unspeakable, it cannot be grasped in language, it is no more than an appeal to the emotions: one look, one kiss, passion. It is at the same time the conclusion, the fulfilment which needs no thereafter; to depict what happens afterwards is boring, wearisome. Efforts to prolong the moment by outlining a future fail because of the dreamer's own lack of interest. Pleasure is only achieved through repetition.

It is also obvious that the linguistic material is sentimental and full of clichés. Listening you sometimes feel that these phrases are consciously and stubbornly chosen for these scenes, that they were the very ones appropriate to the imaginary constructions: I look into his eyes (*Casablanca*) – then passion came – cool beauty. And the images: sitting with your legs pulled up, head on your knees. Or, no one must learn my secret, otherwise I am lost. Did you know what love meant before you chose the long black habit? He raises his eyes and recognizes her for a fraction of a second – he raises his tired eyes without hope, and so on. In other dreams which I have not presented here, women are overwhelmed by passion, aroused by a tender touch; the gaze shows they are meant for each other. Commentaries follow, either written or spoken, full of annoyance at the linguistic sentimentality and the hackneyed images, but nevertheless insisting that they should be there – deploring them, but feeling that they belong together.

Social Relations in Fantasy

Awakening from these dreadful daydreams, we think of those shining resolutions in Bloch's book with a somewhat ambiguous feeling, which we might call triumphant unease. He orientated us towards a better future; he thought of daydreams as anticipations of a better, enlightened world, a utopian strengthening, a will to break bounds. His words sound strangely beautiful as we look at our women's dreams, and at the same time meaningless. Thinking of these dreams we might not trust Bloch's ideas on male dreams either, but we are at least certain of one thing: he was writing about men not about people. In his 'Little Daydreams' he talks about *Knaben* (boys), *Jünglinge* (youths), *erwachsene Männer* (grown men), *alte Männer* (old men) when he wants to speak in universal terms. But the feeling of triumph that we have, on realizing that Bloch uses the generalization 'men = people' as the basis for general statements on the character of daydreams, is by no means an unmixed pleasure. The aftertaste of the dreams is too bitter. Are women incapable of utopian visions of how to change the world? I want to turn this conclusion on the maleness of Bloch's vision into a critique of the lives of women, which make their dreams possible. It will address the social relations which obviously affect not only the external circumstances of women's lives but also take possession of our fantasies, of our very aspirations for a better life.

Erotic Wishes

There is no doubt that all three dreams were erotic fantasies of some kind. Does this support Freud's case that daydreams have an erotic content if dreamt by women, because they devote their ambition to success in love? But Freud also thinks that daydreams are free from external constraint (vol. xi, p. 387), that they are material for poetic production, and that fantasies are only subject to the pleasure principle and are divorced from the activity of thinking. The erotic – or, in our words, wishes about gender relations – are the last word for him, not a circumstance demanding analysis or even to be found shocking. In our dreams we see women suffering, with pleasure. They do not like their dreams but they are addicted to them. The content is an erotic one, the scenes are arranged almost like a sexual event, but we cannot call them free from external compulsion. On the contrary, social constraints are introduced in a systematic way. Also the constructed fantasies are carefully calculated in a very explicit way; the actions and situations are meant to be plausible even when the power of the dreaming women is very different from what it would be under non-dream circumstances. As devious as the erotic element is the reversal of the usual relations of power and powerlessness. The women come into the scenes like men – or as they experience men in their lives; men on the other hand are helpless, dependent, uncertain like women. To demonstrate and ornament this dependence, social powers are deployed: state, church, family, the world of commodities – all become props or part of the gender relation, with which women can cope just as easily as with themselves and others. The contents of daydreams are therefore not merely erotic, but show us a double reversal: the relations of men and women are turned upside down, and the dependence on social forces becomes merely the setting for gender relations. We remember that even the concentration camp serves as the backdrop for the gaze of recognition. Since we know that women are dependent and relatively powerless we cannot be satisfied with Freud's answer that 'women's daydreams have sexual origins'. Instead we are astonished to find that in fantasy all structures of domination are shifted or displaced on to gender relations.

In an attempt to defend female against male morality, Carol Gilligan argues, in *In a Different Voice*, that women's moral development is centred on the growing knowledge of intimacy.[6] 'Intimacy accompanies identity, because the woman recognizes herself by how she is recognized, that is, her relationship with the other.' Recognition, relationship, intimacy, identity – all these concepts match our daydreams, as if they were taken from them. The uneasiness we still feel comes from our consent to situations which we find altogether wrong even when gender relations are reversed. Clichéd sentimentality, cruelty, domination – and not liberation, common humanity and hopeful futures dominated the dream-scenes. Even in reversal, women could not escape from their social relations.

Being reminded of the special moral development of women, it is useful to think of the specific subjection of women in this society. In a lecture at the Berlin People's University I analysed morals as a form of ideology and I explained the specific way in which women are included in moral standards as sexual.[7] The virtue of a woman lies in the purity of her body, and the fight for its normality determines the way she is integrated into society. This body-centredness subordinates women to men and at the same time isolates them. Now, if we assume that the social values – like nurturing, protecting, conserving – which define women's role, are the same virtues which legitimate their subordination, isolating them, centring them on their bodies and thus orientating them towards fulfilment in a relationship with just one man, we do not think that they live this subordination literally and without resistance. In fact, if we look at daydreams as a form of resistance, we can see not only that they involve dreaming instead of changing, fantasizing instead of acting, but also that all wishes remain with, or within, the walls of the ideological: love at first sight; fulfilment in surrendering one's whole life to a single person. The great promise, which brings happiness like a flash of lightning, the moment for which all of life is a preparation – this is fulfilment itself, there is nothing else. Quite naturally, these things occur between two persons. The world is pushed aside, it remains background, or material. In the wishes and hopes presented to us we can easily recognize bad films or cheap novels. We think that these products of the mass communications industry are illusory and stupid and we assume that they are not meaningful for politically active and thoughtful women like ourselves because their clichés and sentimentalism are so obvious. In our daydreams, however, we detect the strange fact that women do have fantasies resisting and changing their powerless, subordinate position within relationships; these fantasies are at the same time required to provide a sort of realization of the promises made by the media industry. The ideological is demanded in the name of the ideological. The fairy tale is supposed to come true. In this context we learn more about the use of linguistic clichés. Not only do they shape our feelings (as is shown by work on memory), but in them women recognize exactly those emotions and experiences which have been promised to them and which they want. This clichéd sentimentalism is revealed as part of the fairy tale which women have accepted as their possible future. We can assume that the reality of relationships, marriages and family has disappointed the women, and yet this experience has only made them look for the 'promised happiness for two' in dreams instead of elsewhere.

Contrary to Bloch's optimistic ideas, we think that wishes are not mere desires for a better future but are themselves products of the social circumstances in which people live. In the case of the women mentioned earlier, their wishes for happiness and freedom from oppression are still dreams of oppression, even when they assume power. Contrary to Freud's simple idea that women's fantasies have an erotic content, we believe that to imagine the whole world as a cosy gender relation is not an adequate explanation; instead it should be seen as a phenomenon which requires further explanation, a sign of how dependent women's lives are.

In spite of extensive reversals, we can see that women, while full of hope, pull the chains of their oppression tighter instead of changing or loosening them. They experience their oppression as being bound to families and dependent on a husband – physically, sexually, economically constantly available. One way of handling this is jealousy and the resulting perception of all other women as rivals. All these aspects have been reversed in the dreams: men are now psychically dependent and sexually subordinate; economic dependence has been turned into a physical dependence of men on omnipotent women. The disposal of time has also been reversed – men have to wait. The places of action are as far from the family as possible in the imaginations of the dreaming women: a concentration camp, a distant meadow, a beach hotel with all its staff. Other women do not exist at all. The world of the dreams is a totally male world. In spite of all these reversals of power, the planning of life, its expectations, its wishes and hopes, remains reduced to a relationship for two. And even there imagination fails to elaborate this being-together in any further detail. There is the idea that the world is really inside oneself and that happiness would consist of drawing the interior to the outside through a single gaze, to meet a counter-gaze. Are daydreams then nothing but effects of the ideological structure, the reproduction or re-establishment of women's oppression at the very moment of resistance and thus a guarantee of its perpetuation?

To Live Contradictions

It could almost be a pleasure to let oneself despair of these daydreams, to condemn them and turn away, were it not for the element of doubt that, the world being contradictory, even dream-answers to its challenge are inevitably also contradictory – and so should not simply be a matter of lamentation or joy. We need a different approach in our analysis. Willis has suggested that we look at the spontaneous understanding of structures of domination that is expressed in practical action.[8] Having studied the everyday resistant behaviour of male pupils in a working-class school, he interpreted it as a sort of partial 'penetration' or understanding, inadequate for devising strategies for change. Acts of resistance point out the areas where both domination and the hopes of liberation are experienced.

If we try to transfer this theoretic framework to our daydreams, we can recognize in them a strange contradiction: in all this reversal, this taking of power, this imagining of themselves as independent, free, important, secure and capable of managing the lives of others, women still pursue the fulfilment of traditional female values. Even by taking prisons and churches into their service, they succeed in being nothing but women: they still rescue, protect, guard, conserve, love, devote and abandon themselves – they are still wives. This is why we regarded ideology as all-powerful. But now we can go further and state that in this reversing, this turning of things upside down, women understand, partially at least, that they need the power held by men and other social powers if they are to live out the virtues that are demanded of them as women. These virtues, to which women want to devote their lives, demand under our social relations that women have power, that they dominate. Even to abandon yourself, you must first possess yourself.

Thus we learn that the construction of femininity both requires and excludes domination, and it transfers this contradiction into values which are supposed to compensate for the effects of domination. We understand that this idea of compensation is too simple. We see that to be good you need money, to rescue someone you need the apparatus of the police, to protect someone you need the church, to give yourself away you must first of all possess yourself – all these contradictions are visible in the daydreams as partial understandings. These demands on women, in the form of values, not only deliver women to subordinate places (households), which do not count because they bring in no money; the demands are also deceptive in their apparent modesty. It is as if the demands could be lived and fulfilled by individual women – 'this poor man, I could rescue him with my love – why not?' – when on the contrary women would need the whole power of society behind them if the demands/values were to be realized. Even as dreams, they lead further into domination structures if they are lived only by individuals. What look like female values are the rules of society at large: to protect, conserve, love and rescue life. It is because these are demanded as actions or attitudes from individual women and not from a social structure, that women are oppressed. For the same reason dreamt liberation becomes tyrannical domination. The dreamed solutions show an almost purposeful indifference towards all other people. Regulation of society and conservation of nature cannot be lived as moral attitudes – this is something we can also learn from these female dreams. At the same time, we learn that femininity, as it is constructed in our society, takes to itself the human hope for community, but in an illusory way. The dream of the realization of this illusion shows us how these female virtues necessarily involve cruel horror when they are lived by individuals.

The dreams of another life display further outbursts/perceptions precisely by remaining within ideological structures. One element has disappeared from the dreamed gender relationships, which is quite dominant in the everyday lived structures of a life orientated towards 'coupleness': the doubt whether the love will be returned, and the uncertainty about exclusive possession of the loved one. All other women as rivals have disappeared. In the glance of recognition itself such doubts play no role at all – that is to say, the reciprocation of the eternal, all-encompassing love is an unquestionable certainty. This linking of personal power and the conquest of doubt about love reveals a further relationship between individual women's private lives and society's structures: insecurity within social conditions, helplessness in the face of outside forces, a lack of participation in political life, are transformed into doubts about attractiveness, a longing to be loved and desired for the sole possession of the loved one. As soon as control of the situation – in the dream for example – is in the woman's own hands, these factors no longer count, no longer exist. We also learn that work is non-existent in the dreams, though all three women did perform paid work in their everyday lives. We see not a single trace of work, no criticism of working conditions, and no connection at all between gender and work relations. Thus the dreamed love relationship is not merely dominant in comparison with other relationships – it is the exclusive content of life.

I have even more difficulties with this finding than with the others. After all, two of the three women had children. Can we conclude that this aspect of being a woman is not as disappointing as other experiences in life; that despite all our theoretical assumptions to the contrary, to be a mother is still the most easily liveable of society's demands on women? We need further research, both for our own plans for a better society and also to be able to say anything at all about the question of children in the wish-dreams of women. I have also not looked at the materials utilized in the daydreams here – the *Zeitmarke*, the mark of (the) time, as Freud called it. Such an investigation should be of particular importance, since we can assume that the intense dreams would only incorporate matter from everyday life which had made a deep and enduring impression on the dreamers. We would also learn a great deal about the socialization of women from this additional research.

Daydream Culture

All these problems and perceptions leave us with the question of what we should do with these daydreams, or what women should do who dream in such a way. It is obvious that we gain an increased knowledge of the situation of women, their socialization, how they appropriate society. We also learn how to criticize mainly male theories on fantasies and daydreams in our society. But these dreaming women are not only material or history. How could they turn their resistant energy into real change in their lives?

The first thought – to tell them to stop dreaming and intervene in society instead – is pointless. It represents a misunderstanding of how women live within social relations, how their wishes are shaped, how their powerlessness is mirrored in their dreamt power. An important issue in women's oppression is their isolation, which shows up in dreams as a solitary struggle. To turn daydreams into more effective resistance would require both breaking with the isolation and retaining it as an important issue to be dealt with. So let us start with the production of these daydreams. Could we produce a daydream culture together? Should we meet in groups, write down our daydreams and work on them collectively? Such a proposal sounds extremely dubious. For one thing daydreams are secrets – to make them public would result in embarrassment and insecurity.

I was unable to get any further because I kept on looking for individual solutions. However, if isolation is a central problem, then simply coming together – to work with dreams collectively – should itself produce some change. To write them down and work on them together could really prepare us to work on the dreams instead of just being addicted to them – a change from dependence to control. We could start with a collective effort to find (a) those points where the dreamt resistance and reversals show contradictions in our everyday demands; and (b) the hopes which, though they chain us as individuals, could liberate us collectively. As another step, we could elaborate the assumed connections between social power and gender relations in these dreams. At this point we could work on real knowledge – for example, what are the correlations between fascist domination, the concentration camps, the church and gender relations? We might be able to work out in detail how masculinity and femininity are built into the maintenance of domination on a large scale. The dreams give us our first clues; we could combine the investigation with our interest in our own lives and socialization.

A further step might be to find out how we consent to the idealization of our desires. Since all the dreams display a kind of concentration on life-fulfilment for two, and a dismissal of society at large, we could try to find all the breaks, new beginnings, restraints and erosions of our former hopes for our lives. We could write stories about what we used to want for ourselves, the hopes, the ideas of a better world, which we as women had before we surrendered and agreed that the whole of life would be poured into a single, fated moment. If we could find out why and when our hopes for life were buried, only to return as the illusion of intimacy, then we could try to take our history into our own hands.

Notes

1. Claudia Honegger and Bettina Heintz, eds, *Listen der Ohnmacht. Zur Sozial-geschichte weiblicher Lebensformen*, Frankfurt am Main 1981.

2. See the comments of U. Holzkamp-Osterkamp in her important article on emotionality, 'Erkenntnis, Emotionalität, Handlungsfähigkeit', *Forum Kritische Psychologie*, West Berlin 1978.

3. Honneger and Heintz, *Listen der Ohnmacht.*

4. All references are to the *Gesammelte Werke*, 18 vols, London 1940–52.

5. All references are to *Das Prinzip Hoffnung*, vol. 1, Berlin/GDR 1960.

6. Carol Gilligan, *Die andere Stimme. Lebenskonflikte und Moral der Frau*, Munich 1984, p. 22; translation of *In a Different Voice: Psychological Theory and Women's Development*, Harvard 1982.

7. Frigga Haug, 'Morals Also Have Two Genders', this volume, pp. 31–52.

8. Paul Willis, *Learning to Labour: How Working-Class Kids Get Working-Class Jobs*, London 1978.

FIVE

Responsibility as Masochism

By female masochism we understand actions which seem to be caused and sustained by self-hatred and which by their very existence compel us to assume that the majority of our sex takes pleasure in suffering. The idea of responsibility, which we hear so much about in public pronouncements nowadays, exists in each of us in an emotionally charged way. If I pause to test the echo it produces in me I find that the word 'responsibility' makes me feel uneasy. Beneath my theoretical doubts about it, unpleasant memories lie concealed. My impression is that in my childhood people always talked about responsibility when I had failed in some way, when I had disappointed hopes that had been placed in me. I remember one occasion when I was spending my holidays with my grandparents – I must have been at least twelve, because in what transpired the adults all insisted that it was my responsibility, since I, too, was already grown up.

One morning, I had gone out with my two younger brothers and three smaller children from the village and wandered through the fields into the alluring green mass of the forest. I went straight ahead all the time, for I did not know my way around the forest and intended to return the way we went. So we did not have to keep to the boring paths but instead just walked directly towards the sun. We planned to be home at noon.

Our idea was that we would just turn round and go straight back home. That was the plan. The village children were less used to long walks and adventures than I had expected. They did not know the area, so they soon began to tire and wanted to go home. My brothers, too, became more and more silent. I suddenly became aware of my own anxiety which had been overlaid by my pleasure in being among the lofty trees. So I agreed that we ought to turn round and go back. The sun was not high in the sky. Had we missed its zenith or was it still early? The strange empty feeling in our stomachs could be hunger; in that case it was late, or perhaps it was fear or ... No, the direction was not a problem. If the sun had passed its zenith, it must have passed over our heads. That meant we should not turn our backs on it but walk towards it. But I wasn't quite sure. One of the little boys had started to cry. I couldn't let them see my own uncertainty. So I gaily took each of them by the hand, struck out in the direction of the sun and got them all to sing a song. Much later we stumbled along in a line without singing. Of course, to the very end I took care not to let them see my own anxiety. Not even in the middle of the night when the men had found us and took the howling children in their arms. I did not need anyone. It was the sun's fault and the fact that it was not possible to figure out its path. I was not given any supper because I had not behaved responsibly. Moreover, the children really had been too slow and weepy. That was just another of my failings. It was a shame that it had to be my grand-parents who until then had always treated me as something special ...

There were other events, too, which come to mind in connection with the subject of responsibility. They are all associated with a dim sense of my irresponsibility, my inadequacy and of a growing feeling of resentment that my character was deficient in crucial ways. I was a failure. It was not until the run-up to my school-leaving examination that I first began to consider the matter from a theoretical standpoint. We had been set a German essay topic on a statement by Albert Schweitzer to the effect that the invention of the atomic bomb made it necessary for all of us to become more conscious of our responsibility as individuals and to act accordingly in our everyday lives. Given the overwhelming display of state power which the bomb represented, and given the fact that only a handful of politicians, at most, could possibly feel that they were called on to make individual judgements, I felt outraged at being required to make a personal response as if I had any actual influence on such matters. The whole issue seemed blasphemous and obscurantist. It transformed my feeling of impotence in the face of an existential threat into a question of personal guilt. The essay I wrote became a contribution to the history of my personal failure, and I tried to forget it.

I became responsible for my life, and then for the well-being of my husband and daughter, for the household and the family, without ever having confronted them as critically as I had done in the case of the outrageous demands of Albert Schweitzer and Western governments. From the point of view of social expectations I failed as a housewife and mother when I took up a profession which kept me away from home for days on end. I failed as a housewife too when I shut myself up in a room to prepare for my exams, and neglected my responsibilities for the household as a whole. This practical responsibility, or rather these multiple responsibilities, generated insoluble dilemmas and feelings of insecurity which I responded to in a female manner; that is to say, I tried to retreat into illness – a highly irresponsible attitude towards my own body. Only much later did my theoretical doubts surface once more, and this time, too, it was in connection with politics.

In 1980 I had written a talk called 'Victims or Culprits?' for the first Berlin People's University, which attempted to tackle the relationship between masochism and responsibility.[1] In it I questioned the thesis, which was popular at the time and which is still widely accepted in a slightly modified form, that women generally possess the status of victims. In opposition to this I argued that women's oppression could only last as long as women actively worked to maintain it. Even the process of self-sacrifice could be decoded as an action. Since I was speaking at a People's University event, I tried to make my talk accessible to a non-specialist audience. In the process I came across a number of jokes against women, including the following one from the transport workers' union magazine, which evoked painful echoes in me. A man and a woman are sitting in a meadow in the blazing sunshine, next to them a picnic basket and the inevitable portable radio. Both of them are extremely out of sorts, and she says to him: 'I told you to forget about the news on a beautiful day like this. But no, you never listen to me, and now you have ruined the whole afternoon because you have to sit there and think about overkill.'

While I still felt that my indignation about Albert Schweitzer was completely justified, I realized at this point that I had conflicting feelings about the joke. I knew that the masculine reaction was the right one. After all, it meant that the man was interested in humankind and its survival, whereas the woman wanted to enjoy a peaceful afternoon by cheating, that is to say, by repressing important information. His moral justification was underlined by her naïvety. Her stupidity was exposed by his desire for knowledge. I found no difficulty in identifying with this man against this woman, all the more so since I too would not have listened to the news during a picnic, anymore than I would have let the idea of overkill spoil the afternoon. But I was no longer eighteen and had been active in political groups for a long time – so I knew what feelings I was supposed to have. Reflecting on this contradiction between my feelings which approved of the glorious afternoon and my knowledge of what constituted appropriate political behaviour, it dawned on me that the joke made an obvious assumption which at the same time guarantees its comprehensibility. This was the realization that it was not just a specific woman who shows herself to be too un-imaginative to appreciate matters which concern the survival of the human race. It was women in general. And the reason for this is that it is their responsibility to ensure that the afternoon should be beautiful and enjoyable, that the food should be tasty and the man should be able to put aside his tragic cares for a short time. It is up to her to provide for immediate survival: for the transformation of his wages into things that serve the needs of living, what might be called the 'culture of life'. She has to devote everything she has to this task – including her own body. So if the man listens to the news on an afternoon off, this does not point to her ignorant belief that the world can be rid of over-kill simply by her pretence that it doesn't exist – after all, his knowledge does not eliminate it either. Her failure is that he should have switched on the radio in the first place. It means that she was unable to make him concentrate entirely on her. But that was her duty, since otherwise he will not recover from the stresses of the world of work.

This scene had led me to accept all sorts of assumptions whose dubious nature I should have long since perceived. My uncritical common sense led me to believe that of course it was men who bore the responsibility for the conduct of society as a whole, for government, knowledge and for public affairs in general. In contrast women were concerned with the sphere of the home, of private life. Their responsi-bility was the limited realm of pleasure. In order to make a study of the obstacles which such a scheme presented to women who wished to become politically active, we set up a project on women and responsibility in a women's seminar in Hamburg. We started, quite deliberately, with our own experience. We wrote stories derived from our daily lives. Many of these stories turned out to be surprising in their combination of the expected and the unexpected, of what we knew already and what we had forgotten. Our aim was to produce contributions with the title, 'How I Once Felt Responsible', in the conviction that these would enable us to work out how each of us understood and constructed the idea of responsibility for ourselves, to discover its meaning and to uncover its components, connections, constituents. Here is an example of the stories that were written in this way. Perhaps it will provide a further insight into the topic of 'women's responsibility'.

It was Wednesday or Thursday – two or three days to the Saturday morning shopping expedition for the whole commune – and there were already great gaps in the supplies in the fridge. The cold meat and cheese were almost all gone, a solitary slice was all that was left in the bread-bin, and only one tin of catfood remained. It was evident that they could not last out until the weekend. She felt the anger welling up inside her; she had frequently gone out shopping in recent weeks, whereas Anita and Werner apparently did not care whether they were well stocked up. If necessary they just went out to eat ... Martina had no time today, but at weekends she had done a lot of cleaning, as she frequently did, and she had already promised to clean the bathroom the coming weekend. Martina was not the target of her fury, since Martina regularly did housework in the commune and also thought about the need to organize duty rosters in advance and to reach agreement about them. Anita and Werner, on the other hand, always had to be reminded that something had to be done. This was the position at the moment. They never thought about the need to plan the shopping. Werner worked very hard. He was out of the house from seven o'clock until around eight in the evening, and usually had to work on Saturday morning as well. What annoyed her about him was that he did not do anything in the house even when he was free – though she could see that he did not have much free time. She was particularly irritated by Anita, who was convinced that she and Martina would take such a grim view of everything. But she did have more time now that she had given up her job.

Her ideal was that everyone would regularly do the chores. Perhaps they disliked some jobs more than others, but it should be possible to arrange matters to suit them all. Even if one or another person was unable to do the shopping, it would be wonderful, if only he or she were willing to cook a meal from time to time, or do something out of the ordinary, like going out to buy the rolls on Sunday, or helping out when someone else couldn't spare the time. She would then really be able to feel at home and relax and it wouldn't be up to her to think of everything all the time. She would sometimes be able to enjoy the feeling that other people were looking after her for a change. She would be particularly grateful not to have to do the housework when she was very busy working for her seminars and study groups.

It annoyed her that she even had to come to terms with her irritation at the collapse of the household routine, instead of using her energies for her other obligations. She could remember how much she had enjoyed it in the commune to begin with. Then everyone had joined in, a meal was ready when she came home and she could enjoy the feeling of being cared for. This was quite different from the time when she lived with her boyfriend.

She went out to do the shopping ...

Our astonishment at the banality of the story turned to curiosity about its construction. Our first question was: What view does the writer give us of responsible feeling or action? After some hesitation we came up with the answer: she goes shopping for the commune. Of course, it was hardly necessary to write a story to prove that point. We all knew that shopping for the commune is a common responsibility. But the writer describes it at length, with much passion and many details. Behind the first answer we discerned a second one: She had to feel responsible because the others failed to do so. So the true subject of the story was the irresponsibility of the members of the commune who made living in it unbearable. Responsibility manifests itself as an irksome compensation for the faults of others. This stands in sharp contrast to the lofty feelings commonly associated with responsibility in Sunday sermons. The writer teaches us that responsibility is closely linked with resentment in our thoughts and feelings ('It's always up to me, because the others are too lazy'), with duties, discussions, organization, planning, arrangements and, above all, with work. The answer to our question about the connotations of responsibility is that the hard taskmasters (duty, organization, and so on) make sure that I must feel responsible. My sense of responsibility comes into play when a gap in the system becomes manifest. It is therefore a kind of emergency measure. If everyone 'performs their tasks regularly', no one has to feel responsible. This leads to our first conclusion that *individual responsibility always appears when general rules stop working. And also, individual responsibility is unthinkable in the absence of other people's irresponsibility.*

The writer suggests two further connections: work and pleasure. Oddly enough, work is not on the same side as responsibility, but is opposed to it. A person who works hard does not need to carry so much responsibility. She writes several times that because she works it is unfair to give her too much responsibility. Alternatively, whoever does not work should bear the responsibility. Hence there is an emotionally experienced division of labour. This is not the simple division into working for money and housework. Behind this familiar distinction, according to which housework should be done by those who do less work outside the home, we see a different idea. The fact that work is done outside the home calls for an organizational solution to the problems of recreation, enjoyment and relaxation. Where this is lacking these aspects of life fall into the realm of 'care', 'anxiety' and hence of a woman's responsibility reluctantly accepted. We arrive at the conclusion that *female responsibility is a mistake, a social deprivation which points to a general disorder in society. What is being neglected here are the basic elements of physical well-being. This disorder consumes human energies.*

Finally, we tried to discover what explanations the author gives for what she perceives as the misfortune that women's responsibility continually reproduces itself. We found three explanations. First, *necessity* ('There is not enough food in the house'); second, *anger* (she constantly reiterates how the behaviour of the others irritates her); and third, *anger about her own anger.* She shows graphically how petty-minded calculations, irritation and non-caring behaviour combine to destroy their communal life, and also that her own anger is itself a source of irritation. We are driven to the conclusion that *the approval of one's own personality and its associated feelings, the desire for living together with others in an enjoyable way and, third, necessity, are three forces which result in the production of a female responsibility which is felt to be undesirable.* This conclusion points to a contradiction in the construction of femininity and a woman's responsibility. We may tentatively formulate this contradiction by saying that the approval of one's own personality and its associated feelings depends on actions which the self feels to be wrong. Thus the story yields three curious findings: that the reproduction of responsibility is rooted in the contradictions of the personality; that (as in the first scene) responsibility is a negative phenomenon; and that women are conscious that their sense of responsibility is based on a disordered society.

I want to pause at this point. To gain a different perspective on the problem, I looked up Freud. Whenever I do this, I discover to my astonishment how little he has to say about the psychological problems that preoccupy me. Responsibility is a subject that he scarcely mentions at all. In one of the few places it occurs he discusses it in connection with dreams. The question that agitates him is whether we are responsible for our immoral dreams. By immoral he understands sexual fantasies which violate the taboo on incest and, following a heterosexual train of thought, include father and brothers in the case of girls, and mother and sisters in the case of boys. This question was much discussed at the turn of the century. Freud gives an account of the vehement disagreements between those who would exonerate us entirely and those who would hold us responsible. Like Solomon, he wisely takes Plato's view and asserts that it is better to commit such shameful actions in our dreams than to do so in our waking hours. The anger and frustration which I felt at such a conclusion was not caused merely by this obsession with sex. I also felt impatient because he had failed to exploit to the full the cognitive apparatus he had developed. Having correctly perceived contradictions between the different dimensions of our personalities, contradictions which emerge in the discrepancies between our claims to morality and our own actions, he deflects them into an alleged conflict between our drives and our moral sense. What gets lost *en route* is not, as I had first supposed, the possibility of unmasking morality as the creation of a dominant ideology, but the perception that opposition to morality can be motivated by factors other than sexual drive or the desires of the id. It is not, it seems to me, the claims of civil society that force us into a compromise with pleasure and sexuality, with the demands of instinctual drives and their gratification. There is something elegiac and seductive about the idea that our society requires us to experience a certain melancholy, but it seems far too spineless as an explanation of the problems of women's responsibility.

Instead, my feeling is that the dominant ideology, of which the sense of responsibility is an integral part, does more than just bring morality into conflict with sexual and other drives. In the last analysis both these polar opposites are frustrated – both the pleasures of instinctual life and the possibility of following the demands of morality. Let us, then, leave the realm of Freudian sexuality and return to the question of women's responsibility in our society. Obviously women are responsible for their own sexuality, but their responsibility for the immediate well-being of their husbands and children is no less essential. The concept starts to become a little fuzzy at this point. It is stimulating to seek assistance from other disciplines, but it is also destabilizing.

According to the philosopher Hans Jonas, the principle of responsibility means restricting our actions to those whose consequences are foreseeable. This choice of words is ambiguous, particularly for women. At first glance what he says seems self-evident, but on second thoughts it narrows things down too much. It is this restriction to the foreseeable consequences which makes responsibility such an unbearable torture for women. It may be true enough that all a woman's responsibilities can be reduced to tasks in the private sphere. But the concept of the private conceals, admittedly in an increasingly threadbare fashion, the fact that she has no real control of the means whereby she is to carry out her responsibilities. How women furnish the home, feed and clothe the family, what education or what involvement in the world outside the home is open to them – these are all matters that depend on her income. Or as Brecht neatly put it: 'The decision about how much meat is to be put in the soup is not made in the kitchen.' We can go even further. Revelations about the pollution of food and the atmosphere and, not least, the above-mentioned threat of nuclear war, make it clear that these are areas where women should assume responsibility, even though they have absolutely no control over the causes of the problem. The virtues which they are called upon to display are really matters for the community as a whole and its regulation. Whenever they attempt to intervene in such matters, to assume responsibility, they either fail or deceive themselves. They thus become guilty. Their personal valour consists in living with this guilt as long as possible; their escape route, illness. So they live as a kind of individual problem in a world which does not function, charged with the duty of making a decent home as a barrier to the disorder prevailing in society. In contrast to Freud's assumptions the attempt to intervene would not just lead to chaos and destabilization; it could also be the basis of liberated action.

Recently, women members of the Green Party have attempted to formulate the concept of political responsibility so as to combine the questions of women's ordinary everyday lives with larger political issues. The point of such a strategy is to improve the opportunities of the next generation.[2] This extension of women's responsibilities seems to me to be the only way to escape from the trap of individual failure and guilt feelings and at the same time to bring about real changes in society. This means that we are not talking about two neatly segregated responsibilities. Our task must not be simply to reject the responsibility foisted on to us, by going on strike, for example (as has been proposed in the women's movement). Instead we must accept such demands and take them further, beyond the limits of the 'foreseeable'. We must restate them as challenges to the established social authorities and seek to gain our point through collective struggle. It goes without saying that we must also extend such responsibilities to cover all the members of society. In this respect women nowadays occupy a key position in society.

Do these reflections really have any bearing on the question of female masochism or with what manifests itself as such? Women are positioned at the meeting point of individual lives and the exorbitant claims of society, and acquiesce without flinching. They would rather be torn apart than give up or enlarge this unreasonable responsibility. They experience this state of being torn apart as personal guilt. They take this guilt upon themselves. The humanity which thereby enters their actions covers up the inhumanity of society at large. Thus women contribute to the reproduction of their own necessary being as these particular women, and in so doing they assist in the very process that tears them apart. Alongside the myth of women's masochism, a myth which anchors in women's nature what really belongs in the structure of society, we witness the emergence of a universal hypocrisy. On the one hand, women embody qualities of goodness, humanity, warmth and the pleasures of life, the qualities which make living worthwhile. On the other hand, they can be blamed whenever anything goes wrong. There are too many examples to cite them all. They can be accused of neglecting their children, of their children's poor performance in school, drug-taking, lack of cleanliness, poor nourishment, ill-health, and even of moral failings within a context of general immorality. It is always women who have done something wrong, whether as mothers, in the family, in education, as lovers, and so on. Their masochism simply describes their efforts to accept this situation, and the fairy tale which transforms such efforts into an essential quality of women is intended to have the function of reassuring us that defects in society can be resolved in women's characters.

Love is one of the crucial factors in this structure, and with it there is the circumstance that in our market-orientated society a large proportion of women are unable to reproduce themselves in terms of the dominant currency. Where everything is exchanged for money, they earn none, or at least less than they need to live. This makes their situation as incalculable and as unconfined as love itself. They feel they always give too little, and sense that they are neither loved nor themselves sufficiently loving to enable them to perform the Herculean tasks of maintaining the social order, tasks which they are expected to carry out within the bosom of the family, that illusion of communal life. Of course, this too is experienced as character weakness and guilt. Women are always willing to redouble their efforts to make up for a flagging love.

Does such an analysis apply only to women, and not to men too, who stand on the other side of that social divide which we term the separation of public and private? I should not wish to assert that the masculine side of this dilemma represents a solution for us, anymore than the feminine one does. But it is absolutely essential not to overlook the element of power in the relations between the sexes, and not to bow to that consensus which has dominated ever since Rita Süssmuth's attempted reforms according to which both sexes should be regarded as equally one-sided gender stereotypes.[3] Even the system of rewards which society makes available to men shows that they can at least deceive themselves into believing that they can control their own lives. The social hierarchy provides men with goals which appear attainable and realistic. The peace which women generate amidst the unrealistic demands that they should individually create happiness, life and a living culture is identical with that very combination of guilt and masochism which is often intensified to the point of self-destruction.

The question of women's masochism led us from the problem of responsibility to that of the demands society makes on women. I have tried to show that women's acceptance of being torn apart by demands they cannot satisfy leads to a stance we may call masochistic. If the attempt is then made to locate the source of this stance in women's inner being, the point of rupture is then shifted – as I have shown with reference to Freud – to the interface between society and individual in general, instead of assigning the blame to specific social formations.

I should like now to go one step further and to conclude with a look at the value of such an account of the relationship between men and women for the reproduction of society as a whole. It then turns out that what has been asserted over and over again and with increasing stridency ever since the emergence of the women's movement some twenty years ago is by no means the whole truth. I am referring to the claim that the work which women do quietly and unobtrusively as individuals makes a fundamental contribution to society and as such deserves to be acknowledged, to be taken seriously and to be revalorized. We have to supplement this account with the observation that the insignificance of individuals in our society makes the sexes experience each other as mutually inadequate. The aspects of life for which women are directly responsible are marginalized by the masculine spheres of production and administration. Simultaneously, activities in the socially favoured parts of society are alienated so that the hopes for the quality of life are likewise displaced to the margins. This explains why women are not only exposed to unreasonable demands but also expected to embody the hopes of a better life, while they themselves are oppressed. All this should be overturned and a new order introduced. That is why in my view we must make efforts to free ourselves from the myth as well as the reality of women's masochism and bring some movement into a social set-up immobilized by the relations between the sexes.

Notes

1. See this volume, pp. 3–12.
2. See, for example, Waltraud Schoppe's article in *Liberal* 3, 1987, p. 61.
3. Rita Süssmuth was the West German Minister for Family Affairs in the Kohl government until December 1988, when she became President of the *Bundestag* – *translator's note*.

PART TWO

Work

SIX

Being at Home in Your Work

The current criticism of the meaning of work for sociological and feminist theory, as well as for social practice, is something that arouses a sense of insecurity in me. For ever since I was a small child, I have thought of work more or less as the magic centre of life.

A Working Biography

It began with fetching the milk from the farmer. My sister, who was two years older than me, was allowed to fetch it. I wasn't. Fetching the milk was work. I had visions of a great adventure full of meaning and importance. I would have to get up half an hour earlier, because I had my task in front of me. I would have to walk a long distance on my own, passing some geese I was afraid of on the way. I would bring the milk home; it was needed and tasted good. I would neither lose my way, nor would I spill any, nor dawdle too long. All this would make me much older than my brother, who was two years younger than me. Fetching the milk – the words conveyed excitement, independence, a sense of the great, wide world and a feeling of insecurity which I could not do without. At last! My exaltation lasted for a few weeks. I discovered short cuts which presented me with other dangers. If I took a different route through a field, I could avoid the geese which stretched their necks and honked at me. But to do this I had to run lest the farmer caught me with his stick. As I clambered over stiles I often spilt some of the milk, but I arrived home five minutes earlier. If I fell down, dirt would get into the milk. Gradually, fetching the milk became an irksome task which I tried to get rid of with as much zeal as I had once displayed in acquiring it. Fortunately, my brother had the same ambition for greatness as I had formerly possessed. I was able to pass the chore on to him. But fetching the milk was just the beginning. I was now of an age when I could take on other household duties. My disappointment about the milk spurred me to look for ways of evading them. I was nowhere to be found when washing-up time came round. At the approach of spring-cleaning I turned out to be unwell. In short, all my energies were directed towards the avoidance of work. At school I developed rationalization strategies. I organized every subject so that I could slip through without work. If my marks began to slide down into the danger zone I became inconsolable, for it meant I had to work. My homework was strictly confined to the train and to the breaks, so that all my 'free' time was available for reading, daydreaming and wandering through the woods. Here, however, there was a lot of hard work, for we had to build huts. We dug trenches and even cut down trees and wove twigs.

During this period I was given the nickname 'the snail', because I had discovered that household chores tended to disappear, if I set about them so slowly and reluctantly that someone else ended up doing them. My entire life was now determined by work, or rather its avoidance. My sense of morality was undermined by it, since I frequently had to tell lies in order to get out of working.

My first experience with the milk was repeated when I went to university. I was in despair because almost nothing happened for the first two weeks. I then threw myself into the excitement of learning. I attended twenty lectures and seminars, and took on seven seminar papers in my first term. I would go to the university at eight in the morning and not leave again before ten at night, when I would go swimming or dancing and become involved in endless discussions. I lived on chocolate. I was in a state of permanent excitement. In the terms that followed I made only minor adjustments to my timetable. A more critical approach led me to abandon some classes and this gave me more time for the library. Only twice did I modify my way of life. On one occasion I was too much in love to spend time at the university at all; on another I became too involved in political meetings and demonstrations to continue attending classes in the history department, which at that time was still unaffected by the political events. The only disruption to my studies was caused by the need to earn money, and this proved soluble in my third semester when I obtained one of the much sought-after teaching assistant's jobs. If only everything could have stayed like this!

After my tenth semester questions about the need to finish my studies began to become more pressing. Many students who had begun their studies when I did were either taking their examinations or had left the university without a degree. The mere thought of a dissertation made me feel ill. I wrote more and more seminar papers so as to avoid thinking about the one big seminar paper. Then suddenly, in an otherwise boring lecture, I heard something exciting. In the early days of the Soviet Union there had been special 'work groups' in which large numbers of people volunteered to spend their Saturdays working for no pay to help in the construction of society. They were called *subbotniks*. Lenin himself took part in them – even he, whom I pictured as working day and night, writing, thinking and making stirring speeches, constantly overworked and exhausted. The lethargy induced by the approaching examinations was now pushed to one side by my memories of my initial pleasure in fetching the milk and building huts when I was at school, and the long years at university. In my mind I now saw a whole nation joined together, sharing in the same enthusiasm at being united and alive in their work.

Work, I had first imagined, is what creates happiness in life. But also: work is boredom, toil, even misery. It takes the place of life – these were the experiences and lessons of my schooldays above all. It remained as a thorn in my flesh. Work, I now felt once more, is the future and it is real and actual today.

A bold leap of the imagination led me to associate the laboriousness of work with the development of theory from Aristotle to Hegel, and its pleasurable nature with the *subbotniks* and Marxist theory. My dissertation subject would fill this framework. It did not fail through lack of effort. I can still see before me, in silent reproach, the rows of books which smothered not only the flame kindled by the *subbotniks*, but also my enthusiasm and with it my ability to finish the work. 'Teaching people to enjoy work' – that was the tenor of the writings coming out of the Soviet Union and the GDR, writings which I had opened with so much hope. All that remained was the musty smell of the classroom at school, the spirit of the chores which I had successfully avoided in childhood. A morality had to be installed. What was assumed to be an innate laziness would be replaced by an education into the appreciation of work. Discipline, obedience, order, would take the place of the joyous, creative, new, vital enthusiasm. To be a useful member of society – that had ceased to be a mystery, a new start, pleasure and togetherness. It was an individual duty, demanded by teachers who wrote about it as listlessly as their pupils apparently reacted to it – if the books were to be believed. The spring storm of living desire had been transformed into the icy wind of duty. The joy of being human had degenerated into the misery of an inmate in an approved school. I gave up. I pushed my dissertation to one side. Its place was taken by the birth of a daughter.

I was driven back to the university by a feeling of restlessness. Eight years later I found the Project on Automation and Qualifications (see PAQ, 1987). Behind the screen provided by this rather sober title I sought once again to uncover the secret of my fetching the milk. Would it not be possible for technological progress to free work from its burdensome nature, from monotony and stupidity? Couldn't workers at long last begin to experience their activities like human beings, creatively and with pleasure? Could work nowadays be structured in such a way that lifelong learning became the norm? Would co-operation lead to mutual encouragement? Would not imagination become a necessity? And would not such a technology necessarily be retrieved from the realm of private profit and rescued for society as a whole? Admittedly, we did not imagine that this would happen as the harmonious and automatic consequence of developments in the means of production. We agreed with Marx on this point and envisaged that such conflicts between the forces and relations of production would take the form of a catastrophe, of questions of life and death.

We attempted to formulate the image of men and women who learn while they work, and who, when they work, work mainly with their heads. We were in search of the 'universally developed individual' and we looked for signs that this individual was appearing in the here and now. Inadvertently we pictured the workers of the future as academics – actually, as participants in our own project. Unlike us, however, they had no bodies – at least not for working with. But this one-sided view of humankind also seemed to point us in a direction in which the culture of bodies became a social action and took the place of the simple using up of labour power. Klaus Holzkamp was a kind of honorary member of our project. We called him the Eddi Merx [sic] of psychology, after the well-known champion cyclist of the day – a name which seemed to point both to the Marxian tradition and to the indefatigable energy which he devoted to the laborious construction of the edifice of critical psychology. Paradoxically, we had chosen an image for this intellectual work which was the very embodiment of measurable, physical labour maintained to the point of absolute exhaustion. This seemed the only appropriate image with which to convey this transformation of vital energy into the energy of change. At that time we intended no hint of criticism. Perhaps it is necessary to experience such a voluntary transformation of lived time into working time in order ultimately to question – as Klaus did in his *Foundations of Psychology* (1984) – this message of the identity of social reproduction and the reproduction of individuals. Even though individuals must re-create society by ensuring their own survival, society still survives when people forget themselves too little, and finally fall sick and die. And society survives even if individuals live parasitically. A culture of individual life is essential precisely because man is a social being.

What is the role of work in psychology in general and in critical psychology in particular? The first part of the question is easily answered. In the various branches of traditional psychology work has no place at all unless its absence in practice – in the form of unemployment – can be cited as the cause of psychic disturbance. In addition, there is the specialized field of the psychology of work – its domain is that of the psycho-physical effects of the use of the human senses, muscles and nerves. But to conceive of work as a specific human activity and hence as a fundamental aspect of every theory of subjectivity – that is the task of critical psychology.

Given this view of the matter, we felt as happy as fishes in water with our automation project in the psychology department. Our hopes that a more human development would result from the emergence of automated labour were reinforced by the concept of 'productive needs', as formulated by Ute Holzkamp-Osterkamp (1975, p. 76). Isn't the wish to act, to give shape to things and change them, to appropriate the world and make it habitable for all, an essential part of human nature? Our unbroken optimism on this score dates back to the time when the announcement of environmental catastrophes had not yet begun to demonstrate almost daily that mankind seems to have made it its goal to render the world uninhabitable. Nevertheless present conditions only make it a more urgent task than ever to create a human race that has the conservation and the peace of the world and the free development of individual capacities at the top of its agenda.

'Productive life, however, is species-life. It is the life-producing life. The whole character of a species, its species-character, resides in the nature of its life activity, and free, conscious activity constitutes the species-character of man' (Karl Marx, *Early Writings*, p. 328). These words of the young Marx seemed to express our very being. We felt unanimous about critical psychology and well equipped for our automation project.

In Ute Holzkamp-Osterkamp's scheme the 'productive needs' include the desire to control the conditions of life in society as a whole. This can be taken to include the protest against the determination of the relations of production by alien goals. The idea that the desire for productive activity could be deemed an innate part of humankind gave a direct boost to psychologists active in social work and education. They transferred the concept without much ado into the real world of nurseries and schools. What emerged was a new idea of 'teaching children to enjoy work'. The inhuman straitjacket created by the musty books from my old dissertation was loosened by the warm enthusiasm of these new educators. The firm grip remained, however. In vain did we strive to revive this new concept at the level of theory. It was far too tempting to use the new critical psychology not just to legitimate the old educational ideals of diligence, discipline, order, and so on, but to imbue them with the spirit of revolution.

In the research project on automation we knew of course that the concept of 'productive needs' was not susceptible to direct empirical application. But could we not discern 'approaches' to them, to the 'motive forces' underlying them and the 'forms' they might assume here and now? To put it in a nutshell, the insoluble problem we were battling with was this: the idea that humankind has an inherent need for productivity, and indeed the idea that we realize our humanity only through our productivity, narrowed our gaze to the point where the only aspects of individual development which we considered were those which concerned the ability to produce – in thought, planning, and in will and capacity. And we did this despite our better knowledge of human beings' social nature. Questions about co-operation had to be tacked on as extras. The impact of alien social influences was considered only as a negative framework which restricted the encroachments of individual desire, not itself a form which governed thought and action.

Thus individuals were reduced in our eyes to consciously active beings. But not only did their consciousness revolve entirely around work; work had devoured their entire existence.

How relieved we were when Klaus Holzkamp in the *Foundations* (1984) not only did away with 'productive needs' as a central category (or rather replaced it with the phrase 'the productive aspect of human needs' [p. 242]), but even ventured to lay hands on the main culprit: Marx's conception of work. Without much fuss the chief authority underlying the many books which wanted to teach people to love work was eliminated from a socialist perspective, together with that historically contaminated sentence about 'work as the primary need of life':

The primary need of life is not 'work' as such, but 'work' only to the extent that it allows the individual to participate in and to control the social process, in short, only to the extent that it makes us 'capable of action'. Therefore our primary need is not 'work', but 'the capacity for action'. The reason for this is that the capacity for action provides the broadest frame of reference for a human and humane existence, and the incapacity for action is the broadest possible term for the human misery which comes from being at the mercy of social relations, fear, unfreedom and debasement.

Holzkamp, 1984, p. 243

Did this put an end, once and for all, to the threat of work-education camps, the joyous process of subjugation in nursery school, the paralysing effects of school, the puritan ethic and the spirit of capitalism, the God who works?

At all events, the concept of capacity for action implies a reference to social relations. Moreover, it is a concept which has the advantage of flexibility. There are degrees of the capacity for action. Were there also degrees of work? Work could degenerate into productivism for its own sake; its social dimension was in danger of being lost. The concept of the capacity for action, on the other hand, brings to mind the struggle for balance, a dynamic that leads to ever-greater capacities for action, the acquisition of these capacities and the control of the conditions which enfold both. Yes indeed, this is without a doubt the primary human need.

Our satisfaction about this turn of events was diminished by too much applause.

To begin with there were the numerous voices from the women's movement. The Marxian concept of work is useless as far as women's liberation is concerned. Even worse, it was expressly devised in order to hide women's work from view. For Marx work is a masculine activity, interference with nature to the point of destruction, production for its own sake, development of technology right up to the atomic bomb, the domination of life by intellect and rationality. The liberation of work from the capitalist conditions of compulsion was conceived as the liberation of the male worker, not the housewife. Can the concept of 'the capacity for action' help us to overcome these problems? We may agree that it creates a space in which to articulate the oppression and liberation of women. It is a practical concept, usable here and now, and it has been rescued from the infinite expanses of Marx's early utopianism and placed in the context of what can actually be achieved. But has it really salvaged what was originally desired?

When I was 'out of work' some years ago, there was a furious debate in the seminar of critical psychologists about my claim that my work made me an integral part of society. The work I was referring to included my political activities, my numerous commitments both at home and in the editor's office and the publishing activities of the journal *Das Argument*. Obviously, no one was so crass as to wish to limit the idea of work simply to 'paid work'. But it was clear nevertheless that social recognition and being part of the social process was an essential factor in one's human status. Above all, it was held that every change in conditions had to come from within, from the productive sector, and not from marginal groups – the unemployed, housewives or subcultures of every kind. The debate became so heated that some were prepared to deny that the unemployed are capable of human development.

At that time – it was the latter half of the seventies – the phenomenon of unemployment was less widespread than at present. Nowadays, when we can look forward to a steady decline in 'productive work' (work in the productive sector) to 10 per cent of the whole by the end of the century, as well as a structural unemployment which grows annually, the sociologists are confronted with the challenge of rethinking the relationship between work and living. This trend does not stop short at the threshold of critical psychology. The latter had collected around itself over the years a number of critical spirits who were minded to use unemployment as a pretext for creating a happy synthesis of psychology and social criticism. The very title of the Second Congress of Critical Psychologists, 'Work and Unemployment from the Viewpoint of Critical Psychology' (1979) was characteristic of its day. The positions taken up at the Congress ranged from the claim that unemployment led to psychological immiseration to the opposite assertion: that freedom from the constraints of work determined by others would result in an unimaginable liberation of creative energies.

In his seminal contribution to the question of unemployment Klaus Holzkamp (1986) was able to apply his concept of 'capacity for action' to create a 'psychological' analysis of people's experience with the aid of the category of 'subjective motives'. In the course of his discussion unemployment becomes just one determining factor among others. The way in which unemployment is dealt with only becomes a topic of interest to psychologists when the unemployed do not know how to gain a purchase on their personal experiences. So the object of scrutiny, as far as psychologists are concerned, is neither work nor unemployment, but only the way in which individuals experience their unemployment. Looked at in this way, work is not just the form of social activity which confers social integration; it is also a field of meanings and hence the object of ideological conflicts and of research into ideology.

This completes a shift in the focus of psychology from the view that work is the defining characteristic of humankind, a primary need, to the view that individual experiences, and hence the change from an 'immediate' relationship to reality to a 'less immediate one', should be regarded as the framework for the individual's capacity for action. This provides a solution to the problem of the normative approach to dealing with people, and refutes the idea of 'teaching them to love work'. Changes become something to be achieved within the framework of what is possible. But what has become of the hopes which stood at the cradle of those ossified concepts of development through work? What did we sacrifice when we abandoned the identity of individual development and work in favour of situating a secure job or unemployment within a general economic and political framework, while investing work with an ideological affirmation which then helps to determine the experiences of individuals? Does this mean in the last analysis that our initial longing for the right to develop one's personality, pleasure and creativity, curiosity, effort and competitiveness also belongs by rights in the realm of ideology?

Marx and Work

It is not just the *Frankfurter Allgemeine Zeitung* and the employers' organizations that have fixed on work as a battlefield of conflicting ideological meanings. The changing value placed on work has also shaken the social sciences, sociology above all. The problem is how to lessen the social importance of work in the eyes of the individual. This permits a greater degree of psychic stability in the face of unemployment, and a less extreme marginalization of people who have no work, when work has anyway become less central than, say, the family. Organizations such as INFAS, which conduct research into public opinion, regularly provide the public with the latest information about the decline of the value of work for the individual members of society – especially its younger members. Society is prudently changing its attitudes. As less labour power is required industrially, workers respond by relinquishing their desire for work. They shed their Protestant 'work-skin' and develop inclinations which do not always exceed the limits imposed by dole money. For example, they experience a need for communication, for friendship and intimacy, neighbourliness and voluntary activities such as looking after the aged or the handicapped. In a 'non-alienated' form – whether in leisure-time pursuits and hobbies or in alternative projects – they develop precisely the hopes that were expressed at the start of my discussion: 'self-activity', 'free activity', 'sensuous pleasure', 'abolition of the distortion of means and ends'. If we follow Dahrendorf's postulation of the 'end of a work-based society', we find that people today are already enjoying the abolition of alienated labour, that is to say, they have entered into the realm of communism without having undertaken a social revolution of any kind.

The 'transformation of work into free activity and the transformation of the earlier limited intercourse into the intercourse of individuals as such' (Karl Marx, *The German Ideology*, 1965, pp. 85–6) is something which according to Marx could only be introduced by a revolution. But it is precisely these categories with which sociologists – such as Habermas – wish to replace the concept of work: free activity and communicative action. Habermas speaks of 'the exhaustion of utopian energies', by which he is referring to projects which aim to free work from the control of others, that is to say, Marx and the labour movement. 'The potential for political stimulation of a utopia based on a working society' is exhausted; potential for resistance in his view is growing 'in consequence of the progressive bureaucratic erosion of communicatively structured life-worlds which have been released from their organic frameworks' (Habermas, 1985, pp. 141ff).

Habermas advises us to give up all hope of a revolutionary transformation of society through the agency of the working class. Nor should we put our trust in the welfare state with its policy of full employment to pacify class conflict. Resistance is to come from the new social movements. In other words, the basis for revolutionary ferment is to be found in people's way of life, not their manner of work. The thrust of Habermas's work is to replace the theory of revolution implicit in Marx's concept of work. But did Marx reduce his project of liberation to the abolition of alienated labour and the emancipation of (presumably male) workers? In other words, how should we interpret the new social movements and the liberation of ways of life in Marxian terms?

Holzkamp likewise refers to a concept of action (and the capacity for action). In his work, however, the centrality of a theory of revolution or social reform based on the labour movement is not questioned. 'Conscious action based on class-specific life conditions' is a fundamental element of his theory. But what role is given to free activity, pleasure and self-realization? In short, what is the role of hope, a quality which Habermas calls 'utopian strength'?

Made insecure by all these questions, I feel that it is time for us to reread Marx. The whole scene is one great battlefield. Different schools of thought appeal to Marx as an authority, while offering conflicting interpretations of his concept of work. They attack each other with assertions that Marx theorized the abolition of work, or conversely, that he wanted to establish its legitimacy in perpetuity. Work, it is alleged, stands in his view in the centre of the development of both the individual and humankind as a whole. It is the foundation stone of social theory and it is a mere synonym for domination and slavery. Those who speak thus have evidently read their Marx. Quotations from Marx adorn their writings like plucked feathers. If you place all their proofs side by side, the conclusion is inescapable that Marx changed his opinions like a weathervane. He has said everything about work, almost as if it didn't matter. How are we to proceed with Marx, if we are not to fall into the trap of interpreting him dogmatically and erecting a single quotation into a permanent edifice, which we would then defend as if it were an article of faith? Would it be any less arrogant to attempt to harmonize all the different interpretations? Or should we just accept that Marx is self-contradictory, that he changes his paradigms in accordance with modern fashion, or that he only proclaimed the truth in his early writings, becoming not wiser with age but more stupid?

In the philosophical tradition and in the more recent developments in political economy (Smith, Ricardo) Marx discovered a concept of work in a significantly controversial sphere. Work was the activity of the poor; it was laborious toil, it exhausted people's lives, indeed, for many it had replaced life. But work was also the source of wealth and of all values.

> But it is the interest of all rich nations, that the greatest part of the poor should never be idle, and yet continually spend what they get.... Those that get their living by their daily labour ... have nothing to stir them up to be serviceable but their wants which it is prudence to relieve, but folly to cure.... From what has been said, it is manifest, that, in a free nation, where slaves are not allowed of, the surest wealth consists in a multitude of the laborious poor.
>
> B. de Mandeville, *The Fable of the Bees*, pp. 212–13, 328; quoted here from Karl Marx, *Capital*, vol. I, p. 765

Work as the connecting link between poverty and wealth, as the contradictory foundation of both – Marx begins by elaborating on the position of work in this provocative contradiction. He sees it as a dimension of domination. According to Marx, 'In the political form of the emancipation of the workers is expressed the emancipation of society' because 'the whole of human servitude is involved in the relation of the worker to production, and all relations of servitude are nothing but modifications and consequences of this relation' (*Early Writings*, p. 333).

In his early writings we find a series of statements which in the language of the day define work as alienation. 'For in the first place labour, *life activity, productive life* itself appears to man only as a *means* for the satisfaction of a need, the need to preserve physical existence. But productive life is species-life. It is life-producing life' (*Ibid.*, p. 328). 'All human activity up to now has been labour, i.e. industry, self-estranged activity' (*Ibid.*, p. 354).

The idea that work is the form in which domination is expressed and by no means the 'primary need of life', leads to the logical conclusion that work itself should be abolished.

One of the greatest misunderstandings is to speak of free, social, human work, of work without private property. 'Work' is by its nature unfree, inhuman, unsocial, activity which is both controlled by private property and which creates it. The abolition of private property, therefore, only becomes reality when it is seen as the abolition of work.

Marx, 1845, p. 25

Finally, from the conception of history we have sketched we obtain these further conclusions: . . . In all revolutions up till now the mode of activity always remained unscathed and it was only a question of the distribution of this activity, a new distribution of labour to other persons, whilst the communist is directed against the preceding *mode* of activity, does away with *labour* . . .

The German Ideology, p. 87

I do not believe for a moment that Marx actually contemplated the abolition of work conceived as man's metabolic interchange with nature, that he promised eternal idleness or that he imagined that the abolition of industry was compatible with the survival of the race. But to think of work as a formal concept compels us to reconstruct what became deformed into the concept of work, and hence what 'substance' remains to be liberated. In its alienated form we find: the free expression of life; enjoyment of life; the activation of the human community; spontaneous, free activity; to know oneself confirmed in love (see *Early Writings*, pp. 277–8); the development of each individual to a whole person; the intercourse of individuals as such (*The German Ideology*, pp. 86–7); free, conscious life activity as species-life (see *Early Writings*, p. 329), and so on.

The emphasis is placed on 'free activity', or 'self-activity' – and this is always connected to the life of the species, as a species-specific characteristic. As species-beings people are active on one another's behalf; this determines their intercourse with one another, the community and their development as individuals. This free activity is a pleasure. Life itself is a pleasurable productive activity. Taking such statements as our starting point we could posit 'self-activity as the primary need of life'; we could conceive of the community as a productive framework; and we could also talk about the development of individuals through their own free activity – but we would never arrive at the modern defensive sociological reaction to the effect that work should no longer stand in the centre of social theory (as it allegedly did in Marx), but should be replaced by communication or way of life (lifeworld).

It is crystal-clear that Marx did not make a distinction between the life-world and the workaday world, or rather that he was concerned to revolutionize what nowadays is called our 'way of life'. He understood this to be the collectively enjoyable, active union of the individuals of a community. And he includes in this the forms of intercourse, love and life itself, although by life he means as always, active life. Our way of life is distorted by the relations of production, the ways in which people produce their material lives. To over-simplify they do this throughout the course of history, initially so that some can indulge in free activity while the others produce material existence (see also *The German Ideology*, pp. 84ff).

Self-activity as a perspective on liberation is related to the production of material life – this relationship is essential in order to be able even to conceive of the possibility of a life without domination. The production of material life passes through a number of stages –

one form is that of work. It is the most direct form of perversion, the 'negative form of self-activity' (*The German Ideology*, p. 84). Thus life becomes divided against itself. In this negative form Marx unfolds analytical categories which he retains later in *Capital.*

> Thus through *estranged, alienated* labour the worker creates the relationship of another man who is alien to labour and stands outside it, to that labour. The relation of the worker to labour creates the relation of the capitalist – or whatever other word one chooses for the master of labour – to that labour. *Private property* is therefore the product, result and necessary consequence of *alienated labour*, of the external relation of the worker to nature and to himself.
>
> *Early Writings*, pp. 331–2

We can already see here his later linguistic usage. In the later writings it is not work which is the formal concept; its place is taken by 'alienated labour'. About labour Marx has this to say:

> Labour, then, as the creator of use-values, as useful labour, is a condition of human existence which is independent of all forms of society; it is an eternal necessity which mediates the metabolism between man and nature, and therefore human life itself.
>
> *Capital*, vol. I, p. 133; and in almost identical words in
> *A Contribution to the Critique of Political Economy*, p. 36.

In its alienated form work is dual in nature. On the one hand, it is a producer of use-values, purposive and in that sense independent of social formations. On the other, it produces exchange-values and creates wealth. This it does only under certain social conditions. The distortions or alienations arising from this are thoroughly analysed in *Capital.* The insight into the dual nature of work is fundamental for capitalism as a form of society that produces commodities. But the production of material existence as a form of free activity – that remains the decisive point of view. It includes the idea of production without domination and hence the elimination of private property (the accumulation of exchange-values) as a regulative principle, as well as a reconciliation with nature which comes from understanding her laws.

The idea of 'free activity' is conceived as a process. At stake is the relationship between freedom and necessity. As an aspect of material production the bounds of necessity should be pushed back as far as possible in favour of free activity. In the realm of necessity work is a problem of distribution – everyone should perform an equal share of necessary labour. In the realm of freedom there is activity of a different kind, in which the traditional division of labour, and above all the division into mental and manual labour no longer holds good. The road from one to the other passes via the development of productive forces which will moderate the aspect of necessity in the production of material existence. And it passes likewise through the division of human labour, its alienation. Alienated labour has to be overcome by force in a process in which human beings finally take possession comprehensively of the productive forces they have themselves created. The entire relations of production have to be overturned, since these relations have distorted the human species to the point where all development, all wealth, culture and the actual conditions of work turn into objective realities that divide the workers and obtain power over them. This contradiction can only be resolved by a rupture.

In the *Critique of the Gotha Programme* Marx sketches the co-operative phase of society (social ownership of the means of production) which – precisely because it has emerged from capitalist society – bears the birthmarks of that society 'in every respect, economically, morally, intellectually'. He goes on to describe a more advanced 'communist society', a community which has overcome the distortions of labour, and it is only in this context that we encounter the phrase about 'work as the primary need of life'.

> ... when the enslaving subjugation of individuals to the division of labour, and thereby the antithesis between intellectual and physical labour, have disappeared; when labour is no longer just a means of keeping alive, but has itself become the primary need of life; when the all-round development of individuals has also increased their productive powers and all the springs of cooperative wealth flow more abundantly – only then can society wholly cross the narrow horizon of bourgeois right and inscribe on its banner: From each according to his abilities, to each according to his needs!
>
> *Critique of the Gotha Programme*, in *The First International and After*,
> p. 347 [translation altered]

These remarks have led to widespread misunderstandings. On Marx's authority individuals could be accused of a 'workshy' mentality and then 'educated' into people for whom 'work is the primary need of life'. Even worse, it was the final proclamation, 'to each according to his needs', that triggered both hopes and fears. Had Marx not expressed his yearning for a society in which needs were moulded by capitalism and superfluous production on the one hand, and by poverty on the other? And would not those needs become the standard by which society would be controlled? Nevertheless, the context makes his meaning unambiguously clear. If men and women succeed in liberating themselves from material want and domination, the production of material life will become a source of productive pleasure and an opportunity for people to develop their abilities. They will then be able to experience this primary need and to that extent they will realize their humanity. This would include the abolition of those divisions of labour which had turned the division of human labour into the foundation of social formations: the divisions into manual and mental labour, men's and women's labour, labour and non-labour. Let us apply these arguments to the question raised earlier on.

The Concept of Work

It is self-evident that when we are speaking of work we should take its formal character into account – something which is constantly overlooked. The failure to make distinctions when we talk and think about work is the source of the majority of misunderstandings. We speak about wage labour, imagine that it is the be-all and end-all of the matter and are critical of the talk about work as the primary need of life. And conversely, to educate people to this primary need is not only senseless; it is for the most part no more than educating people to accept wage labour in its various guises, an education which is indistinguishable from teaching them to submit to the discipline of industrial companies. When we speak of the 'substance', which in our society has assumed the form of paid work within the division of labour, we ought really to use the cumbersome phrase 'self-activation in the production of material existence'.

Work as a Systematic Concept?

The attempts, particularly those by Offe (1984) and Habermas (1985), to shift work away from the centre of social theory become more easily comprehensible, if we suppose that Marx had devised a social theory in the Hegelian mode in which Hegel's emphasis on the spirit was replaced by work. (See, for example, Rüddenklau, 1982, but also, with reference to Engels, Bischoff, 1973, p. 323: 'The development of the concept of work holds the key to the understanding of the entire history of society.') Marx, in contrast, wrote about the social relations in which self-activity assumes particular forms. He shows the impoverishment of individuals, their extreme alienation through work, their deformation into a state of negativity. The division of labour plays a crucial role in this. Within a system of domination such divisions become 'natural', they attach themselves to chance physical characteristics, that is to say, they become bound up with people their whole lives long, become an integral part of them so that even the consciousness of a 'free activity' disappears. A utopia based on work has lost its power over us, claims Habermas, it is our way of life that now becomes the centre of attention. In all Marx's writings it becomes clear that his central concern was with the revolutionizing of people's ways of life. Admittedly, these were determined by modes of production. If we put the ambiguous concept of work to one side and replace it with its 'substance', such farewells to Marx begin to sound as strange as they in fact are. According to such post-Marxism theories, our task would be to give a lower priority to the production of material life, or rather, life and the means of life, and that this would be the new foundation of social theory. Behind such post-Marxist positions lurks the question of whether human development and happiness can be made a real possibility, even though the production of material life is still confined within systems of domination. In that event liberation would be restricted to certain aspects of life. Such theories are intended as solutions to the difficulty of even imagining a revolution in our capitalist societies or of making a less class-ridden society a reality. The fact that new social movements with alternative projects do exist today seems to lend support to such sectoral solutions. However, the logical development of capitalist societies with their increasing tendency to move towards catastrophe on a universal scale is enough to destroy the illusion of a future worth having, unless we make the attempt to influence the framework within which such trends operate. In this connection it seems to me by no means an accident that the women's movement is usually listed as one of the relevant social movements, and is then promptly forgotten. For women's issues are not soluble without the abolition of all domination and the division of labour.

The Question for Critical Psychology

Both my autobiographical notes and my theoretical studies lead me to conclude that both the enjoyment of work and the dislike of it are rooted in the same soil. *Subbotniks* and shirkers are made of the same stuff. In the structures of society we see the emergence of a blind dialectic. In an unforeseen and uncontrollable way enthusiasm for work turns into its opposite. The practical solution of looking for real life outside one's work comes up against barriers at every point, and also leads to transgressions. The theoretical solution of separating work and way of life in our minds betrays the promise of free activity by trying to provide it outside the framework of alienated labour. Holzkamp's concept of a (universalized) capacity for action could – since it implies the possibility of movement – bring some movement into the blind dialectic of work and laziness. The divergence of work and way of life could be regarded as the product of history and this would imply the possibility that it could be superseded. But that could only be achieved if the elements that Marx had in mind when he spoke of 'the primary need of life' were to be reclaimed and revived. An enlarged freedom of action is undoubtedly the prerequisite for 'free activity', but how and in what circumstances can people so earn their material existence that they do not lose it immediately? So that it becomes enjoyment, pleasure, love, development, community? Work and pleasure have been separated by the division of labour, it is maintained in *The German Ideology* (p. 44). Reuniting them would bring the prospect of liberation.

How much is needed before that happens can be seen in literary terms in the work of Volker Braun who writes as follows on the subject of the enjoyment of work – in so far as this is made possible by the development of the forces of production – and the difficulty of engaging in it in a pleasurable way:

If work no longer costs you your life, it sheds its serious side and people will do it for pleasure. Then everyone will scramble to get more of it, but the opportunities are limited. You will have to keep people away from the machines by force to stop them playing them and making the most of it. There will have to be a completely different consciousness. Nowadays it's a struggle and so compulsion and material stimulus are needed, but in a peaceful age the whole business would have to have a meaning too.

Braun 1985, p. 106

Women's Issues

What are we to make of feminist worries that Marx developed a concept of work which excluded women and prevented them from perceiving the reality of women's oppression? Feminist criticism focuses primarily on Marx's arguments about the 'dual character of work'. The idea of work as a force which can create both use-values and exchange-values is fundamental to his analysis of capitalism and its dynamic, as well as for his theory of revolution. A society which is driven by the desire to turn living labour into dead (to use Marx's own imagery) and then to give this dead labour power over the living in the shape of capital, machines and factories – such a society will manoeuvre itself into a catastrophe unless radical steps are taken. Such radical action would destroy the basic structures of social activity: profit as the driving force and with it the domination of incremental value over living labour on the basis of the division of labour and the rule of property. In his analysis of the dual character of work he focuses on wage labour as the dominant method of deforming life activity. A first step towards change would be the abolition of the private ownership of the means of production. These arguments had the effect of making the sociologists focus too narrowly on the male worker in his historical role as breadwinner of the family and on the working-class movement as the subject of politics.

Women's protests appear justified at first glance. For even if we agree that this situation is the creation of capitalist society and not Marx's analysis of it, his discussion is remarkable for a certain vacuity and silence on the subject of women. But instead of hurriedly consigning Marx to the rubbish bin, we should take a step back and see whether the women's movement could not make good use of his formulation about 'enjoyable free activity in the production of material existence'. In reality Marx places the question of women's oppression squarely in the context of alienated labour: 'This latent slavery in the family, though still very crude, is the first property, but even at this early stage it corresponds perfectly to the definition of modern economists who call it the power of disposing of the labour-power of others' (*The German Ideology*, p. 44). At one point Marx even draws attention, admittedly only in a footnote, to the household work involved in the reproduction of that commodity 'labour-power', a topic he allegedly neglected. He refers to 'the family labour necessary for consumption' (*Capital*, vol. I, p. 518, n. 38).

The first advanced deformation occurs with the arrival of production for the market. This both socializes work and foregrounds the quantity and exchange-value of products. In this context, initially workers of both sexes are equal. As soon as the stage of production for immediate subsistence has been surpassed each sex works for itself and to produce a surplus for the market. The special position of women stems from the fact that a large part of their production – pregnancy, birth, child-rearing – cannot be marketed. Nowadays we begin to see signs – in the shape of surrogate mothers and modern birth technology – that women will start to catch up. Of course, it is being done with a violence familiar to us from the process of 'civilizing primitive peoples'. Any concept of the self-determination of society is as alien to the former as to the latter.

Is not the framework which Marx proposed for human society and the individuals who live in it so constructed as to enable the oppression of women with its mixture of 'natural' and social origins to acquire a tremendous dynamism? The sexual division of labour is inscribed in an altogether diabolical fashion in the division of labour between the production of life and the means of life, and in the further division between work and free activity. The sphere of actual life is marginalized from the vantage point of the social production of the means of life, and with it the people, women, who largely inhabit it. At the same time, at the centre of society activity is alienated so that all hopes of liberation are displaced towards that living activity on the margins of society. Women, who are still being oppressed, are irrationally expected to bear the weight of society's hopes for a better life, for enjoyment and sensuous pleasure.

In Marx we find the formula that 'the worker is at home when he is not working, and not at home when he is working' (*Early Writings*, p. 326). Not without some justification this remark, too, was made the butt of feminist criticism. Does he not speak here from the standpoint of the male worker, while overlooking the situation of one half of humankind which does indeed work at home and therefore is at home when it works (see Ivekovic, 1984)? However, this criticism overlooks the problems hinted at by Marx. It overlooks the double cleavage: first, the separation of sensuous pleasure and the meaning of life from work; and second, the division of work into paid work and work that counts for nought. This is the implicit point in the metaphor that 'he is not at home when he is working'. In this deformation women occupy the home, the marginal realm which is also a refuge, a deformed place of hope. The oppressive idealization of women becomes essential for the survival of the male wage labourer. And it is made permanent in the co-operation of the two sexes within the family.

Would it not be a revolutionary act to introduce some disorder into this system in order to establish the basis for a new order? If we are to salvage the marginalized areas of life, they must be universalized and hence revalorized. Simultaneously, the realm of social labour which is now privileged must be occupied by women and its authority weakened. Once the two sexes share the various spheres of activity, this will deal a blow to an element of domination which up to now has confirmed the old destructive order. In my view this is a precondition for bringing love back into the realm of work. With that the women's movement becomes crucial for the humanization of society.

References

Bischoff, J., *Gesellschaftliche Arbeit als Systembegriff*, West Berlin 1973.
Braun, V., *Hinze und Kunze. Roman*, Frankfurt am Main 1985.
Dahrendorf, R., 'Im Entschwinden der Arbeitsgesellschaft. Wandlungen der sozialen Konstruction des Lebens', *Merkur* 34, 1980.
Habermas, J., *Die neue Unübersichtlichkeit*, Frankfurt am Main 1985.
Holzkamp, K., *Grundlegung der Psychologie*, Frankfurt am Main 1984.
——— , *'Wirkung' oder Erfahrung von Arbeitslosigkeit?*, West Berlin 1986.

Holzkamp-Osterkamp, Ute, *Grundlagen der psychologischen Motivationsforschung*, Frankfurt am Main 1975/76.

Ivekovic, Rada 'Noch einmal zum Marxismus und Feminismus', *Projekt Sozialistischer Femininismus: Geschlechterverhältnisse und Frauenpolitik*, Argument-Sonderband 110, West Berlin 1984.

de Mandeville, B., *The Fable of the Bees; or Private Vices, Publick Benefits*, 1714, 5th edn, London 1728.

Marx, K., 'Über F. List's Buch "das nationale System der politischen Ökonomie"', 1845, in Marx/Engels, *Kritik der bürgerlichen Ökonomie*, West Berlin 1972.

——, *The German Ideology*, Lawrence & Wishart 1965.

——, *The Penguin Marx: Early Writings*, Harmondsworth 1977.

——, *The Penguin Marx: Capital*, vol. I, Harmondsworth 1976.

——, *A Contribution to the Critique of Political Economy*, Lawrence & Wishart 1971.

——, *The Penguin Marx: The First International and After*, Harmondsworth 1974.

Offe, C., *Arbeitsgesellschaft – Strukturprobleme und Zukunftsperspektiven*, Frankfurt am Main 1984.

Projekt Automation und Qualifikation (PAQ), *Widersprüche der Automationsarbeit. Ein Handbuch*, West Berlin 1987.

Rüddenklau, E., *Gesellschaftliche Arbeit oder Arbeit und Interaktion?* Frankfurt am Main 1982.

SEVEN

The Age of Privatizations?
The Impact of Social Change
on People's Work and Way of Life

1. The Problem of Crisis

The assertion that patriarchy and capitalism are connected has become a political truism. But the precise nature of the link is still a matter for investigation even though it continuously impinges on our everyday lives. If, as truly radical feminists, we question whether the great questions of humankind can be answered without a solution to women's issues, we cannot but observe that these problems are constantly addressed without reference to us. I shall attempt in what follows to think about the opportunities for, and obstacles in the way of, a socialist project and about the effects on women and workers of the world economic crisis and the implications of modern technology, the political shift to the right and the consequent political mood of resignation. I shall proceed empirically, basing myself on case studies, and I hope to be able to generalize from them, not by means of any statistical approach, but with the aid of the insights gained from a theoretical grasp of the conditions under scrutiny.

I shall begin with a quotation from Stuart Hall, in which he formulates the problems of mobilizing the masses in terms of a question about the nature of democracy:

Everything thus depends on how, in relation to the issue of democracy, the present crisis is understood. It has gradually dawned on the left, face to face with the crisis, that ... the possibility that the crisis may now be seized, and shaped so as to create favourable conditions for an advance towards socialism, is inextricably linked with the deepening of democratic life, and the widening of popular-democratic struggle. In that way alone lies the possibility of dividing the classes along the line of the exploited and the exploiters, which, in turn, alone might provide the conditions for a more sustained socialist advance.

Stuart Hall, 1980, pp. 158–9

The fact that we are living through a profound crisis is so integral a part of our understanding of the contemporary social situation (at least in the Federal Republic), that it scarcely appears necessary to specify what we mean by it. There are the great world crises (the danger of nuclear war and the threat of ecological catastrophe), which menacingly overshadow the economic crisis. There is mass unemployment and our habituation to the poverty of the Third World. In the capitalist nations of Europe restless sectors of the population are perceived as a 'problem.' We have a 'woman problem', a 'youth problem' and an 'ethnic minority problem'. Since these 'problems' exist worldwide they begin to be part of everyday normality. At the same time, the similarities between these various crises point to a larger and more general reordering of capitalist societies. Since the crisis takes many different forms, it becomes difficult to see where we should look for solutions. What makes the situation even more opaque is the fact that all these crises are enacted on different planes and involve different actors and arenas. We can attempt to give them a unified pattern by asking, in Lenin's words: What can the exploiters no longer do and what will the exploited no longer endure?

The simple answer, namely that the exploiters can no longer make sufficient profits and the exploited can no longer endure working so that others may garner the profits, was always misguided. It points to the general direction of the historical forces, but it fails to specify the elements of friction which impede them in their path.

In what follows I shall leave to the specialists the question of how far the great capitalist industries and their profits are really in crisis and whether Keynsian credit and interest policies are still capable of functioning, and shall concentrate instead on the other side of the equation.

In other words, I shall confine myself to what the exploited will no longer endure, what they are doing about it and the opportunities for, and obstacles in the way of, a socialist project. (I shall not restrict my understanding of the term 'the exploited' strictly to the wage-earning class, but shall use it to refer to oppression in general.)

If we hold fast to the idea that the crisis is a general disorder, experienced as the feeling that things cannot go on like this, it will be obvious that the sites which are felt to be unbearable will also be the points of conflict from which new construction can begin. We cannot, therefore, simply look to those areas in society which are improving, if we wish to identify the impact of new forces, but we must rather look at those where problems and disasters are mounting up. We can be sure that, at such points of conflict, we shall already find the right installed with new projects and proposals. Any attempted left-wing action will therefore find itself threatened not only by the *conservative* powers of tradition, but by the dynamic interventions of the new right. These external enemies will be joined by internal ones. In a sense, the left is conservative too, and in the confusion of day-to-day politics the differences between the factions may dwindle. When we come to consider the social formations which might help to promote a future left-wing project, we find that it is usually the 'new social movements, and above all the women's movement' that people have in mind. Would not a labour movement that is struggling with the consequences of the new technologies be strengthened by an alliance with the radical energies of the Greens or with the feminist interrogation of the structures of society?

I do not wish at this point to discuss the relationships of the different social movements to each other, nor do I wish to comment on the question of the dominance or otherwise of the labour movement. Instead I want to discuss aspects of a problem of common interest to all the radical movements. One important factor in times of change seems to me to be the extent to which individuals can be mobilized and in which of the available paths they have invested their hopes and their utopian desires. I wish to inquire, therefore, into the structures that are about to collapse and into the wishes and plans of those who are in a state of flux. I wish to inquire into the ways in which individuals insert themselves into their new conditions of life, how they change and what interventions they contemplate. At the same time, I shall investigate the work of the right in the reconstruction of the conditions of life of workers and women. In particular I wish to show how people come to terms with the clash between those forces which draw them into the realm of the social and those which consolidate the privacy of the individual. I would hope that my analysis would enable me to put forward proposals for cultural revolution.

2. The Socialization of Work and the Privatization of the Workers

Marx formed the view that capitalism continuously revolutionizes the forces of production and thereby drives work from the restricted sphere of the private into the social realm. This process culminates in a threat to the ultimate barrier, the private ownership of the means of production, which governs the laws of the capitalist social order. In his eyes the gathering together of large masses of workers in the *factory* was the visible evidence of the socialization of the work process. This phenomenon could become the starting point for the organization of a counterforce and the factory workers would become the agents of the necessary radical historical change. This revolutionary development of productive forces has unquestionably taken place. Almost all work today is 'socialized', and yet the hopes of a socialist victory on the part of the workers seem to have been buried by the very latest revolution in the productive forces, namely the electronic, automated mode of production. Although socially productive labour seems to continue to take over more and more spheres of activity, the exclusion of large sectors of the population from a working life appears to make it impossible for those still in work to acquire a direct relationship to progressive politics. Furthermore, the new processes of automation appear to have neutralized the build-up of workers under one roof, something which Marx had welcomed, by a new isolation of individuals sitting in front of a computer screen. Segmentation and isolation are negative trends, in which the climate of radical change and new departure has evaporated.

During the last ten years it has been replaced by the gloomy prediction that under capitalism automation would lead to deskilling, polarization, Taylorization and the intensification of work, in short, a thoroughgoing dehumanization of the conditions of work. More recently, a different view has emerged (see Kern and Schumann, 1984, and a critique in Haug, 1985). We seem to have moved from the frying-pan of the theory of the immiseration of the proletariat, to the fire where we enthuse about the positive implications of the new technology for those still in work. The Social Democratic Party has adopted a modern outlook and is conducting an aggressive technological policy in alliance with 'progressive employers'. Whilst I can see the historical legitimacy of both one-sided points of view, it is important not to allow them to thwart future action. For this reason I intend to look at the contradictions that have been created by this latest development in the forces of production and at the crises it has caused, in order to discover the points at which battle must be joined.

I shall bring together a number of theses which have emerged from our research in the Project on Automation and Qualifications (PAQ). I shall start from the very beginning in a rather didactic fashion because automation has introduced uncertainty into many beliefs hitherto regarded as inviolate.

By the forces of production we refer to the ways in which human beings act on nature. In other words, to socialized labour. These different ways correspond to different social formations, that is to say, a new technological basis gives rise to new formations. Nevertheless, a single mode of production may result in different social formations. Today we see what is essentially the same technological basis in both the capitalist and the socialist countries or, in other words, the technology of the first industrial revolution has produced two different social formations: capitalist and socialist, to which we must add the variously structured societies of the Third World and the corresponding delays in introducing automation. We have socialist societies based on primitive technology. The advanced capitalist societies are superior to the socialist societies in terms of technology and labour productivity, and so on. We have countries which have carried through technological revolutions, but where social revolutions have failed to materialize. Conversely, there are countries where social revolutions have taken place and the technological revolutions stubbornly refuse to meet the planned objectives year after year. So history does not progress in a neat linear fashion. In the Third World, where neo-colonial capitalist societies have been superimposed on pre-capitalist ones, and where the resulting formations have been overlaid by the

East–West conflict, the complexities are of a magnitude which often defeats our imaginations and our ability to grasp them intellectually.

Class struggles in capitalist countries are often fought out in the force-field created by their technological over-development and the simultaneous time-lags in the development of many socialist nations. Hence it is probably safe to assume that a further development of productive forces would trigger radical change at every level, a great reorganization in which the specifically revolutionary elements need to be identified.

The automation of production, distribution and administration revolutionizes society at the point where Marx discerned both the basis and the result of domination and the existence of classes: in the division of labour, and specifically in the separation of physical and mental labour. The process of automation consists essentially in studying the mistakes of an objectified theory of regulation. It analyses processes with a view to developing them further. The radical changes in the demands made on the workforce affect their entire knowledge and abilities, their attitudes, the division of labour and the form in which they co-operate. On the one hand, the technical revolution hits the old producers hard, with their experience, expertise, virtues and their familiarity with the old ways of doing things. On the other, it is these old ways of doing things that have now developed a revolutionary impetus. If the process of production is to function at all it will be a challenge for both sides of industry. The employers will, of course, attempt to escape cheaply for a while. But the cheapest response is not necessarily to rationalize the workforce, to exploit the remaining workers more intensively and to save as much as possible on training costs. On the contrary, the further training of individual production workers proves to be a useful investment for the company. In that respect the workers' organizations – the unions above all – experience these new productive forces as a stimulus, as well as a threat. Emancipatory demands for the further training of the workforce and claims on behalf of enhanced learning and co-operation can be justified on the grounds of the functioning of the entire process. Conversely, the employers make vigorous efforts to win the support of workers in automated processes. Personnel management has become a flourishing branch of management training. Company politics has become a major theme of sociologists' conferences. Furthermore, the growing threat of unemployment relieves the employers of some of the burden of their psychologically schooled efforts at integrating the workforce. In a battlefield so defined, it is vital to observe how individual workers interpret the factors governing automation for themselves. We have an opportunity to study the cracks in the entire edifice, and to focus on the bases and points of resistance for a socialist project, on a small as well as a large scale.

An important division in the lives of individual wage-earners is the split between work- and leisure-time. Although this division is conceptually problematic, it has its practical value for individuals, as something which marks their entire lives and which they jealously guard. The recent breaking-down of barriers resulting from the automation of production is experienced as both a threat and a liberation. Long before automation, management devised strategies for merging elements of *working* life with that of *leisure-time* and enabling each to make use of the other. Even the language used occasionally betrays as much. The company family [*Betriebsfamilie*] is an example frequently encountered. A patriarchal authority attempts to transfer to the firm feelings and attitudes appropriate in the family – such as loyalty, trust, self-sacrifice, in short, obligations which are not obtained for money. Such transfers, which try to win the loyalty of the workforce for the firm, may be regarded from a capitalist standpoint as a possible solution to the problems of responsibility, obtaining the necessary commitment and the optimization of people's efforts, which emerge with the introduction of automation. For the trade unions, of course, for the workforce to adopt the company's point of view can be a grave disadvantage.

In one firm we studied (see PAQ, 1981b, pp. 588ff) the workers were regularly sent to trade fairs. Having been selected to represent the firm, and singled out by the opportunity of being able to report back 'at home' about what they had experienced, and perhaps to make recommendations about new machines, they learned to look at the means of production through the eyes of profit makers. This is made easier at the fairs where the production plant is arranged to look like a purely technical apparatus.

In an oil refinery the principle of *self-supervision, that is to say, the adoption of another person's standpoint* was introduced. This means that the workers could take part in a public meeting presided over by the foreman which even discussed fixing wage levels. As individual workers come to think of themselves and their workmates from the point of view of achievement, they judge themselves with the quantifying gaze of the valorizers of capital. This disrupts their old structures of solidarity and at the same time organizes a new group of individual fighters. It also undermines the old cultures of workers' solidarity, which made possible such actions as the collective withdrawal of labour. At the same time these techniques of inducing workers to judge themselves are even more successful when the workers' views of one another are made an integral part of the process (see PAQ, 1981b, pp. 560ff).

We also found simpler methods of persuading workers to adopt their employer's point of view. In 15 per cent of the cases we investigated the device used was that of profit-sharing, something which is as old as the working class itself. It aims to combine the *self*-interest of those in subordinate positions with the *alien* interest of those in control. Other workers were entrusted with various managerial tasks and since they were given 'a free hand', they were able to consider such matters as profitability and what action should be taken 'to improve the product and its marketability'. In general, keeping an eye on the market and the cost-effective use of the means of production frequently forms part of the tasks given to workers in automated plant. The employers we questioned interpreted the workers' successful change of standpoint as a matter of character and expressed their 'confidence' in the workers concerned. 'We can rely on them.' Even in such descriptions of successful integration you can hear echoes of the problems employers have with those of their workers they cannot rely on, and you can guess at the efforts that have gone into this battle for the right standpoint.

The most important insight which we gained from the possibility of occupying an alien standpoint was the exploitation of the 'private' interests of individual workers for the successful prosecution of the private goals of the enterprise. The *community* is one that has shrunk to the dimensions of the family whose *outer* limits are defended in order to protect the private *interior*. Under capitalism this allows the opposite situation, one in which it is the *private nature* of production that is used as a lever to mobilize communal energies, and not (as we had first assumed) its *public, social dimensions*. The employers formulate this in the following way:

Obviously each worker also has a private life and is well aware that everything costs money. He can therefore be persuaded to be thrifty. If we make him feel that the machine that he is working on is *his*, he will instinctively do his best with it.

PAQ, 1981b, p. 454

Workers who had previously been small businessmen are often the best suited to working in expensive automated plant:

He is expert at figuring out the cost of everything and adjusting to the needs of the market-place. After all, he used to own his own farm.

Ibid.

They even rely on a sense of 'good-housekeeping' in calculating the costs of steam, fuel oil and crude-oil distillates. We have seen how the process of automation under capitalism had begun to erode the strict separation of work and leisure with its centring of 'real life' in leisure-time. We now see how the domestic view of things is imported into work.

We have seen how the exploitation of family attitudes and habits for work in the factory was one way of breaking down the dividing line between 'private life' and 'working life'. We suspected that the other side of the equation was the effects of radical change in production on people's way of life. Does this not create an unbearable tension between these new methods of production and the various customary ways of life, and lead to crises in the ways in which individuals are socialized?

Work presents a series of major tasks; they call for a commitment to work that can be impossible to reconcile with a careful division into a regulated, self-contained working day and place of work. We had guessed that this would inevitably lead to difficulties in family relationships, especially when the workers were women. The elimination or avoidance of difficulties poses challenges that call for a flexible attitude towards lessons that have been learned and an openness towards new skills. This applies generally to the ever-faster pace of technological innovation (see PAQ, 1980, pp. 100ff). What disruptions will the need for lifelong learning bring to people who are accustomed to finishing with their studies while they are still young and who regard these studies as establishing their right to a job? The self-contained nature of the working day has a corresponding organization of time which is structured in work that predates automation by the assignment of particular tasks, breaks at specified times and inspection. In contrast, unfilled periods of time, unforeseen tasks and control of one's own time are what characterize automated work. All these factors help to obscure the boundaries between time controlled by *onself* and time controlled by *others*. These necessary elements of autonomy in the work situation threaten the traditional link between self-determination and working at one's hobbies. This leads to the question of how the workers actually experience conditions that have been destabilized by the new tasks imposed by the changes in productive forces. How do these changes affect relations between the sexes, the relation between work and leisure, studying and professional training, between self-determination and determination by others in the work process itself?

In the course of hour-long group discussions (with programmers) on the subject of 'private life' we found that they came back to the topic of work again and again. Wherever the conversation started, it ended up back at work. The discussions were defined by the opposite polarities of fascination and indifference. It is well known that workers are fascinated by the new means of production and above all by computers. What is important, however, is the way this fascination is expressed. Almost every statement seems to suggest that the fascination is somehow contemptible; it is a striving for senseless competence. It brings stomach pains and sleepless nights in its wake; people forget the need for food or relaxation. Fascination, then, adds up to a kind of *incompetence* in private life.

This threat to *private life* forms the starting point; the desire to protect it structures people's perceptions of the changes taking place in their *working lives*. In this way people experience a discernible interest in work as an alienation 'from themselves'; it is expressed as a condition of being dominated. 'You keep having the feeling of doing something new.' This statement by one programmer is no paean of praise to human creativity, but describes a kind of obsession. 'You are taken over by an idea.' 'I dislike this sense of fascination because it leaves no room for anything else' (PAQ, 1983, p. 26). In statements like these we see the contradiction between the private individual, dependent only on him- or herself, and an alienated socialization expressed in terms of the excessive demands of the forces of production. These programmers wish to escape from the fascination and discover 'the centre of life' – which lies 'outside my work'. They insist that their work should become *more of a matter of indifference to them.* Marx had another 'indifference' in mind when he wrote:

> The fact that the particular kind of labour employed is a matter of indifference is appropriate to a form of society in which individuals easily pass from one type of labour to another, the particular type of labour being indifferent to them and therefore a matter of indifference.
> *A Contribution to the Critique of Political Economy*, p. 210, translation modified

The metaphor of 'indifference' established itself in the older sociological research into industry because its criteria were relevant both to the relations of production and their subjective evaluation by individual workers. In our context, on the other hand, everything seems to have been turned upside down. The programmers' work is not a matter of indifference to them; there is no question of their passing easily from one type of work to another, and production relations do not even enter the picture. If a flight from work does not succeed, in other words, if they succumb to the fascination, competition and the class struggle are displaced into a struggle with the machine:

> *Otto*: For all that, computers are a terrible temptation. They are perfect. They are absolute. They are complete in themselves.
> *Inge*: I think there is a power struggle with the machine, to see who is better.
> *Otto*: The computer is absolutely merciless, unfeeling, and when what you have done works out, and the program has worked, that is the most objective authority you can imagine. There is nothing better. No one can be as efficient as the computer. Because the computer is so absolutely merciless. A full stop instead of a comma and the whole thing's useless, just because of a little detail like that. That's just one small example, but it is quite typical. Just a minute detail in a gigantic system and it destroys everything you have done.
> PAQ, 1983, p. 26

In our society learning is usually organized as a competition. Only one person can come top. Marks are given from above. The dependence on one's superiors opens the door to both caprice and opportunity. Within this framework the programmers' attitudes seem surprising, even though they are quite consistent within the limits of the existing relations of production. In addition to their sense of their own competence, the theme that runs through the interviews like a kind of leitmotiv, is their complaint about the absence of recognition by superiors, whom in other respects they regard as incompetent.

The programmers utter an incisive critique of capitalism, but in a contradictory form. They do not just want to work for money, 'because that is not a concrete form of confirmation'. They complain about the fact that their work seems to have no social value, and in the same breath as asserting that 'it's of no interest to anyone', they suggest how proper management relations could be re-established. They call for better leadership: their superior should praise them from time to time. Thus they express criticism of capitalism, but *this criticism assumes the form of recognizing its worth.*

The whole terrain is full of contradictions. The work demands a high degree of autonomy, but at the same time they have no say about the nature of the tasks they are to perform, nor any sense of their value. Their work is not subjected to supervision from above. The programmers can organize their duties and their time as they see fit, and they have to interpret the tasks given to them as best they may. What is missing and what finds expression in their complaint about the absence of praise from their superiors, was expressed by one of the women programmers who sought to compensate for it at home by frequently praising her son's efforts 'because it is an essential part of the process of humanization ... and motivates him for further actions' (PAQ, 1983, p. 33).

In their subjective meanings work and private life are constructed as opposite poles. The first is felt to be determined by *others*, the second by *oneself*. In their work the fascination of the computers gives the programmers a kind of self-determination within the general system of determination by others. They play off their private lives against this unbearable paradox and try to protect them from interference by the world of work. One of the programmers went so far as to abandon hope of any recognition at work. 'I am given enough recognition in my private life.' The incompatibility between work and private life leads to a complete confusion. The problems of work are perceived through the spectacles of private life and in the last analysis are subordinated to the private realm and are downgraded in importance instead of being analysed.

Conclusions

The programmers experience a series of conflicts which arise from the fact that the forces of production are developing, while the relations of production remain by and large unchanged. They interpret these conflicts as conflicts between work and private life.

Their activities as programmers call for a conscious commitment which should entitle them to a say in the social utility of their work. The programmers do not demand this right to influence what is done, but protest instead at their own commitment because they (wish to) locate their consciousness and their sense of the centre of their lives in the private sphere.

The fact that they can organize their own work, both the time they take to do it and the sequence in which it is done, ought to imply that they regard their own lives as precious, as a part of the total labour-time available to society as a whole, and hence as something to be filled with a meaningful life. Such a relationship to time is in conflict with the mechanistic division of time into work-time and what is left over. The programmers interpret this demand that they should organize their time autonomously, neither as part of a campaign for a shorter working week, nor as the route to a genuine independence on an individual basis. Instead they interpret it as their right to live a quiet life and not to use up too much energy at work, so that they can conserve their strength as far as possible for their private lives.

Their work requires of them that they should introduce ideas of their own and develop systems, so that their role is not just the passive one of following instructions. Instead of challenging their dubious 'superiors', they clamour for external praise. They do not want to have ideas because these ideas could take possession of them. They seek to oppose a 'private self' to this state of being possessed, something 'of their own' which makes the ideas worked out in the interests of their employer seem alien, even though they are their own ideas.

In this way we see how, in the interest of their private lives, the programmers structure and displace all the problems which come up against the boundaries of the private relations of production. That means that it is not just the interests of *private ownership* that militate against changes in the relations of production, but also the *private lives of the producers.*

3. Women's Identity and the Privatization of the Women's Movement

If the private experience of the producers constitutes a barrier to the forces of the social, both in a good sense and a bad, it may appear pointless to investigate the private aspect of women's lives. After all, women are in a sense synonymous with everyday private life. It was this very confinement to the private sphere which was of such crucial importance in the emergence of the women's movement in the sixties and seventies. 'The personal is the political' – this was the slogan that reverberated round the world and which set out to demonstrate the centrality of the private sphere within the debate about society as a whole. At the same time, it insisted on the crucial role played by a separate private sphere in contributing to the maintaining of the system as a whole. Politics is made in and through the private sphere. A large proportion of feminist activities can be seen as an attack on those walls which seal off the private from the public sphere. At a *practical* level these activities include everything which asserts the importance of work in the household, down to and including the demands that housewives should receive a wage. It also includes efforts to socialize childrearing (in children's nurseries and play-groups) and, above all, the publicizing of violence in marriage, the establishment of women's refuges and, finally, the attempts (now successful in the United Kingdom) to use the law to make 'rape within marriage' a punishable offence.

On the theoretical plane an attempt was made to incorporate housework into the Marxist theory of value. Housework had to be seen as an aspect of a still-enduring primitive accumulation of capital, and subsistence production had to be inserted worldwide into the centre of social theory and the critique of political economy. The efforts to drag women's issues from their private cells into the public eye, and hence to decode this twofold division into private and public life as the soil from which domination grew – these efforts did not bring women directly into society, but, in the first instance, into the realm of government administration. Women discovered here, if they had not known it before, that the private is not just a prison, but also a shelter, admittedly one which has long since been organized by the state. Compulsory school attendance, custody and protection until marriage, are regulated by the state and are permanent structural parts of women's lives. Unlike men, women are not subjects of the state who associate economic independence with adulthood as much as with a profession. Women become citizens of the state by becoming housewives. For the state to take an interest in women's issues means involving them even more deeply in its structures, instead of liberating them from it. But the situation is double-edged. The effort of bringing the fact of private domination to the attention of the public has actually created an awareness that such major aspects as life, sickness and death, the preservation and maintenance of nature have been marginalized into private preoccupations, while the public interest was reserved for the production, circulation and consumption of commodities. The fact that these are concerned with profit on a large scale is something which can assume a general measure of acceptance, partly because small households are accustomed to thinking and acting on a private plane (this is the starting point for an understanding of, for example, Margaret Thatcher's populist, monetarist policies).

The protests of women have brought contrary trends to light. For example, their own oppression, which has been given permanence by their co-option into the realm of the private, and by the extent of the private throughout a society which promotes class rule as the universal interest. What is felt to be unbearable – to recall Lenin's question once more (see p. 114 above) – is that life and nature, human welfare and happiness, should be regarded as marginal issues which can be easily ignored. This is the source of the proximity to, and partial identity of the women's movement with, the ecological and peace movements. At present it is the discussion about birth technologies that has effected an alliance between the women's movement and other protest groups.

In the meantime, conservative governments have come to power in a number of Western countries and one of the effects of this has been to return those women's issues with a public or governmental dimension back into the home. Finances for women's refuges have been reduced, outside supervision and control has been strengthened, university chairs for women have either been cut or the teaching load so rationalized that courses in women's studies have had to be dropped. But these policies have not had it all their own way. In the Federal Republic of Germany, for example, resistance to the privatizing ambitions of the Christian Democrats has been organized by women within their own ranks. Conservative, red and green alliances have emerged and have succeeded in, for example, blocking an attempt by Christian Democrats to make abortion more difficult.

The administrative policy of rollback on women's issues is accompanied by massive propaganda in favour of the family, for the need for wives and mothers to be willing to make sacrifices and for women's values, such as caring and love (see Hauser, 1985). Even the 'feminization of society' has become a slogan that can be deployed by the right, whereas ten years ago, that would have been as unthinkable as it would be today to propose that homosexuality should become the norm in our society.

The women's movement was not entirely unprepared and taken aback by this positive reevaluation of the feminine. In a sense the groundwork had been laid for an acceptance of these trends. 'Feminine values' had also been rediscovered in at least parts of the women's movement, where they were promoted and celebrated, either as the voice of the future or as a source of resistance, just as if such values were an inherent part of women and not merely social expectations. The qualities associated with motherhood, for example, were traced back to matriarchal religions with maternal goddesses, and revered as an eternal principle. The meaning of the family, of the work associated with 'reproduction' and relationships became a long-standing theme. How could the seductive calls of the Christian Democrats fall on entirely deaf ears?

Was it reasonable to expect resistance from those in the women's movement – and there were many of them – who were less exercised by the need to develop their 'feminine' qualities than to conquer all realms of activity for women? After all, it is not the case that all women live mainly or exclusively within the confines of the 'reproductory sphere', nor do they see it as their future goal. The expectant gaze directed at these sectors of the women's movement encounters a different kind of reluctant acquiescence in government intentions: widespread resignation and disillusionment and the defiant desire to abandon politics and go back into the home, a reprivatization. In short, a desire for children, a home of one's own and a partner have again become the dominant goals for many women (see, for example, Meulenbelt, 1985).

Even though such a retreat from society and politics can be motivated by a desire to resist, it appears to us as though the wish to fetter oneself is the predominating motive. Our research led us to the conclusion that the desire for subordination to a man, and hence a lack of faith in one's own competence and in the possibility of bringing about social change, can still be part of the constitutive elements of a woman's identity, even where women have a career and are (still) politically active. As we pursued our researches into the construction of 'femininity', we encountered evidence that a whole series of elements of subordination within the family are fed not by women's conformist acceptance, but precisely by their resistance to being forced into those parts of the social structure traditionally reserved for women. Resistance to their parents drives women to establish their own, 'better' family – an action which is often regarded as a step towards freedom. Resistance to the organization of their time by others leads them to object to timetabling in general – something which often ends with their subordination to other people's timetables. The fact that young girls see their mothers as having been made responsible by the division of labour for the physical and emotional well-being of the family, not uncommonly leads them to react by rejecting any concern for their *own* well-being. But this very neglect of their own interests is what fits them to slip into the role of the self-sacrificing wife and mother.

Equipped with hopes and desires born of this resistance to the process of socialization, women come to terms with the inhospitality of society by treating it as a challenge which they will make good in the family circle. At the same time, there remains a generalized restless feeling that they would like other things too. They retain this restlessness as a kind of lifelong schizophrenia. Most women think or feel that they are really somebody else, that they are deceiving their fellow human beings, or that they have failed to gain recognition for what they are. By retreating into the private sphere, they console themselves with the thought that they will have a different life, not now, 'but later', 'sometime'. They hope that this new life will manifest itself as a sort of discovery. This hope is reinforced by the illusion industry.

4. Life and the Means of Sustaining It

We have seen how the productive forces of work have been paralysed by the perception of society from the standpoint of the private sphere, leisure-time, the family, in short, of people whose socialization has directed them into the realm of the private. We have witnessed the diminishing energies of one of the important new social movements, the women's movement, which has been doubly ensnared in the toils of the private sphere. Where can we hope to discover new revolutionary impulses which are sufficiently ripe to form the building blocks of a new society? On the one hand, we are probably right in seeing the controversy about the private sphere as a sign, if not of the dissolution, at least of the loosening and the restructuring of its fetters. The forces are distributed in a crazy fashion. On the one hand, the private nature of the producers becomes a barrier to exploiting them for purposes of profit, as well as to the aggressive acquisition of technological expertise which would be to the advantage of the workers themselves. On the other, the privatization of women's issues takes place despite their integration into the state and as a protest against the inhospitality of society.

The crisis affects the realm of work and also of the private sphere which is split off from it, as well as the connection between the two. The great issues affecting society are experienced as immediate threats to the individual. The neat separation into a sick society and an intact private world no longer functions. This crisis is articulated as a problem of ways of living. This is why the protests of the new social movements are enacted in these arenas and not directly in the sphere of production, even when these protests are aimed at the new technology. This fact leads Habermas to conclude that 'a particular utopia' has now come to an end, 'a utopia which in the past had crystallized around the potential of a society based on work' (Habermas, 1985, p. 145). This concept includes in his view such varied phenomena as Marx and the European labour movement, 'the authoritarian corporatist movements in fascist Italy and Nazi Germany', as well as 'social democratic reformism in the mass democracies of the West' (*Ibid.*, p. 146). He recommends 'the communicative society' as a way of formulating utopias, facilitating the use of the communications media for alternative strategies and constructing a 'self-acting, autonomous public sphere' (pp. 158ff). In Habermas's view of social theory hitherto, the main thrust has been an emancipatory movement leading from the abolition of heteronomous work in the direction of free activity. Confronted with the crisis in the welfare state, the new labour-saving technology with the consequent growth in unemployment, and in view of the new social movements at the periphery of the process of production, he sets out – and this has been the general object of discussion at two recent sociology conferences in the Federal Republic – to remove the concept of work from the centre of social theory, while retaining the claim to individual activity as a way of achieving 'liberation'.

From what Marx called 'the standpoint of ready-made phenomena', this mode of argumentation may be convincing. And the concept of individual activity should not be left to the populist movements of the right, since it is a necessary component of every liberation. Needless to say, individual activity must go hand in hand with self-socialization, with the growing collective supervision of the conditions governing the social process of life. In itself, simply doing things for yourself is neither a goal, a path nor a true satisfaction. Moreover it has constantly to live with the threat that others (including other social forces) will seek to lay down rules for your activities. Thanks to the dynamism of the new technology, everything is now caught up in a process of radical change. It is possible to discuss the struggles about ways of life and the frontiers of the private, as if the elimination of the concept of work were at stake. Why not stick to those sentences of Marx's that Habermas finds particularly unconvincing.

> Thus things have now come to such a pass that the individuals must appropriate the existing totality of production to achieve self-activity.... The appropriation of these forces is itself nothing more than the development of the individual capacities corresponding to the material instruments of production. Only at this stage does self-activity coincide with material life, which corresponds to the transformation of the earlier limited intercourse and the casting-off of all natural limitations.
>
> Quoted from Habermas, 1985, pp. 145ff[1]

Marx certainly did not picture this process of the development of the forces of production as one which would take place automatically and without struggle. At the stage of the electronic mode of production we have reached, that would mean universalizing the ability to make use of these productive forces, something which – given their nature – would necessarily include the possibility of applying them directly right across the social scale. At the same time work itself would have to be universalized. If each woman or man needed only to work for four or perhaps five hours a day to earn their living, this would set free the time which everyone could make good use of for social or political activity, further education or for individual cultural reproduction. This would make it possible to overcome the old divisions of labour. Needless to say, this situation could also lead to the further consolidation of these old divisions, since an army of housewives could be used to make good the cultural plight of specialists or the unemployed. Similarly, a growing state apparatus might attempt to keep specialists from applying their expertise to production as a whole, just as it strives to compensate for the impoverishment of the unemployed. This appears to be the programme of the new right.

We, on the other hand, should do everything in our power to use the crisis for restructuring. One important political task would be to establish a universal right to a working life, but a working life differently conceived. We should discuss a new model consisting of work for material gain, political and social work, and work for individual maintenance and improvement. Proposals along these lines should be worked out in detail with particular attention to those aspects that could be implemented at present. The debates about shortening the working week could then at long last be given positive content. Such models should be introduced into groups, institutions and political organizations of every kind. At the same time the new forces of production could be adapted for use in alternative projects. The aggressive use of the new media could also help to link up this huge proliferation of self-activating projects with a view to universalizing these models for a new distribution of working and living. The very fact that the crisis has involved so many different people in so many walks of life means that there is a greater opportunity for achieving a breakthrough in a general socialization project, which would consider the question of what we produce and how we produce it to be a condition of our lives.

In connection with our findings that the private realm has a paralysing effect on those whom it affects, we now conclude that their privatization is not just a shackle left over from the old days, but that it also represents a challenge to our political organizations. The questions raised by the problem of ways of life are just as much in need of political articulation, as it is vital for those who have withdrawn into the private sphere to learn how to occupy a larger political space.

In this we are building our hopes on the forces of self-socialization, and upon the desire and the necessity to regulate society collectively. In our 'utopia of a work-based society' (to use Habermas's phrase, but in opposition to his belief in its demise), we imagine that, initially, the collective energies of the community will be tied into the market model of capitalist socialization, but in the form of resistance movements. At any rate, they will not exist independently in a freely disposable form, but will be bound up with particular institutions whose dissolution we shall experience as a crisis. What I have in mind here is above all the *factory*, where social production takes place, and the *house* and the *family*, which are responsible for regulating the other aspects of life. We would designate both these sites – and not just the state – as community forms, and their agents as the incarnations of utopian aspirations. The new forces of production are subverting these bodies, destroying their institutions and creating insecurity among their agents. What we need are new ways of living and working together. We now have the possibility of abolishing the old divisions into work and leisure, and between men's and women's functions, in such a way as to enable us to aim at a collective organization of life – consciously and in all its aspects.

From the standpoint of the reproductive functions of society both questions are crucial: that of the production of the means of subsistence and that of the production of life itself. The fact that the capitalist marginalization of the questions of producing and sustaining life can erupt in crises does not mean, in my opinion, that questions of production can be treated as marginal. We should rather say that the time has arrived when the effects of the capitalist mode of production have become so intolerable and destructive 'that the individual must appropriate the existing totality of productive forces to achieve self-activity'. At the level of the electronically based mode of production this requires a model of civilization in which social labour-time, the time needed for making politics and the time required for individual development and sustenance, can be redefined. The definition of society's large-scale goods can no longer be undertaken behind people's backs as a sort of afterthought to the profit-making activities of industrial and commercial production.

The contemporary crises in Western industrial societies led us to infer a connection with the role of the productive forces and the electronically based mode of production. We found the appropriation of those productive forces to be both determined and impeded by the private lives of the producers. The economic crisis is also experienced as a crisis in people's way of life. Here women are doubly affected. In industrial societies it is they who are given the responsibility for people's way of life in the broadest sense. Private space, the privacy of the family, would be unthinkable without the role played by women. They experience the crisis as a threat to the private sphere. Even the women's movement, with its efforts to overcome the limits of the private and to occupy the public sphere, was unprepared for this shifting of the crisis into the realm of the private.

The old debate about whether workers' problems and women's problems are connected or opposed can and must be posed today in such a way as to ensure that they both reach the agenda together. The catastrophic logic of the capitalist mode of production is destroying humankind's prospects of survival. At the same time it creates the conditions in which the full participation of women in the definition of the whole life of society will become a necessity. Our ideas about what is central and what is marginal within capitalist societies must be overturned. But also – and here we find ourselves in opposition to Habermas's view – the question of how society is defined in terms of work must remain central, as long as work remains one of its own defining factors. To that extent the project of socialism has as great a right to a place on the agenda as the fact that the workers must play an essential role in the overthrow of the old order. But that 'the measure of universal emancipation' can be inferred from 'the degree of women's emancipation' (Marx/Engels *Werke*, vol. 2, p. 207), is an idea that has been given a new relevance in our day. To that extent women's issues are not merely issues for women; in them is expressed the issue of the survival of humanity as a whole.

THE AGE OF PRIVATIZATIONS?

Note

1. Habermas is quoting from *The German Ideology*, but without a page reference and in a highly idiosyncratic manner. Since it is not my concern here to point out in detail the various qualifications and additional comments, I shall confine myself to quoting the entire Marx text in order to give readers the opportunity of assessing the situation for themselves (the italicized passages are those omitted by Habermas):

> Thus things have now come to such a pass, that the individuals must appropriate the existing totality of productive forces, *not only* to achieve self-activity, *but, also, merely to safeguard their very existence. This appropriation is first determined by the object to be appropriated, the productive forces, which have been developed to a totality and which only exist within a universal intercourse. From this aspect alone, therefore, this appropriation must have a universal character corresponding to the productive forces and the intercourse.* [The omission of this passage from '*but, also*' to '*intercourse*' is indicated by ellipses in Habermas's text, but the other omissions are not similarly signalled – *author's note*] The appropriation of these forces is *itself* nothing more than the development of the individual capacities corresponding to the material instruments of production. *The appropriation of a totality of instruments of production is, for this very reason, the development of a totality of capacities in the individuals themselves. This appropriation is further determined by the persons appropriating. Only the proletarians of the present day, who are completely shut off from all self-activity, are in a position to achieve a complete and no longer restricted self-activity, which consists in the appropriation of a totality of the productive forces and in the thus postulated development of a totality of capacities. All earlier revolutionary appropriations were restricted; individuals, whose self-activity was restricted by a crude instrument of production and a limited intercourse, appropriated this crude instrument of production, and hence merely achieved a new state of limitation. Their instrument of production became their property, but they themselves remained subordinate to the division of labour and their own instrument of production. In all expropriations up to now, a mass of individuals remained subservient to a single instrument of production; in the appropriation by the proletarians a mass of instruments of production must be made subject to each individual, and property to all. Modern universal intercourse can be controlled by individuals, therefore, only when controlled by all.*
> *This appropriation is further determined by the manner in which it must be effected. It can only be effected through a union, which by the character of the proletariat itself can only be a universal one, and through a revolution, in which, on the one hand, the power of the earlier mode of production and intercourse and social organization is overthrown, and, on the other hand, there develops the universal character and the energy of the proletariat without which the revolution cannot be accomplished; and in which, further, the proletariat rids itself of everything that still clings to it from its previous position in society.* Only at this stage does self-activity coincide with material life, which corresponds to the development of individuals into complete individuals and the casting off of all natural limitations. *The transformation of labour into self-activity corresponds to the transformation of the earlier limited intercourse into the intercourse of individuals as such.*
>
> *The German Ideology*, pp. 84–6

Setting aside the question of philological accuracy, which creates the impression that Marx had intended the meaning conveyed by the sentences as Habermas has juxtaposed them, we may note that the following points have been omitted: the relationship between individual development and mode of acquisition, on the one hand, and the necessity of maintaining the individual's own existence, on the other; the unconditional dependence of individuals for their own development upon the development of the instruments of production (this is an aspect of the mode of production in the electronic age, about whose effects Habermas explicitly writes, and which should have been emphasized; see on this point Volker Braun's elaborations in his play *The Great Peace* [*Der grosse Frieden*]); the resulting possible development of the proletariat itself (an aspect which Gramsci developed further with respect to worker-intellectuals); the need for a social revolution to make this development possible, and, finally, the role of intercourse, or, to use the modern term, communication in this context, a factor which Habermas himself sees as an alternative.

References

Habermas, Jürgen, *Die neue Unübersichtlichkeit, Kleine politische Schriften*, vol. V, Frankfurt am Main 1985.

Hall, Stuart, 'Popular-Democratic vs Authoritarian Populism: Two Ways of "Taking Democracy Seriously"', in Alan Hunt, ed., *Marxism and Democracy*, Lawrence & Wishart, 1980.

Haug, Frigga, 'Automationsarbeit und Politik bei Kern/Schumann', *Das Argument* 154, 1985.

Hauser, Kornelia, 'Die CDU und die Frauenbewegung', *Das Argument* 153, 1985.

Kern, Horst and Schumann, Michael, *Das Ende der Arbeitsteilung?*, Munich 1984.

Marx, Karl, *The German Ideology*, Lawrence & Wishart, London 1965.

—— *A Contribution to the Critique of Political Economy*, Lawrence & Wishart, London 1971.

Meulenbelt, Anja, *Die Gewöhnung an das alltägliche Glück*, Munich 1985.

Projektgruppe Automation und Qualifikation (PAQ), 8 vols:

—— Vol. 1, *Automation in der BRD*, Argument-Sonderband 7, 1975.

—— Vol. 2, *Entwicklung der Arbeit*, AS 19, 1978.

—— Vol. 3, *Theorien über Automationsarbeit*, AS 31, 1978.

—— Vol. 4, *Automationsarbeit: Empirische Untersuchungen 1*, AS 43, 1980.

—— Vol. 5, *Automationsarbeit: Empirische Untersuchungen 2*, AS 55, 1981a.

—— Vol. 6, *Automationsarbeit: Empirische Untersuchungen 3*, AS 67, 1981b.

—— Vol. 7, *Zerreissproben – Automation im Arbeiterleben, Empirische Untersuchungen 4*, AS 79, 1983.

—— Vol. 8, *Automation im Widerspruch, Ein Handbuch*, West Berlin (in preparation).

EIGHT

Microelectronics and Subjectivity

The Problem of the Socio-Psychological
Study of Work

At the present time about 70 per cent of all jobs are connected directly
or indirectly with microelectronics. It is essential, therefore, that when
we come to consider the tasks facing a psychology of work, we should
not fail to include the changes brought about in consequence of this
fact. They concern people's relationship to machines, nature and
science, and thereby their relationship to themselves and others. In
what follows I argue that the need to consider the psychology of work
as an aspect of scientific psychology has arisen for the first time as a
result of the emergence of the microelectronic mode of production.

I approach that subject obliquely, from the subject of the scientific
study of work in the narrower sense: as an aspect of economics. The
various branches of this science have undergone an unprecedented
expansion, thanks to the radical changes in production and in the
service sector. At the World Congress for Work with Display Units (in
Stockholm in 1986) it was possible to obtain an idea of the work done
in these fields. Three hundred scientists from thirty nations presented
the results, in figures and other data, of comprehensive studies carried
out in depth.[1] The analysis of the products of such research are of
inestimable value for the process of critical learning.

Even on a cursory examination it becomes evident that these studies are based on a view which treats humankind as a stimulus–response mechanism. Nevertheless, even an approach of this sort can yield useful information about the damage resulting from the one-sided use of people as sources of labour power. We can go further and work out the dimensions of a critical psychology of work if we look to see what is missing in this ergonomic research – for example, in its investigations into the harmful effects of working with computer screens. The logic of the effects implicit in the stimulus–response model omits the following elements which are essential for a field concerned with studies with and about working people: men and women themselves as active beings; their experiences; their position in the labour process; their relations with the means of work – the computer (do they use it, or does it use them?); the content of work; the organization of work; the position of their work within the overall task; and, naturally, the social context in which this work is carried out. These omissions give us some idea of how the socio-psychological study of work should proceed. But beyond that, the scrutiny of such international research reveals another interesting phenomenon. The damage caused by working with VDUs differs considerably from one country to another and also according to sex. It is mainly women who are affected.

In Australia a sudden paralysis of the arms seemed to be spreading like plague in the Middle Ages. This disease, which affected women, was first diagnosed as tenosinovitis, but later became known as RSI – repetitive strain injury. The symptoms often last months or years. Whole armies of scientists were on the move in the attempt to discover explanations. The women who suffer from it have absorbed it into their sense of time: 'That was before I had RSI . . .' The situation in Sweden was quite different. There they discussed miscarriages and deformed babies. In Finland it was mainly people's eyesight that was affected. Neck and shoulders are also sites where intolerable strain comes to the surface. It would certainly be valuable to test critically the assumptions which give rise to such findings.[2] At this point I should like to emphasize something else: it would be useful to regard these different findings, these national variations in the consequences of a similar set of changes in working conditions, as a practical and illuminating critique of the traditional sciences of work. These findings compel us to go beyond the ergonomic approach and view work with VDUs – like all other work – as a social phenomenon, and hence to include the elements of culture and gender in the investigation.

Within this field (of work with VDUs) our initial question is: What changes are introduced into the work process by the computer (as the relevant means of work), and why do women in particular suffer from work-related illnesses?[3]

The Work Crisis

It seems reasonable to describe sudden changes in the conditions of action as a crisis, when it is unclear how these changes should be handled. The internal work crisis (as distinct from the 'external' one involving the amount of work available and its distribution) has four aspects: shifts in the proportion of physical to mental labour; the blurring of the boundaries between work and leisure; the relation between men and women, and the question of learning.

Physical and mental labour

As soon as work becomes a matter of processing information, the old division between manual and intellectual, practical and theoretical labour in production and administration becomes untenable. This raises a question about the legitimacy of hierarchies and co-operative relations as well as the relationships between particular groups of workers. In terms of substance, at least in our society, hierarchies seem to lose their *raison d'être*, though their authority remains unimpaired. This gives birth to a new contradiction. People in subordinate positions become more competent than their superiors, while remaining inferior in the hierarchy. But it is not enough simply to define computer work as mental work – an information-processing activity. For the elements of work confront the individual not just as information, but in the form of a theory about the labour process. To that extent people's distance from their work is increased. We automatically tend to think that distance from one's work is something negative, an increase in alienation. But in so doing we overlook the other side of the coin – namely, that an excessive closeness precludes the possibility of an overview and of criticism, both of which are essential for progress.[4] The greater the distance, the easier it is to reflect on the relationship to work. When compared to the typing work it succeeded, this holds good even for simple tasks of inputting data, and all the more so for interactive processing and systems analysis. Computer logic provides a specific kind of access to language and information. You can submit to this and try to learn the commands by heart and live in constant fear of being ejected from the system. Or you can appropriate the system, in other words, you can test it, extend it and develop it further. The resulting relationship is essentially experimental. The work grips you and holds you fast – this is well known, although the nature of the fascination is not always understood.[5]

The shifts in the relations between physical and mental labour give rise to new tensions and contradictions. The development which had begun as early as the first industrial revolution is now coming to an end. The workers stand outside and above the actual process of production, without having achieved the right of control appropriate to that position.

Absorption in work becomes more intensive and concentrated, and also more enthusiastic as the distance to the object of work increases. Empirical studies which lament this growth in intensity and concentration, and use it as evidence that a specific type of work is particularly undemanding, overlook the fact that work demanding enthusiasm and strong motivation is always associated with an increase in intensity of which the workers themselves are subjectively conscious.

The forms taken by the division of labour are less directly hierarchical here, even though the hierarchy does not actually disappear. The workers' superiors are less competent than their underlings, but without losing their authority.

Work and leisure, men and women

One of the major divisions in the life of working people is that between work- and leisure-time. During their free time they are at home, private people escaping from work. But it is also true that they escape from the narrow privacy of the home into the sociability of the workplace. Various changes take place with the introduction of the computer.

Since the work is mental work it does not stop at the factory gates or the office door. The problems can be taken home. They infiltrate what had once been free time. Computers are also hobbies. When computers break down, the majority of companies use the difficult state of the labour market to force their employees to develop greater flexibility in their working practices. The hours missed because of the breakdowns have to be made good as overtime. Such practices affect family life if they become general. Work breaks out of the limits laid down by office hours. The introduction of flexitime creates chaos in the ordered life of the family. If the office workers affected are women, either they find they cannot do the overtime required and have to take on a part-time job, or their partners change their attitudes and behaviour and take over some of the household chores – could this be a further step in the direction of equal rights for women? In our study of computerized offices the men and women we interviewed reported unanimously that such sharing relationships were normal.[6] Admittedly, when we looked more closely at the way the duties were divided up, it appeared that the women had not really put this to the test. They did no overtime and their position in the firm was correspondingly fragile. In all the changes we have outlined between work- and leisure-time, and between physical and mental work, we have noted a weakening of the traditional sexual division of labour. At the same time, the main question has not yet been answered: Is computer work 'masculine', technical work or is it 'feminine', clerical work?

Learning

Here, too, I want only to outline a number of features. There can be no doubt that the introduction of computers has changed the relationships between learning and working, theory and experience (the relation to practice is itself a matter of theory). We must begin by asking a series of new questions: How can it be possible to finish learning, if working implies constant further development? What 'training' is really needed, if learning is a lifelong activity? Can work be so arranged that learning becomes an integral part of it, and what about the current fashion for learning by doing?

I should like to argue that work in the microelectronic mode of production makes it necessary to think of the general conditions of work as changeable and developing, and that workers have to take on the responsibility for this themselves. The divisions of labour, the organization of work and above all the relations of production stand in the way of the appropriate ways of dealing with these new means of production. Lastly, questions about work culture and work identity must also be placed on the agenda.

The Crisis of Subjective Identity at Work

The experiences of workers with the new conditions of work and the way they come to terms with them in their everyday lives must form an essential part of the psychological study of work. After all, the traditional structures, divisions and organization of labour, forms of training and the acquisition of skills, concealed both capacities for action and their organizational underpinnings, as well as obstacles and shackles (the latter above all in the case of non-male, unskilled workers).

When we included workers' attitudes in our studies we found that they mainly experienced the new conditions of work as a kind of fascinating catastrophe.[7] On the one hand, the work was as enjoyable as a hobby, on the other, as threatening as a burglary. On the whole, it can be said that working with computers is culturally indigestible. I should like to support this contention with a number of arguments:

1. Work is perceived as non-work – much as the work of intellectuals used to be perceived by the workers. Work has so changed its character that it is now unclear what should be described as work. The traditional yardsticks no longer apply. Is the time spent learning also work? Is the search for solutions, trying things out, work, or does it prevent work from being carried out? What about idle periods? Is looking for mistakes work?

2. When manual work becomes mental work the attitude of practical workers towards intellectuals becomes problematic.

3. If it is unclear what is man's work and what is woman's work, identities that are strongly bound up with work experience a crisis.

4. Cultural habits in and around work are destroyed. For example,

there is an impact on the consumption of alcohol at work, banter, the feeling of strength, all of which safeguarded 'masculinity' and were based on physical labour.

5. Modes of co-operation, the relations between the sexes and attitudes towards family and leisure are altered. The dangers sensed with the introduction of flexitime – the reduction of friendships to those whose work-time and leisure-time coincided with yours, and the reduction of the social to the internal organization of the family – all these are just the beginning.

Subjective Ways of Coming to Terms with Objective Changes

In an empirical study of 240 office workers involved in inputting data, interactive processing and systems analysis, we analysed the various components of our subjects' relation to the work process and attempted to discover the specific experiences of individual workers with the new means of production. That is much more easily said than done. We inquired into their qualifications, the variety of their work, the division of labour and the hierarchy, the forms of solidarity and co-operation among the workforce and, finally, the opportunities for further study and training. We at once encountered two remarkable features.

First, we observed that our subjects were quite sure that in general the effects of working with computers were negative. The work was mainly monotonous; computers had, if anything, reinforced the division of labour, they led to isolation, and opportunities for further study did not really happen. Admittedly, all this applied in the main to *other people*, who for that reason were assumed to feel no solidarity with one another because they had nothing to lose.

Second, our subjects were no less certain that a knowledge of computers in *one's own work* meant better qualifications, more varied work, integrated work assignments and more effective co-operation, as well as being bound to lead to better study opportunities. They were convinced they were different, and this boosted their self-confidence; at the same time it left them feeling very alone.

This finding points to a problem which has methodological implications. When our interviewees described the negative effects of

143

working with computers, they were apparently not describing their own experience, since they regarded themselves as exceptions. The dominant opinion had prevailed in the teeth of their own practical experience. Its divergence from their own practice was interpreted as a separation between them and everyone else. Instead of rejecting the dominant view, they consciously isolated themselves. The fact that interviewees can react in this way casts doubt on the value of empirical methods that simply accept the answers at face value and present their results as a collection of facts free of contradictions.

We encountered such self-isolating strategies and similar phenomena again and again. The new technology was perceived as a threat to the private individual, the sphere of privacy, and the existence of the private as such. We can be sure that this retreat reflected a resistance to the real improvements, as well as to the actions taken by employers and the alienated work conditions. This resistance takes the form of fleeing into one's own private fortress.

All these radical changes, which objectively could be seen today to represent an enrichment, were perceived from the vantage point of the old situation and people as they used to be. For example, a group of programmers who had a greater say in disposing of their time, interpreted this as a gap and a defect in the system, and longed for the previous set-up. Again, they reported on the incompetence of their superiors with a certain pride, but at the same time complained about the absence of social recognition which accompanied this decline in competence. It was this complaint which had led even conscientious and politically committed programmers to shift the focus of their lives to the family, transferring their own unmet need for recognition and socially meaningful work to their children, in the hope that they, at least, can become real human beings. And lastly, the fascination the new technology exerts on the individual is seen as a seduction to be resisted, as a temptation to forget the realm of the private.[8]

In general we may conclude that the introduction of the new technologies has produced an increase in anxiety and a tendency to withdraw into private experience.

The Implications for the Psychology of Work

If we take stock of the typical tasks tackled by industrial psychologists we find that they advise employees in so-called personal matters, such as the family, marriage and bringing up the children. In addition there are questions about job-suitability and the development of aptitude tests. Sometimes they are consulted about questions of training and workload. Very rarely they are also involved in matters concerning the organization of work.

At first sight these questions have little connection with the changes we have been discussing and the problems that result from them. But in times of radical change they acquire a new importance. We must abandon the thesis that the work situation directly determines the situation in the family. This thesis was popular years ago and was based on the simplistic idea that oppression is simply passed on – the male worker is oppressed at work and passes the oppression on to his family by way of compensation. The opposite hypothesis, that the family disrupts the tranquillity of the workplace, also seems too simple and linear. Our studies showed rather that the way in which problems are formulated and solved in the private sphere – namely, singly, hierarchically and by eliminating any contradictions – also determines the way problems are solved at work. But here, under the new conditions, it fails to function.

'Way of life' and 'way of work' should be seen as interconnected. The urgent task facing any effective research into work is to help to rebuild the workers' ability to act more creatively and at more demanding tasks in response to conditions of rapid change. But it is important not to treat workers as the objects of such research, for the problem is not to have one group of people diagnosing the problems of another. Instead the new methods of production imply that employees will only be able to act effectively if they can master their own work situation. One of the basic preconditions for this is that the work processes should be analysed by those involved in them. Doubts about one's own identity and the problems arising from the resultant lack of self-confidence call for a historical analysis of one's own work and its meaning for society. How else can meaning and significance be discovered when one's daily tasks are described (as our programmers insisted) in terms of shifting a decimal point or a hyphen within a general context where work and the professions are being radically redefined?

The theoretical and practical control of one's own field of work implies the ability to learn how to learn, to introduce changes, suggest alternative modes of action and make criticisms. Even if such ideas sound abstract and utopian, they are a reality at the different levels of computerized work and can be observed there. Instead of simply adapting oneself to preordained work structures, the task now is to appropriate them.

Project Research

Learning stands at the heart of a new kind of work. All radical changes in the conditions of work require new forms of learning and active efforts, if one is not to be swallowed up by attitudes which are in any case inadequate ways of coming to terms with the new technologies. Any study of work which aims to be more than descriptive, and hopes both to intervene actively and also to include within the new work structures the idea of self-critical subjectivity, inevitably calls for new methods. From among the methods tried hitherto the most promising seems to me to be the idea of the project. It combines an exploratory process of learning as an essential prerequisite for all learning, with the possibility of involving the workers in the relevant field in the analysis of their own situation. For such a procedure collaboration between politically committed academic research and the trade unions seems to me to be absolutely indispensable.

Methodological Considerations and Initial Findings

Changes in the work situation are often experienced in contradictory ways. Ways of dealing with these contradictions can include denying them – which of course brings only temporary relief – half-suppressing them or retreating from such a conflict-ridden arena. Getting to grips with them collectively is something which is steadfastly countered by the efforts of both employers and the government to strengthen the isolation of the individual – the autonomous individual celebrated in neo-conservative strategies – and the subjective approach to dealing with the experience of privatization.[9] I have already reported on our remarkable finding that individual office workers believe that their own jobs are interesting and have been enhanced by the introduction of computers, but that on the whole this did not modify their negative view of the effects of computerization. In short, they followed the common practice of making sweeping statements, while denying their application to themselves, even though they adhere to the general opinion of their own field of work.

This contradictoriness at the individual level led us to formulate a method which would provide support and encourage people to discover in contradictions a way of moving forward.[10] We started from the premiss that the need to be capable of action even in contradictory situations means that people must be in a position to recognize and explain contradictions, to articulate them instead of evading them. We had begun by setting up (mixed) groups of people occupying various positions, with the aim of presenting a number of themes for discussion, but only intervening if the discussion turned into a monologue which threatened to exclude the other participants from the collective production of ideas. Our guidelines explicitly asked for a discussion on the basis of the participants' own experience, although we had not reckoned with the fact that everyone would suddenly start to make conjectures about what they supposed other people's experiences to be. They communicated in such stereotyped phrases that they were unable to generalize from their own experience. We became depressed by the thought that we would never get beyond the level of a pub conversation, whose various moves we could well have predicted in advance. We therefore resolved to apply our method. This was to confront the official view of what work is like with people's actual experience of it.

We set out to explore the contradictions in people's minds between their own good experiences and other people's bad ones. We therefore presented the official view and opposed to it what people actually experienced and got our participants to discuss it. What they did was to focus on its verbal aspect and not the underlying contradictory reality. They regarded each contradiction as a challenge which they had to eliminate through a form of words, rather than to confront head on. The discrepancies between their own individual experience and the received views that filter down through society led to such statements as 'unqualified computer work' (other people's, that is) was 'simply a question of character' – something they found reassuring since it singled them out from the masses. The only disturbing factor in this black-and-white picture was the loneliness of the qualified computer specialist compared to the cosy solidarity of the unqualified mass. 'These are the people who have no chance of a career in the fast lane; they stick together and develop a feeling of solidarity,'[11] said one gloomily, a specialist who had no prospects himself of such a career, but who was describing the lack of solidarity he experienced and thought was unique to himself. Once a contradiction had become an agreed part of such a discussion, its various implications were followed up, as if they had a life of their own. New dimensions were revealed and the discussion became more exciting for the participants. They felt they were making progress and even breaking new ground.

With the computerization of the office, the group moved from isolation and loneliness at work to a greater collaboration, as the group itself noted, and an increase in co-operation. They insisted, however, that this did not alter the loneliness. We may therefore describe their situation as a transitional one of *co-operation while remaining isolated.* Hitherto we had assumed that all co-operation between people at work was to be seen positively. The benefits of co-operation in terms of efficiency and productivity are undeniable. Marx believed that the more sensuously people experience it, the greater the spur to new efforts. But even from the standpoint of the workers themselves we had seen co-operation and the experience of it as the starting point for solidarity and as the vitality of socialized human beings. This was why we felt that the question of the fate of co-operation in computer work was of strategic importance. On the whole the conclusion was inescapable: while there was in fact an improved collaborative structure, this was experienced as a decline in co-operation. Further discussion revealed that co-operation had not actually decreased, but that its increase was felt to be something forcibly imposed on them, sometimes even a threat, at any rate as an intensified heteronomy. Both subjectively and objectively the new collaboration took the place of the earlier *personal relationships* at work. By personal relationships they meant birthday celebrations, conversations about weddings, christenings, illness, the death of relatives, and celebrations of all sorts down to token gifts, such as flowers, to colleagues at work. They described such 'personal relations' as the foundation of solidarity. In short, they missed these relationships whose non-work content we are inclined to explain in terms of the fact that the forces and above all the relations of production do not permit work-based relationships in the same place and among people of the same status, or, alternatively, do not allow relationships which go beyond work.[12] Conversely, our office workers were incapable of perceiving office relationships as real ones between people. The fact that they were thrown together in the office was felt as a double threat – as a threat both to personal work relations and as a threat to oneself as a private individual because of the relationships forced on one at work, relationships against which there is no defence.

At this point I shall cautiously formulate a number of hypotheses. In competitive situations work relationships that are imposed on you constitute a paradox which is experienced as a threat. The exposure to heteronomy is intensified, rather than attenuated. What could be a self-determined co-ordination of individual pieces of work, appears as its opposite, as the exposure to strangers in an undefined horizontal and, therefore, all the more competitive, collaboration. 'I have had enough of my colleagues during the eight hours' work and I just long to be at home with my family and be able to do what I want.... This close co-operation which exists in part at work is about as much as I can take. I don't want any more of it ... least of all after working hours.'[13] The most important lesson of this co-operation was a truism. Co-operation is tied to decisions by individuals; it cannot simply be an arrangement ordained from above for individuals to fit into without losing their self-confidence. And in fact at some point in all our group discussions people would start talking about 'real co-operation' and tell us excitedly about 'subversive acts' – how, by acting together, they had bypassed the rules, circumvented regulations, and so on. We can now add to the thesis proposed above: where the work is determined by others, co-operation is experienced as a subversive act.

Since we regarded the old demarcations between different kinds of work and workers, as well as the boundary between work-time and leisure-time as obstacles to the development and humanization of work relations, we at first thought of the dissolution of these boundaries as an opportunity. Our study very soon revealed, however, that our interviewees consistently regarded these 'opportunities' as a threat, one which they tried to ward off by drawing new boundary lines or extending old ones. Their main purpose seemed to be to prevent leakage between the two realms. For example, work should never be taken home – if it had to be they 'saved' the situation by renaming it, by refusing to classify thinking, turning over of ideas in their minds as 'work'. The reverse is even more important. Private matters, their existence as private individuals, must never enter the workplace. What becomes crucial is the ability to control information about oneself.

Once again we encountered the phenomenon of increasing isolation. Since this was reported as something new, we assumed it was not 'only' the product of the relations of production, but that it must be connected with the productive forces, in other words, the introduction of the computers. We asked about the specific requirements in computerized offices and of the experience of individuals with these requirements. Even though the jobs people were doing differed considerably, they started by agreeing that the need for better qualifications had increased and that more knowledge and greater skills were necessary. However, they all saw this negatively. In answer to our questions about how this necessary knowledge had been acquired, they had surprisingly little to say. And this in turn pointed to differences between the sexes. There had been introductory courses, principally for men. Women mainly gained the necessary know-how on the job. Were there established procedures for teaching people about computers? This question was met by blank incomprehension, that is to say, the number of people who failed to respond was unusually high. Since further training had always been one of the normal ways of obtaining internal promotion we tried in the group interviews to discuss this method of learning. We arrived at the surprising conclusion that acquiring computer handbooks for using at home and secretly studying them after working hours was not seen as a form of training or education at all. More often it was regarded as a way of eliminating character deficiencies. This was essential if they were to make themselves more saleable in a deteriorating labour market, or escape rationalization in their own company.

Learning by doing is not a very good method if the activity is not comprehensible in terms of ordinary everyday activities. Computers have a different logic from everyday common sense. This calls for a way of dealing with them which places the user theoretically above the actual work processes and treats the computer as 'stupid'. In other words, the operator assumes a 'thinking' stance towards the machine.

Initiated by way of inadequate introductory courses, which, moreover, came at a time when their male colleagues already possessed the necessary know-how, and they themselves for the most part did not have enough time in the evenings to catch up properly, the women reacted mainly with panic. They learned the commands by heart and this meant that they constantly felt they were living in a prison in which incomprehensible catastrophes might erupt at any moment. We found a host of signs suggesting that in countries all over the world it was women who were most likely to find working with computers unbearable.

Do women generally work at less well-qualified jobs than men, and are they therefore more at risk than their male colleagues? In our sample we found that there was a relatively high proportion of men working at inputting data, and almost half the interactive process jobs were filled by women. This meant that this theory looked a little flimsy. Exploring our preconceptions still further, we wondered about another popular explanation: women are more hostile towards technology. An aversion towards technology in general might easily cause anxiety and make for difficulties in learning and working with VDUs. However, our sample – which did after all amount to 250 people – contained very few men or women who did not have a positive attitude towards the new technology in their own work. Despite this there was still a gulf between people's opinion of themselves and opinions about women's attitude towards technology. The younger men (those under thirty-five) and the married women were generally of the opinion that women are not well disposed towards technology and that this is perceived by their superiors, who act accordingly.[14]

Once we were on the track of gender distinctions in the problems arising in automated offices, we were alerted to the extent of the dissatisfaction experienced by women employees. In our view this was connected with the character of their work. They frequently complained that they had not achieved anything. They wanted the gaps that arose in the periods when the computer was not functioning to be filled by other tasks. We had actually assumed that women's social character would be particularly appropriate to a type of work which involved the ability to deal with sudden crises, waiting times, criticism and experimental cautiousness, because women are used to similar demands at home from their families. But in fact it was they who felt such work to be peculiarly unsatisfying. They looked at themselves through the eyes of their superiors and judged their work, which in some ways resembles housework, inadequate, indeed not work at all, but simply wasted time. They 'might just as well have stayed at home'. The remarkable fact is that women do not attempt to evade work because it is alienated and paid; rather they regard it as a mark of favour to be allowed to work for money at all. This also explains why they wish to be kept abnormally busy.

It would be astonishing if the male takeover in computerized offices should be accomplished without notable signs of conflict. Office work is generally characterized as 'feminine'. It is physically undemanding and clean; it is a form of typing and not dirty or predominantly technical, as would be appropriate for men's work. In our group discussions a kind of anxiety surfaced among the male participants about the prospects of further technological advances. Their fears were that the future belongs to women because technology itself is being 'feminized'. This went as far as the vision of 'rose-tinted computer screens'. Ultimately such fears were neutralized ideologically in a way that redefined this type of work. They concluded that working with computers is not actually the same as typing. It is technical and therefore it is proper men's work. This conflict about the gender-specific meaning of work, and hence of particular jobs, is being fought out everywhere. Women look like losing it unless they take energetic steps.

It is both difficult and necessary to compensate for the inadequate training facilities on offer at work. In this context we inquired about cooperation with colleagues, about catching up and obtaining advice. The replies showed evidence of women's cultural exclusion. Whereas 80 per cent emphasized the need for such advice, the men evidently had networks for passing on information from which women are largely excluded. Women regularly form networks when they are definitely in a minority. A relatively high percentage of women even thought of handing in their notice on this account. At the same time – at least in our sample – women had a remarkable influence on the structures of solidarity in general. Whenever there was a high proportion of women in the workforce, there were scarcely any individual attempts to resolve conflicts, while the collective attempts which had previously amounted to 20 per cent, now rose to 70 per cent of the total. Interestingly, the male and female information networks were not regarded as gender-specific by the participants, nor as a way of sticking together. We can conclude from this that solidarity structures exist in practice which are not consciously recognized as such, and which, therefore, are unable to develop any conscious strategies or objectives.

A brief run-through the changed working conditions after the introduction of computers highlighted a series of problems, contradictions and paradoxes:

• A type of work which could in theory attenuate the vertical hierarchies and the hierarchy between the sexes, work which has an egalitarian tendency, is in reality felt to be divisive. Masculine work cultures exclude women. Where both sexes are represented in more or less equal numbers – for example in various specialized positions – new divisions of labour develop. Women let themselves be pushed, or they move 'voluntarily', into less ambitious jobs or into positions which offer less recognition. In addition they always take on the chores of watering the plants, making coffee, running errands, photocopying and filing.

• Training for the more advanced qualifications, the need for which is now generally recognized, is not equally available to all. It is true that information sciences have now been introduced into schools in a number of *Länder* in the Federal Republic. But here, too, we find that it is the boys who show more initiative in grasping their opportunity. Doubts about the value of co-educational education are on the increase.

• A type of work which ought to increase the all-round competence of the workforce in terms of their access to the work process and their overview of it is leading in practice to increased control from above. Even the question of ownership of the means of production and the product is becoming unclear. The theft of data and software is now an everyday occurrence. And yet this dissolution of one of the major props of our society, the inviolability of property, has still led to intensified competition.

These paradoxes are experienced personally as a state of being torn apart by contradictions and they lead to isolation and anxiety. Both are essential causes of the somatic effects of cultural incompatibilities. The relations of production become indigestible and within them the same holds good for the relations between the sexes, customs, values and, in the last analysis, the very identities of the members of the workforce themselves.

In this field it seems to me that the ability to deal with contradictions is fundamental. The subject of men, women and computers is a mine-field, in which we finally discovered how to overcome the usual evasive tactics for dealing with contradictions. I have already described how people are accustomed to tone down contradictions, fasten on one side of them or ignore them completely, replacing them with a spurious harmony. The participants in our discussion had evidently had much practice and showed great ingenuity in arguing contradictions out of existence. Their efforts were aimed principally against understanding them and hence against the need for change. Men and women were equally adept at this. We proposed contradictions; they outdid them-selves in disposing of them. They changed them into mere differences, argued that different people had different characters, or simply changed the subject. This process proved trouble-free until we reached the question of gender. Our argument that computer work was both masculine and feminine, but for opposite reasons, was met by long speeches from the male participants on the equality of the sexes, culmi-nating quite quickly in sublime statements about man in general and his inalienable rights ... At this the women lost patience.

> I really had to keep a hold on myself.... I really only held back because I know what work you do, on the computer, and that you really belong in the evaluating department of computer work, which is partly women's work, so that maybe you don't see the difference. But that's not how I see it. There are enormous differences between men and women on the computer ... Women are just shoved in front of them, their typewriters are taken away from them, because the boss has simply decided that the computers are more profitable ...[15]

Interventions of this sort brought about a strategic change of direc-tion. The nature of the discussion altered; the active woman became something of a spokeswoman in the group. The themes were now treated rather differently. After the first act of denial everyone suddenly began to speak clearly and analytically about all manner of contradictions. The topics discussed included profits, the arbitrary decisions of employers, the relations of production, capitalism – the old questions were now seen in a new light and this led to new insights. We drew the following conclusion from our experience.

It is obvious that there are contradictions that reach so deeply into the public consciousness that it is no easy matter to deny them. Cracks in the façade lead to the comprehension of other issues too, such as those arising from the relations of production and their contradictions. Our interpretation of the world becomes more full of conflict and clearer. A key contradiction in our day is that of relations between the sexes. This can be articulated by women. They no longer tolerate its being ignored. This enables them to become a force for larger and expanding actions that themselves bring further changes.

Lessons for the Socio-Psychological Study of Work

The basis of the socio-psychological study of work is the analysis of the socially dominant conditions of work. These determine not only the work of the future, but also the sectors not yet directly affected – whether it be in the tempo of work, the composition of the different kinds of work, or the anxieties of workers who fear for their future. An essential 'object of study' must be the actual experience of the workers, how they are affected, how they adapt. Lending support to their ability to act is a practical task of the psychology of work. In so doing it must take account of the fact that individuals participate in several, often mutually contradictory 'worlds of experience', whose coexistence is an individual balancing act, which in our society is stabilized with the aid of the daily elimination of contradictions. Wherever the experience of work makes change necessary people react by inwardly distancing themselves, instead of rejecting the official interpretation of these changes, which initially seems far less important than one's own activity. Our experiment with contradictions should be extended as a strategy for including workers in the research project. The habit of analysing one's own conditions of work, appropriation instead of adaptation, appears unavoidable in the age of microelectronics. It represents an opportunity which is also a challenge to industrial psychologists. After all, a research project undertaken together with workers, instead of with workers as its objects, means that academically qualified social scientists should also work towards their own abolition at the very point at which they take their function as intellectuals seriously.

An important result which must determine every methodological approach is the historicity of the individual subjects, processes and even concepts with whose aid knowledge is to be acquired. The object of research, as well as a practical problem, is the way in which workers of the 'old' type of worker are 'inserted' into the established structures with their advantages and disadvantages. To work their way out and break new ground, in so far as it seems emancipatory, or declare their opposition to novelty where the existing sense of insecurity leads to a more intensive process of subordination, calls for a strategy to deal with the increasing pace of change. The problematic areas must be sought out with the co-operation of the workers themselves, and solutions must be attempted which look to the expansion of the collective power to act. Knowledge is an essential prerequisite for researchers and the objects of their research. This is a characteristic of the new productive forces. By which we mean the collaboration between people and the technical and organizational conditions of work. New forms of knowledge are developed, which remain technical and internal to the system even though their function is to think about systems. New demarcation lines excluding those without this knowledge intensify the contradictions in the individual industrial nations. A psychology of work in the interests of the workers must also include the analysis of the solutions proposed by employers and governments. Isolation must be fought by exploiting the opportunities for collective action. The tendency to withdraw into the private sphere must be countered by strengthening the meaning of the social project. And, finally, people's self-confidence in their ability to act must be fortified so as to overcome their fear.

Notes

1. B. Knave and P.G. Widebäck, eds, *Work with Display Units 86*, Amsterdam/New York/Oxford/Tokyo 1987.

2. For example, another study of the effects of work with display units in Sweden showed that the frequency of miscarriages, the news of which sent panic waves through the country, should be blamed less on computer screens than on women's work in general.

3. In the Federal Republic of Germany the proportion of women working with computers rose by 64 per cent in the period from 1970 to 1982; since 1982 it has been slowly declining, while the proportion of men has been growing over the same period.

A comparative study of differences, or even the different relations of production would require a huge empirical investigation which would go beyond the scope of the present discussion. In my empirical account I shall confine myself for this reason to questions of the work culture in West German businesses and offices.

4. In his play *Der grosse Frieden* [The Great Peace] Volker Braun establishes a connection between the work of the farmer – eyes on the furrow – and the impossibility of ruling the country and abolishing domination while in that posture:

> But in peacetime he is on his own
> Separated off by his work, which bows him down
> Behind the wooden post that he forces into the ground
> A little empire, isn't it? From one morning to the next
> That's all he knows. This dinosaur
> never lifts his eyes from the furrow. Where
> is his office?
> The farmer cannot represent himself.

5. On this point see the detailed account in Projekt Automation und Qualifikation, *Zerreissproben – Automation im Arbeiterleben*, Chapter 2, 'Arbeit und Privatleben. Programmierer', 1983; and also, *Widersprüche der Automationsarbeit*, 1987, Chapters 11 and 15.

6. See G. Brosius and F. Haugh, eds, *Frauen\Männer\Computer. EDV im Büro: Empirische Untersuchungen*, Berlin 1987.

7. See on this point Projekt Automation und Qualifikation, 1987, particularly Chapter 11.

8. *Ibid.*

9. On this point see my 'Zeit der Privatisierungen? Über Verarbeitungsformen gesellschaftlicher Widersprüche in Arbeit und Lebensweise', *Das Argument* 156, 1986 (this volume, pp. 113–36).

10. As early as 1973 Holzkamp proposed a similar experiment in his book on 'sensuous knowledge'. He started from the very assumption that people do not mirror the real contradictions in their everyday thoughts. Via 'experiments with contradictions' in which 'subjects' are explicitly exposed to such contradictions, he hoped to shed light on the nature of subjectivity in bourgeois society, as well as to stimulate understanding in his subjects. See *Sinnliche Erkenntnis – Historischer Ursprung und gesellschaftliche Funktion der Wahrnehmung*, Frankfurt am Main 1973, pp. 216ff.

11. See Brosius and Haug, eds, *Frauen\Männer\Computer*, p. 88.

12. On these different types of relationship see especially Klaus Holzkamp, *Grundlegung der Psychologie*, pp. 326ff.

13. See Brosius and Haug, eds, p. 88.

14. We were puzzled by the surprising finding that it is above all the younger men rather than their fathers who have strong prejudices about women's suitability, and have tried to explain it in terms of the deteroriating situation in the labour market.

15. Brosius and Haug, eds, *Frauen\Männer\Computer*, p. 65.

PART THREE

Politics

NINE

Men's History, Women's Liberation and Socialism

Pre-history of the Topic

To come out with it right from the start: I found it very difficult to get to grips with this topic. Instead of problems resolving themselves neatly as I worked, new ones constantly made their appearance. And although I have only been thinking about the question intensively for the last few months, I now find it hard even to recall the time in which the entire matter seemed self-evident and the relationship between the two movements altogether natural, not at all a problem to which one ought to devote much effort. The self-evident nature of the relationship was a part of my political life. As a Marxist of over twenty years' standing I have thought of myself as being a part of the labour movement and scientific socialism. For the last twelve years I have been active in the women's movement. The fact that I could find the existence of two independent movements with similar goals unproblematic has taught me to realize that it can be dangerous to take anything too much for granted. That aside, I should like to ask your indulgence if you find that my theses are rather too provisional and that my arguments have not been fully thought out. Further debate in the women's movement will be needed to bring greater clarity into the issues at stake.

If the relationship between the two movements was so unproblematic, why did I start to question it at all? I was invited to give a talk on the subject and thought at first that I would refuse. In my letter declining the invitation I began by saying that unfortunately I could not come because the subject was not one I had specialized in. The word 'specialize' looked a bit silly when I was talking about whole movements and so I looked for an alternative: it was not one of my 'interests'. That was even worse. My changing the word brought home to me the scandal inherent in the subject. The fact was that I had not really thought much about it, or rather the problems it raised. I changed my letter of refusal into one accepting the invitation and began to work on it. I brought down from the book shelves the debates that had been going on internationally on the topic of feminism and Marxism, or feminism and the labour movement over the previous three to four years. I had been saving them up to read in the vacations. One of the first questions in these debates was concerned with the emergence of 'new social movements'. Women active in the labour movement generally express their amazement that society should contain such a huge untapped critical potential, one which had previously gone unnoticed and which the labour movement had not yet been able to turn to its own advantage. This led to questions about the mobilizing power of the women's movements (about which I shall have something to say later) and about political forms of activity. At the centre of the discussions was the question about what the labour movement could learn from the women's movement and, conversely, how women could formulate their demands in such a way as to enable them to effect an entry into the political realms now occupied by the parties.

These questions, regardless of whether they were answered in a positive or negative way, presupposed a connection between the women's movement and the labour movement, while denying such a connection in practice.

The Gulf between the Labour Movement
and the Women's Movement

What does 'denying the connection in practice' mean? In my view it means a form of politics based on distinct interpretations of the meaning of oppression in the two movements. To take the labour movement first. Marxism assumes that liberation will come in more or less independent stages. The main thing comes first – that is to say, the economic revolution, the liberation from the capitalist domination of wage labour. This is to be followed by other changes, such as dismantling men's subjugation of women. As the women's movement grew in strength the separation was accompanied by a phenomenon which I would describe as 'the opportunistic incorporation of women's demands' into the general programmes of workers' organizations. This can even go so far as to include setting up women's sections. These changes can be thought of as 'opportunistic', because we are talking about concessions which have been made under external pressure, perhaps so as to win over women voters, for example. They do not spring from a fundamental rethinking of an entire strategy. This piece-meal approach has the further disadvantage that such additions can be discarded again at any time, without disrupting the rest of the programme. Such a policy tends mainly to concern itself with the question of how to enlist the support of these women who have suddenly become aroused on this or that issue. It tends to ignore the question about what is wrong with a policy which does not automatically cater for the specific needs of half the population.

The women's movement, too, tends in practice to deny the connection between the two movements. In their case it is a question of the patriarchy thesis. This assumes that men's domination of women spreads beyond the barriers of class. Historically, it antedates capitalism and will outlast it. In its more radical formulations (such as in Millet 1970) the patriarchy theory dispenses with class struggle entirely. (For a discussion of the crucial concepts in the women's movement, see Barrett, 1980.)

But there is also a third position which in practice denies the connection between the two movements, while giving the impression of doing the very opposite. Its representatives, women for the most part, can be seen eagerly attempting to establish that connection by expanding the concept of class. Either they argue very radically and proclaim the female sex to be a class so as to inscribe themselves into the class struggle; or else they quite reasonably question the restriction of the Marxian class concept to the workers and try to extend it to cover white-collar workers – a strategy which allows them to include a larger section of working women in the working class.

These conceptual redefinitions, which of course do not elaborate on any changes that would be needed to combat capitalist oppression in ways specific to women, also include the attempt to forge a link between women's oppression and capitalist exploitation in another way. It is claimed that if women stop doing the housework capitalism will collapse, or alternatively, it is argued that unpaid housework is the foundation of economic exploitation. It is not my concern here to assert that nothing would be changed if housewives went on strike, but only to ask whether justice can really be done to women's issues by situating them like this in the class struggle between capital and labour. What it overlooks is that the history of capitalist production is one in which women have never made more than guest appearances, and that the conflict between the two classes has essentially always been a conflict between men. Of course, none of us has any difficulty in thinking of important labour disputes involving women, or of the role of women textile workers in the Russian Revolution, and of other like events. But the very fact that such actions are emphasized and can be singled out in this way shows how far from obvious it is that women should play a part in workers' struggles. Furthermore, the attempt to establish a connection in theory contains the tacit admission that there is no direct link between the two movements. Thus all three attempts end up by demonstrating the gulf that exists between the two movements in practice. However, by the same token, at a very general level they reveal an abstract overarching relationship. Both movements have as their goal a society without oppression and exploitation and both are projects which aim to transform their own living conditions.

Unity in Diversity: Socialist Feminists

Alongside these general interconnections there is also a specific link between the women's movement and the labour movement. As I intimated in my opening comments, this is a connection established within individuals. Because of the practical divergences it expresses itself as an internal contradiction, possibly over a period of time. Or it may manifest itself as the fate of someone caught 'between two stools' – smiled at condescendingly by authentic political activists whose ideas are so developed that they work only in the labour movement, and denounced as traitors by true feminists because they refuse to devote their entire efforts to the women's movement. I am referring to socialist feminism and its representatives, such as myself. If we ignore for the moment the question of inner conflict, we can examine the politics actually pursued by socialist feminists. I shall make such politics my starting point because it must yield a practical answer to our question about the link between the women's movement and the labour movement.

Let me begin with the political activities of the Socialist Women's League [Sozialistischer Frauenbund], of which I have been a member since 1969 (when it was still called Action Committee for the Liberation of Women). My account will be (self-) critical and in the interests of comprehension, a little exaggerated. (I would ask fellow women-members to overlook the exaggeration. Simplification is necessary in order to highlight the problematic nature of political activities for which I, too, bear some of the responsibility.) So what I shall describe is not what a socialist women's politics should be, but what we actually did.

Back to the year 1969. I was a member of the League of German Socialist Students [SDS] and by socialism we meant the necessary framework of freedom and emancipation. It meant the abolition of capitalist domination, the expropriation of the owners of the means of production and the socialization of those means. Those were the goals we were committed to. That the 'woman question' is older than capitalism was clear to us. That the labour movement, the parties and trade unions, fail to represent the cause of women properly, that women are inadequately represented in those organizations and hence are unable to speak for themselves, indeed the fact that unless they have jobs they have no right to be a part of the labour movement at all – all this inspired us, since we thought of ourselves initially as just being 'politically motivated', to organize ourselves into a women's organization in addition to the labour movement. Since we had no desire to abandon our political aims it had to be a socialist women's organization.

How did we conceive of the relationship between socialism and women's politics? Committed as we were to political organizations which failed to represent our interests, we saw it as our main task to educate women to play their part in their political activities. This included training them to speak out at political meetings, to write pamphlets and to realize that, in addition to their membership of women's groups, they should join a 'genuine political' organization too, a trade union at the very least. Our statutes, for example, contained a clause making membership of a union mandatory. Apart from that, we saw our task as encouraging women to go out into the workforce, to liberate themselves from economic dependence. The double activity which we expected from all our members, the genuine split between official political activities and women's issues expressed itself again and again in the complete overloading of all women's organizations, as well as of their individual members. Vietnam, South Africa, the proposed legislation on universities, nuclear armament, peace, the proposed emergency laws — we had to react to every issue, since after all we were a women's political organization.

But when were we supposed to discuss the women's issues which, looked at in this context, always seemed less urgent and less vital, matters which could always be postponed until tomorrow? We had more to do than ever before and were able to do less for women's issues than was necessary. All around us the non-socialist women's movement formed so-called 'autonomous' groups and organized large-scale activities on 'home births', 'consciousness-raising' and 'self-examination' — we took no part in them. Finally, we took the decision to confine our activities in the women's organization to women's issues and apart from that — since we were a socialist organization — to take part in May Day, the day celebrating the workers' struggle. In general terms we found ourselves in the mid 1970s roughly at the stage defined by Ottilie Bader in 1908:

> There is no further need for special organizations for fellow women comrades; women everywhere will join the Social Democratic Party. However, this common organization does not spell the demise of other institutions set up by our comrades in the light of prevailing conditions and with a particular end in view. These institutions have proved themselves to be an excellent means for providing the female members with a theoretical training, for winning the allegiance of women from the masses for the political and economic struggle of the proletariat and recruiting them for the party organizations.
>
> Quoted in Niggemann, 1981, p. 70

On 1 May, therefore, we took our banners for equal wages, more education for women, more equality of opportunity, and so on, and joined the march. But because the working class 'as such' was marching, we were not allowed to display the banner of our organization. This meant that our banners with our particular demands to do with women's issues – for nursery schools, for example – were unable to make much of a show. As usual, they were just appendages to weightier demands. Who can be surprised if hardly any of us marched with the women? Since the majority were members of both organizations, they mainly preferred to carry the more dignified banners reflecting the concerns of the working class as a whole. Who can be astonished if the Women's League did not increase in size? Many joined our ranks; but just as many abandoned us in favour of the 'real', 'grown-up' organizations, once they had learned from us. Once there, some of them even spoke up on behalf of women's interests. Why did we not interpret this loss of members as a criticism? Because we thought it right that they should leave us to work in the 'political organizations'. The fact that some of us remained, myself included, seemed necessary to provide continuity and because, as usual, not enough was being done for women.

It was political activity of this kind that leads me to the conclusion that we basically conceived the connection between socialism and feminism as a non-connection. We looked for and found mistakes in ourselves and wanted ·to correct them so that we could be more successful politically. But we had put our trust in the belief that the way to achieve socialism was by expropriating the owners of the means of production. We did not hold with the view that women's problems would be solved subsequently, nor that women's politics were superfluous. But we did believe that we (that is to say, over half the population) were needed to help bring about a liberation and that change in social conditions would of itself lead to a change in people, a transformation in people who had grown up and were trapped in (the realm of) private social relations.

But what we did not question, or even venture to contemplate, was the proposition that a movement which sets out to overturn the entire system of master and servant relations calls for a different kind of politics from one in which just one part of the population makes the decisions about how all this should be achieved. Basically we believed that real politics was a serious business. Whenever politics became fun – for example, we carried a placard on 1 May which said 'Everyone Must Know Everything' and were pushed to one side and told to remove it – whenever politics became fun, we were dismissed as petty bourgeois, a criticism we never came to terms with. Nor did we ever lose our bad conscience about the absence of real proletarian women from our organization, a criticism which one petty bourgeois always uses as a stick with which to beat another. We attempted, rather clumsily, to defend ourselves against this accusation by pointing out that our League had doctors' assistants, technical draughtswomen and bookshop assistants, and that our organization did contain at least some proletarians. In other words, we twisted the theory in ways already mentioned to give the impression that our struggle was a direct class conflict. In short we did believe that the two movements were directly related, and we did not question Lenin's advice not to split our forces and not to divert forces from the economic struggle and into the women's struggle. We thus confirmed that it was right to do first the one thing, and then the other.

Quite apart from the question of feminism, the fact that we simply accepted the economic struggle uncritically as the only real political struggle is all the more astonishing when it is recalled that at a general political level our discussions were very much concerned with *connections*, such as those existing between the monopolies and the state. But how should we go about fighting against the power of the state if it is assumed to be in league with the monopolies, and where exactly is that power to be found? For example, is not the state the sponsor of the family and thereby also of the actual condition of women? Does it not involve itself in questions of education? Why then did we fail to direct our political activities to matters such as these?

The Campaign against Paragraph 218

The abortion campaign is one instance of a particularly misconceived politics on our part. It is instructive to see how we conducted the attack on Paragraph 218 because it proves that personal involvement is not an adequate basis for action. In our case it produced some fairly dull and uninspired politics. I shall make the fact that we conducted the campaign against Paragraph 218 mainly out of a sense of duty the starting point for an examination of our political activities and our way of thinking, but my intention in so doing is to show that its defects can be overcome in a constructive way. For all my criticisms it should not be overlooked that the new women's movement as a whole was brought into being by this campaign and that the Socialist Women's League can take the credit. The first advertisements in *Stern*, ('I too have had an abortion') were placed by members of the Women's League – taking their lead from Alice Schwarzer, who had imported the idea from France. Likewise it was we who organized the first great conference in Berlin and it was our spokeswoman who spoke at the parliamentary hearing on behalf of a movement which by then had expanded to more than forty groups. But we soon found ourselves mired in a paralysing discussion about which groups we should actually choose to ally ourselves with.

The question of alliances was urgent because the SPD with its mass organization was willing to join in the fight as long as we agreed to call for the modification of Paragraph 218. But we were radicals and demanded complete abolition. We posed the issue as follows: Did we prefer a mass campaign that would call only for modification of the existing legislation or would we rather remain uncorrupted and keep our numbers small, while going all out for complete abolition? The choice confronted us with the great dilemma of obtaining mass support, but at the cost of laying ourselves open to the charge of pandering to petty bourgeois conformism. We conducted a broader theoretical analysis of the entire problem and came to the conclusion that the right to one's own body, which seemed to lie at the heart of the debate was basically predicated on the idea of the private, bourgeois individual. Such a right was doubtless indispensable as a campaign slogan, but had not really advanced beyond the French Revolution of 1789, when citizens demanded their rights as individuals.

Having reached this point, that is to say, having realized that we were following the route laid down in the French Revolution, the path taken by the private, bourgeois individual, we appended a further complicated piece of analysis explaining why it can be progressive in a capitalist system to fight for individual bourgeois rights. Individual rights, we maintained, and in certain circumstances the rights of society too, had to be defended against the encroachments of the state.

We followed this up with a rather unimaginative and dour campaign which we conducted from a sense of duty, all the time with the feeling that genuine politics had somehow passed us by – and this despite our very real personal commitment, since almost all women have had something to do with abortions at some time or another.

Roads to Socialism

How was that possible? I do not believe that we had come up with a mistaken answer to the question we had posed, or that we should have analysed it differently or drawn different conclusions. It is my belief that we asked the wrong questions, and that to debate the question of whether this or that demand is socialist, or whether it leads directly to socialism, is misguided because it renders us incapable of action.

I should like now to take up a number of ideas as formulated by Sheila Rowbotham (1973) for the English abortion campaign, and expanded by myself, in order to show how productive other forms of political activity can be. Rowbotham asked herself what questions are raised by abortion and how consciousness is changed by campaigns for repeal of the legislation restricting it or making it totally illegal. Unlike us, she wastes no time discussing the legitimacy of the right to one's own body. Instead she realizes that the abortion question leads us to reflections

- on fertility and motherhood;
- on the general question of man's sexual domination of women;
- on people's relationships to their own bodies and to the question of sexual pleasure;
- about parliament and the legal system;
- about a democratic and social health service;
- about a comprehensive system of childcare;
- about the power of the state in population policy;
- about the technology of contraception and profits in the chemical industry, and – to extend her list:
- about the role of the church and justice in general;
- about the connections between sexuality and politics;
- about family policy and national budgets;
- about the role of science in legitimating domination, and so on.

Thus the ramifications of an apparently personal matter like abortion turn out to involve more or less the entire system. We can learn from this that power relations are a diverse and complex business and that our earlier, deductive thinking presupposed a movement which only existed in our minds, and not in people's actions. We posited *one single* movement where in reality there were many. We overlooked the diversified nature of relationships of power and domination. All this means that we should not have asked whether this or that was a socialist policy. We should have asked instead: What will change or be changed, how is something experienced, what is it linked with, how are posts and positions connected with each other in reality? This example has implications for the general question of the relationship between the labour movement and the women's movement and of the different kinds of political activities.

The Connection between the Labour Movement and the Women's Movement: A Proposal for a Socialist Women's Politics

I shall now formulate a number of theses which will emphasize the features common to the two movements and amount to a plea for a change in socialist policy. My ideas are by no means fully clarified and will be set out in somewhat abbreviated form. Genuine clarity can only be obtained in the course of actual political struggle. My arguments are based on the following assumptions:

1. The power of men over women, in other words, women's oppression, is older than class oppression.
2. The social structure of our society is based on the oppression of women. By social structure I understand the system of the division of labour operating throughout society, the gender-specific ascription of the role of reproductive tasks (caring for the family), and the system of cultural values and norms.
3. In the process of achieving liberation from exploitation by capital, the working class is the historical subject and women's liberation plays no part in it.
4. All attempts to import women's issues into the programme of

class struggle, despite what was said above, lead to unsatisfying and forced attitudes, a scale of important and unimportant priorities and an artificial link between women's liberation and the economic conjuncture. (By this I mean the attitude that in times of economic crisis we simply cannot afford the luxury of fighting for women's demands, but have instead to stick together on the main issues.)

5. I am proceeding from the assumption that attempts by parts of the women's movement to establish a direct link between women's oppression and capitalist exploitation are sterile games which serve to fill people's minds with complicated problems but change nothing in practice. In addition, my experience with the abortion campaign leads me to include a further observation. A general policy of the kind that we have been considering, one in which attention is focused on the capitalist exploitation of male workers, while ignoring other oppressed groups, such as women, who at best come last in the list of priorities, is, to say the least, of dubious value. This is not just because it omits to include half the human race in its struggles, but because it claims to want to abolish all domination, while failing to tackle all sorts of other power relationships. In other words, it is not concrete, but abstract and declines to intervene in processes which cause human happiness or misery. Paramio (1982) goes so far as to assert that the future of the trade unions in the Western industrial nations depends on whether they are prepared to make equal pay for women their first and most important objective.

The Personal is the Political

In order to overcome this political abstractness I should like to begin with the thesis with which the new women's movement made its appearance on the historical scene: the personal is the political. It is a motto everyone is familiar with. Its utility in practical politics is often overlooked by 'real politicians' who point to a common misinterpretation. Its justification, in my view, is threefold:

1. Everything that passes for the personal, the private sphere, is so inextricably interwoven with power that it functions as the breeding ground for the maintenance of existing social and political structures.

2. The separation of different spheres, of politics and private life is itself a manipulation of power, and its consequences, including the very existence of professional politicians, constitute a division of labour which makes it impossible even technically for us to make a natural transition from the private realm into public life.

3. The abolition of hegemony is a programme which must extend down to the smallest details of private life, only then is it possible to wage a radical, committed campaign on a mass basis and to transform our own conditions of life.

With these three interpretations it became possible for women to enter history as political subjects. But the validity of the thesis necessarily extends into politics as a whole. We might say somewhat critically that any politics that disregards such basic assumptions presupposes that the men who are engaged in such politics do not themselves have private lives, but are just public persons and not people with private dimensions which affect their lives as politicians. Jane Jenson is very informative about the clash between the feminist approach to politics and the traditional agenda-setting of actions which are held to be politically useful. Her history of a women's group of the Communist Party in a Paris *arrondissement* is very instructive. In it Jenson discusses, among other things, the question of which women's books should be offered for sale at the bookstall. This involved decisions which the men in charge wanted to deny women the right to make. And the most important issue to emerge – at least in my view – was the women's refusal to distribute a leaflet on the grounds that it appealed to the stupidity of the women it was aimed at. It contained very general and hence completely vague questions such as, 'Would you like a better life? Would you like a better life for your family? Do you think they are badly treated?' This was followed by an invitation to vote for the Communist Party which had solutions for all these problems ready to hand. The women's commission justified their refusal to distribute the leaflets not just because it reduced women to their role in the family, but above all because 'it all came from outside, without making the slightest effort to lead women to reflect on changes *they* might want to introduce' (Jenson, 1980, p. 140). The women's commission in contrast wanted policies 'in which women would be made responsible for the changes in their own lives and in which it would not be left to politicians and parties to define what improvements should be made' (*Ibid*).

Overlapping Structures of Domination

I shall summarize my previous arguments and conclude with a specific proposal for political action. What we were looking for was the link between the labour movement and the women's movement. The aim of the labour movement is freedom from capitalist exploitation. It is therefore economic in nature and centres on the day-to-day struggle for wages and better working conditions. Beyond that it looks forward to a mode of production not based on the profit motive and envisages relations between people which are not based on exchange and competition. Women's demands are directed at changing social structures. The attempt to derive the one logically from the other leads to reductionist solutions which have not proved viable. They include the extension of the concept of class, or the assertion that the private sphere of the reproduction of the working class is essential for profit. Here the Nordic nations are well on the way to socializing large parts of the realm of production (and in our society, too, fast food, canteen meals, and so on, are a growing source of profit), without ceasing to be capitalist. It is not possible to deduce the labour movement from the women's movement or vice versa; neither movement can be reduced to the other. (Not that it would occur to anyone to deduce the labour movement from the women's movement, whereas the reverse happens all the time.)

The need to establish a connection despite all this becomes even greater when we reflect that the problem of women is older than capitalism and older therefore than the problem of the workers as well. Can the connection be established in a non-reductionist way? Let us investigate the origins of the various bonds that fetter both workers and women. This is a way to discover how the two oppressions are related to each other in practice and how the various elements of domination are interwoven.

Since the two oppressions do join forces in various ways we must rule out every one-sided historical account of women's oppression of the sort suggested by the patriarchy thesis. The critique of patriarchy does provide a sharper picture of women's oppression, but at the price of rendering invisible the workings and the ramifications of the power relations that operate today. Instead of a precise investigation of what is taking place in our time, we are given illustrated proof that women's oppression is always with us. In such accounts clitoridectomy is assigned the same significance as marriage, and the links with concrete socio-political operations of power are obscured.

It is easy to study the collaboration of power structures as long as they follow class lines, in other words, as long as the economic relationship parallels the man/woman relationship, and the man is the superior in terms of class and the woman the inferior. This coming together of the two forces leads to the brutalization of both. This can be seen when the industrialist sexually harasses his female apprentices, the boss makes advances to his secretary, or the man of the house sexually abuses his servants. (Paramio shows that in the reverse situation male workers attempt to rape their female superiors. A worker I am friendly with confirmed that at the very least they dream 'of showing her that she is just a woman'.)

It is also well known that right-wing movements prop up their appeal by promising men the possibility of obtaining power over women, in other words, they use the oppression of women as an instrument for securing power in general. I find evidence of this, for example, in Reagan's moral campaign against abortion, or in the CDU's family policies which make use of conservative values in their campaign, all of which are based on the subjugation of women. In the process the bigoted parliamentary speeches, all by men, about how lucky women are to bear children and rear them, go so far beyond what is bearable, that our fury prevents us from using this fairly explicit emergence of the alliance between conservative politics and the oppression of women as a starting point for a progressive politics.

Even more problematic, however (and hitherto completely neglected), are the ways in which the different dominant structures overlap and become interwoven in the course of day-to-day activities. To scrutinize them in the trade unions, in traditional political organizations, in the workplace and in all other spheres of daily life is an urgent task for socialist women's organizations, because the combination of economic exploitation and women's subjugation paralyses the struggle from both sides. I shall give some examples of this. They

are intended to show that the traditional politics of the labour movement enfeebles itself, if it ignores the women's movement, precisely
because the various power structures are intertwined and build on
each other.

Let us consider the fight against unemployment. That fight is
weakened in the first instance by an apparent strengthening, by
excluding women from the right to a job. This is achieved by the ideological claim that the man is the main breadwinner, a claim which of
course reflects an actual situation – the man earns more than the
woman. The exclusion of women is justified by the idea, prevalent in
union circles as elsewhere, that for women to have work in hard times
is a luxury, the first thing we have to renounce. The most important
thing is that at least the men should have work. These attitudes then
find their place in the unions' shopping list of demands and encourage
workers to compete with each other on the basis of gender.

An intensified version of the same problem can be seen in the
question of automation. The printing industry can provide us with an
illustration of the way in which the oppression of women and economic
exploitation reinforce each other, although this is an area where feelings ran so high that it is difficult to reach a balanced judgement. At
issue was the introduction of photo-typesetting. Everybody knows by
now that the printworkers lost the fight against photosetting and that in
this fight the jobs of highly skilled, male compositors were lost over-
night and they were replaced by female workers. Photosetting became
the norm, together with the employment of women workers, the re-
introduction of home-working, piece rates, jobs without security, and
so on, and so on.

In my view a number of the features of this battle are characteristic
of the problems of automation in general. In all such cases the trump
cards pass from the unprepared and prejudiced union representatives
to the employers who are then able to dictate their own terms without
difficulty. To begin with, there is the question of what constitutes
skilled work. It is masculine and physical. If it can be performed by
women, it must be unskilled, since women's work is unskilled by
definition. It must have been a terrible shock when the employers first
announced their intention of employing secretaries (typists) as type-
setters, because for centuries women had been thought unsuited for
compositing, which was classified as skilled work. These events did not

persuade the union to examine the actual skills required in photo-setting, or indeed in those needed in order to master computers, and to make appropriate demands for specialized training. Instead they came to agreements with management to block the employment of women in the first instance. The old compositors were simply put in front of the new machines on the theory that since this was regarded as light, women's work, no special training was thought necessary. (Bürger [1978] gives a graphic account of one printworks where workers who had previously been well organized experienced an anarchic collapse of solidarity as the result of such a policy. These workers secretly acquired the necessary skills and concluded individual agreements with the employers.)

The general deskilling campaign which accompanied the move towards greater automation could also build on a further source of anxiety among workers. The new work was not only women's work, it was also mental, not physical. The employers were able to exploit what was a double humiliation for skilled male workers and set what conditions they wanted for the new women workers who were now employed. The friction between the sexes gave the employers an easy task, but the damage would have been smaller if the workers had presented a united front and if the men had not been so prejudiced about women's work.

Wage struggles, too, are a matter which cannot be isolated from relations between the sexes. For example, they are tied in with the structure of the family. It is a well-known fact that workers cannot strike indefinitely because they have families to look after. It may be supposed that they have not fought as hard as they could for equal pay for women because they see themselves as the main breadwinners. It is probable that women do not fight as hard as they could for equal pay because ideologically they are still imprisoned in the dominant values of family and motherhood.

A further fruitful field for study would be the question of whether individual groups of workers can be played off against each other because the sexual division of labour inside the factory makes the 'natural' hierarchical division into skilled and unskilled, physical and mental labour, credible and effective and prevents the unification of the working class. (In a study group of the West Berlin People's University, 'Everyday Victories and Defeats – Diaries of Women Trade Unionists', a number of women shop stewards, shopfloor representatives, and other union members attempted to write the history of their day-to-day political work with a view to providing an answer. See *Das Argument* 135, 1983). Instead we have privileges for men: secondary exploitation, bribes, using the private structures for pacts with the boss, the I-am-master-of-my-own-house syndrome, the tacit agreements about who is responsible and who isn't, the kind of self-confidence in dealing with subordinates that is practised in the family; and conversely, on the part of women, you find self-denial. (On this point see the story about a retired couple in Haug, 1980, pp. 51ff.) Willis (1979) shows clearly the extent to which masculinity is associated with physical hard work, so that the 'affirmation of masculinity' implies the voluntary acceptance of subordinate jobs.

All this means that workers' consciousness cannot simply be described as either progressive or reactionary; it is both at once (see my 'Report on the Engineers' Congress', *Das Argument* 127, pp. 416ff). Our ability to act depends on our understanding of the specific concrete connections established by the various power structures. The separation of spheres and struggles into 'economic' and 'private' makes it difficult to perceive the possibilities of mutual assistance. Hence the exclusively 'economic' struggle is largely unsuccessful, partly because it fails to take into account the ideological dimensions of a conflict between behaviour patterns which are determined by socially valid norms, and partly because it ignores problems thrown up by the sexual division of labour. Conversely, any struggle which confines itself to the subjugation of women by men will remain ineffectual because it disregards the real support given to men's power by the existing economic set-up – by the interlocking of different forms of power.

The difficulty of conducting separate struggles does not in my view lead to the conclusion that the two campaigns against oppression should simply be added together and complemented by mutual assistance. There are three reasons for my conviction that it is not possible to integrate the demands of the women's movement into the labour movement.

1. The battle against the exploitation by capital, the history of labour struggles and the history of the working-class movement are the history of a male-determined productivity. For this reason – as I have

argued above – women's demands are always just tacked on at the end; they are also-rans.

2. Men are also the beneficiaries of women's subjugation (a man's life-plan rarely features the tasks of bringing up children, even if he wants to have children). This remains the case today, even though it is the same power structure which forces them to attenuate their struggle against exploitation and exposes them to internal divisions and corruption.

3. The prevailing modes of representation by people who make politics, change conditions, make provision, put demands – all on my behalf – are wholly unacceptable to the women's movement. The movement's claim that the private and the personal are the political brings with it a different form of politics. When women make their appearance in the political arena each one has to be political in her own right. The women's movement is an activity which encompasses everyone, and that is its strength.

Women's Autonomous Socialist Organizations

What is the position with the socialist women's organizations which I began by criticizing? How should they change their strategy and what political forms should they embrace? Let us take a final look at the specific realms in which the oppression of women becomes socially visible. I asserted above that the existing structure of society is founded on that oppression. This refers above all to two realms of activity. It refers first to the division of labour (including the sexual division of labour), in which women are assigned the role of caring for the family (rearing children and looking after relationships in general). Secondly, it refers to the realm of ideology, values, consciousness and science. Within these realms there are all sorts of undercurrents and cross-currents of power which call for resistance and reorganization. Up to now the struggles of the self-styled autonomous women's movement have focused on values, role models, taboos, prejudices, habits and interpersonal sexual and mental practices. They are, in short, cultural struggles, attempts to discover a different culture and a different system of values. Furthermore, what had previously been the functions of the state are now reappropriated into society. Self-help groups provide services such as women's refuges, health centres, and so on. These actions are directed against state control and at the same time they represent alternative models of social intercourse. Other groups in the autonomous women's movement have busied themselves with rewriting masculine history and masculine science and scholarship. They have unearthed neglected fields of study, forgotten realms of knowledge, untried or hidden alternatives, and tried to make them viable.

If we review all these activities, it becomes evident that it can scarcely be our task to abandon them and replace them with un-ambiguously socialist ones. Nor is it obvious that socialist groups should attempt to dictate what activities these groups should under-take. Conversely, it would also be a complete misunderstanding to interpret their criticism of the politics of 'socialist women' and their reports on feminist activities as a call to block socialist demands for more state welfare benefits and campaigns for better wages, higher standards of living and better working conditions. There is no absolute solution. All struggles have multi-faceted dimensions and causes. To replace the universal solution there are many different kinds of solution and the task is to bring them all together. The single historical subject has to be replaced by one with many voices. It would be self-defeating to force the various forms of resistance under a single umbrella. Even if we do succeed in joining them all together, we shall only generate a tension, which will be all the greater, the more varied its individual components are. The idea that a political movement must concentrate all its efforts on a single platform, and will be enfeebled if it fails to do so, underestimates the manifold and decentred nature of domination; it misunderstands the nature of the system.

The socialist wing of the women's movement and the autonomous socialist women's organizations provide a constructive answer to the problem of the split between the women's movement and the labour movement. The connection they experience between socialism and feminism is calculated to provide an impetus to research into the ways in which the two power structures – of politics and the economy on the one hand, and patriarchy on the other – function in tandem. This casts a completely different light – and for the first time – on the alleged absence of working women in the women's movement. Their absence should not be regarded with nostalgia or bad conscience. Nor do women any longer want to change conditions for other women. Instead, working women occupy a key position in such research, but they do so as subjects who carry out their own investigations. Their experiences are indispensable for an understanding of the way in which the different power structures interlock. They are not women who can safely be reduced to the two main issues that preoccupy the reformist labour movement: wages and working conditions. They enter into history in their own right as investigating subjects, not as the objects of historical research.

Research can scarcely be the sole preoccupation of socialist women's organizations. But here, too, I believe that we should consider in all seriousness the claim that socialism is either scientific (in the Marxist sense) or it is nothing. And this insight should be carried over into our day-to-day politics. Admittedly, this means changing our understanding of 'science'. It cannot mean simply obtaining a knowledge of the general structures governing our society and attempting then to implement an unchanging policy towards them. We must instead study minutely the forces at work in each situation before embarking on every new campaign. The arenas in which we make political interventions are by no means one-sided and unchanging. Indeed, in the case of women's politics the actions of feminists themselves continuously have an impact on and modify the existing forces at work.

Let us take the question of women's refuges as an example. The establishment of a safe house for the benefit of women who have been battered or raped can be classified as a piece of social work which relieves the state of the need to provide the relevant welfare. Such work has no socialist dimension of itself and is, at best, social reform. We might also prefer the specificity of such a concrete task to a more general demand for more state expenditure on welfare, and even drop this from our programme. Consistent with this, we might fight to have more and more services carried out by private initiative in the movement. The one-sidedness of such a policy is obvious. In reality there is no good reason for rejecting the promotion of women's refugees. It is equally important to make demands on the state welfare budget. The contradiction is a challenge to thought, not to political action. The fact that women's refuges have been set up independently makes possible a different policy in the state sector. It highlights the scandal of state policies towards women and strengthens the case for improvements –

every woman can see what is involved here. At the same time, the existence of women's refuges makes it possible to put them forward as models for a more humane welfare policy, and hence to press for change on a broader front.

Studying the varied and multi-faceted initiatives taken by others before launching one's own can liberate a great flood of creative ideas. It is also a pleasurable activity and helps to bring about a culture of political discussion. Moreover, it humanizes the whole terrain of political action. It means that we no longer expect ourselves to sit in judgement on other activities, forms of struggle or slogans, or to ignore them. Their inclusion in the political struggle allows us to develop more humane forms of political behaviour. For example, let us suppose that someone proposes objectives, such as 'wages for housewives' – a proposal we would never adopt ourselves because we think it mistaken. We would now set about asking the following questions. What are the implications of such a policy for the housewives who might be impressed by it? How do they cope at present with their duties as housewives? What questions occur to them? What questions could we put to them that they might be willing to listen to? Who inspects their work? Why is work inspected at all? What exactly is one paid for? Should every housewife be paid the same, regardless of skills? What skills do housewives actually have? What is the relationship between domestic work and factory work? And so on, and so on. The catalogue of possible productive discussions will be as long as the imagination of the participants.

In these discussions socialist women will focus their questions on the interface between actions by the government or the employers and their implications for women's subjugation. The forms of political action will be as varied as the political discussions. The wealth of ideas buried in people's minds has only been blocked by the boring debate on political representation. At the same time the socialist women's organizations will not be able to avoid the question of the need to educate women in the fundamentals of political economy. But in this new environment the problems of economics will have to be formulated in a much more concrete fashion.

By and large I see an opportunity for the autonomous socialist women's organizations to forge an alliance between feminist radicalism and irreverence and the socialist perspective. I believe that they are capable of combining a politics 'from below' with a high degree of conciliatoriness and that they can harmonize their own spontaneous feelings with an awareness of the need to assemble collective experiences and to use them to develop a new politics. In the process they can marry the lack of deference characteristic of the autonomous organizations with the realization that they must play a part in politics of every kind.

References

Barrett, Michèle, *Women's Oppression Today, Problems in Marxist Feminist Analysis*, Verso, London 1980.

Bonacchi, Gabriella, 'Esiste una theoria feminista?', lecture given at the Congress 'Die neuen sozialen Bewegungen und die heutige Politiktheorie', Oaxaca, Mexico, April 1981 (published in *Internationale Sozialismusdiskussion 2*, Argument-Sonderband 78, Berlin 1982).

Bürger, H., *Einsatz der neuen Technik in der Text- und Datenerfassung und -verarbeitung, Betriebliche Erfahrungen und Interessevertretungen der Arbeitnehmer*, Bielefeld 1978. Projekt 'Arbeits- und Lebensbedingungen der Arbeitnehmer als Gegenstand der Hochschulforschung', *Arbeitsmaterialien 2*.

Frauengrundstudium, Argument-Studienheft 44, Berlin 1980.

Frauenstudien. Theorie und Praxis in den USA und Grossbritannien, Argument-Sonderband 71; *Gulliver* 10, 1981.

Haug, Frigga, 'Welche Bedürfnisse steuern die technische Entwicklung?', *Das Argument* 127, 1981.

—— ed., *Frauenformen. Alltagsgeschichte und Entwurf einer Theorie weiblicher Sozialisation.* Argument-Sonderband 45, Berlin 1980; enlarged and updated edition under the title *Erziehung zur Weiblichkeit*, 1991.

Jenson, Jane, 'The French Communist Party and Feminism', in *The Socialist Register*, Merlin 1980.

Millet, Kate, *Sexual Politics*, New York 1970.

Niggemann, Heinz, *Emanzipation zwischen Sozialismus und Feminismus, Die sozialdemokratische Frauenbewegung im Kaiserreich*, Peter Hammver Verlag, Wuppertal 1981.

Paramio, Ludolfo, 'Feminismo y socialismo: raices de una relacion infeliz', source as for Bonacchi.

Pasquinelli, Carla, 'Movimento feminista nuovi soggetti e crisi del marxismo', source as for Bonacchi.

Projekt Automation und Qualifikation: *Automationsarbeit – Empire* 1–3, Argument-Sonderbände 43, 45 and 67, Berlin 1980 and 1981.

Ravaioli, Carla, *Frauenbewegung und Arbeiterbewegung. Feminismus und KPI*, USA Verlag, Hamburg 1977.

Rossanda Rossana, *Einmischung, Gespräche mit Frauen über ihr Verhältnis zu Politik, Freiheit, Gleichheit, Brüderlichkeit, Demokratie, Faschismus, Widerstand, Staat, Partei, Revolution, Feminismus*, Europäische Verlagsanstalt, Frankfurt am Main 1980.

Rowbotham, Sheila, *Hidden from History*, London 1973.

Samuel, Raphael, ed., *People's History and Socialist Theory*, Routledge & Kegan Paul 1981.

Sölle, Dorothee, '"Vater und Mutter unser im Himmel": Anfragen feministischer theologie', *Das Argument* 129, 1981.

Willis, Paul, *Spass am Widerstand. Gegenkultur in der Arbeiterschule*, Frankfurt am Main 1979.

TEN

The Women's Movement
in Germany

The women's movement in the Federal Republic of Germany is every-where and nowhere. This ubiquitous non-existence has perhaps long been a feature of the new women's movement, but the recent shifts may be best understood in the contradictory terms of a *successful defeat*. The state, initially under the Social Democrats, but currently also under Kohl's right-wing coalition, has treated the question of women as a legal, financial and symbolic issue. There are now linguistic rules, such as that which stipulates that job advertisements must refer to both sexes; there are experiments making it easier for women to learn male professions; thrifty yet irreversible measures are being taken to finance refuges for battered women; new agreements have been reached between universities to improve the proportion of female teaching staff; the law obliging a married woman to seek the consent of her husband before taking up employment was abolished long ago. The Green Party has a female leadership in parliament. In southern Germany, thanks to a local electoral law, women in the Social Democratic Party (SPD) and the Christian Democratic Union (CDU) have made some headway against lowly placing on candidate lists for the *Landtag*. Yet the stronger women's position becomes in public life, the weaker the women's movement appears. Similarly, just as the importance of 'new social movements' in general is increasingly emphasized on the left, the actual *self*-confidence of the women's movement seems to diminish accordingly. Women's bookshops, women's newspapers, women's publishing firms – none are escaping the crisis. Although events with feminist themes still attract a growing number of interested visitors, there is nevertheless a certain atmosphere of resignation. The energy drawn from many different sources seems to be yielding to a centrifugal force that is pulling it into the void.

The problem of writing history

In this situation, to reconstruct the history of the new women's movement also involves a kind of reconstruction of the movement itself. This may sound presumptious, but I feel it is important to bring out the strengths and the weaknesses of the movement for the benefit of future action. This option necessarily puts the character of the historian, namely myself, into the foreground of initial considerations. Commissioned to write a survey of the history and current prospects of the West German women's movement, I initially reacted with pleasure. At last there would be an account in which the role of socialist feminists, who from the beginning constituted a major part of the movement, would not be passed over in silence or at best mentioned briefly and negatively, like a kind of historical error. It was my intention, therefore, to write an 'objective' report. As a socialist feminist, and a member of the new women's movement from the outset, I imagined this would not be difficult.

Yet my first attempts to analyse what seemed to me important events, actions and ideas were not successful. A sense of modesty precluded giving undue prominence to those experiences in which my own participation, or that of my group, found some echo or had a lasting effect. Where, on the other hand, numerous accounts of the German women's movement ignored our role, I was plagued by doubts as to whether they might not be right to have done so. Finally I came to the conclusion that the history of a movement in which one was and still is active always requires a construal of the meaning of one's own actions. One arrives at a history by grasping oneself historically, at least in retrospect. Therefore my aim could no longer be just to reproduce the multifarious record of the movement as objectively as possible. On the contrary, I would have to work my own partisanship into the story in such a way that the socialist and feminist perspective would be identifiable as its procedural material. Thus I write as a feminist among socialists and as a socialist among feminists. I think this standpoint is fruitful and appropriate to the subject, for the new West German women's movement emerged from the start against the grain of 'socialism' as then understood: whether as the 'real' variant in the German Democratic Republic, the 'theoretical' variety on offer in the West German student movement, or the 'traditional' conceptions championed by the labour organizations of the German Federal Republic.

The early history of the contemporary women's movement was characterized by nervous attempts at distance within an overall attachment (such as autonomous women's organizations or groups in left parties). Then there developed angry demands for acknowledgement of its basic political legitimacy (in reply to the accusation from some quarters that women's groups would *split* the labour movement). Finally there came scathing criticism of Marxism (a small book entitled *Bebel and Engels: Fairy-Godfathers of the Women's Cause* appeared as sacrilege to forces of the student left rallying to female emancipation). Ultimately the women's movement developed new forms of struggle, expressly intended to be different from the traditional labour practice of strikes, demonstrations and leafleting. Amidst tortuous political disagreements – right-wing objections to the new women's movement as a manifestation of the left; left-wing suspicions of bourgeois influence in the new women's approach to their own liberation; non-socialist women's opposition to socialist women – the situation of women in East Germany was a constant reference point. For some, their high level of employment (90 per cent engaged in the workforce) could be triumphantly cited as the fruit of a socialist transformation of society; for others, their continuing absence from political or economic positions of authority, and their omnipresence in housework and child-rearing, demonstrated that the oppression of women was independent of the suppression of class.

Thus the specific dynamic of the women's movement in West Germany has been determined by the country's peculiar reaction to East Germany, as well as by Social Democratic policies of the 1970s. But at the same time the women's movement – even more than the student movement – is an international phenomenon. Political forms, theoretical debates, practical routines, institutional projects, even the most important literary, sartorial or behavioural patterns, have in some respects been similar the world over, as if there were no more spatial distances, no different cultures, no language barriers and no national limitations. One might say that in this regard the women of the world seem to be realizing what the workers of the world have been unable to achieve. Since the women's movement does transcend national frontiers, I intend to sketch only briefly those phenomena I know to be uniform and to concentrate instead on national peculiarities in this chapter. This procedure seems the best way of highlighting the strengths of the West German movement, and of showing that its weaknesses are surmountable – indeed in favourable circumstances can be consciously transformed into conditions for political action.

1. The Beginning – Sexual Politics and the Left

It is usually difficult – even arbitrary – to pinpoint the exact beginnings of a movement, but in the history of the West German women's movement there was one spectacular event which was heard and understood by many as a signal. In September 1968 Helke Sanders made a now-famous speech at the delegate conference of the League of German Socialist Students (SDS) in Frankfurt. She was speaking on behalf of a small women's group from Berlin, calling itself the Action Committee for the Liberation of Women and appearing for the first time in public. Amid growing commotion she sketched out the themes which to this day are the main concerns of the women's movement: that we live not only under capitalism but in a patriarchy; that we have to 'perceive oppression in our private lives not as private but as politically and economically conditioned. We need to change the whole quality of personal life, and to understand the process of change in terms of political action' (*Frauenjahrbuch* 1975). 'Personal development must converge with a practice that prefigures a future society – which at once eroticizes all existential relationships and renders aggression productive.'

Why was this attempt to formulate a dominative nexus between the private and public/political dimensions of life derided by our own comrades? After all, the student movement articulated and lived much of its own protest in this same sphere. In the student revolt various dimensions overlapped: outrage at the US war in Vietnam quickly extended to solidarity with the peoples of the Third World and thereby to a protest against imperialism abroad and the power of monopolies at home. The newspaper king, Axel Cäsar Springer, became a symbol of the monopoly of capital and manipulation of the masses. The student revolts in Berkeley and above all the Cultural Revolution in China further influenced the nature and direction of the student upsurge in West Germany. Sexual liberation and collapsing authority in the universities, alternative communes and mass sit-ins in lecture halls, were just as much part of student tactics as demonstrations, spontaneous riots and street-fighting with the police. So why did the argument that personal oppression in the private domain is an element of the ruling system as a whole meet with such ridicule? The spectacle of it reached its peak when Berlin women found it necessary to bombard their male comrades with tomatoes.

The breathless extent of student protest, reaching from US aggression in Asia to events in private bedrooms, had inspired a large proportion of women, who now constituted 34 per cent of the student body. They met again in political centres to make coffee, to type leaflets, to duplicate and distribute, for those engaged in all-night discussions. Their contributions to debate, when they ventured to make any, dispensed with the standard rhetoric. Moreover they recognized that sexual liberation, in so far as it was practised, was a male privilege and could only be damaging for women who tried it. (A widespread saying at the time was: 'whoever sleeps with the same person twice / is already in the establishment's vice.') By accusing male comrades, friends, brothers, fathers, in short the entire sex, and exposing them as the practical beneficiaries and agents of day-to-day oppression, women gave a new shape and direction to political struggle. They were to unite independently and resist the customary supremacy of men, in order to strike at the foundations of the two-headed domination of a capitalist–patriarchal system. This turn also implied a critique at the level of theory. In the nexus of power relations, oppressors were identified who were at the same time oppressed in other contexts. Domination was therefore not simply a pressure exercised from the top down; it was more like a net woven through the whole society – in which all women were trapped like fish.

Enmity towards men

Subsequently women began to behave in a consciously hostile manner towards men. Alongside the West Berlin Action Committee for the Liberation of Women was founded the Frankfurt *Weiberrat*, which by its name alone promised to shock the bourgeoisie. *Weiber* (a term for 'women' with no single English equivalent) traditionally denoted women as the objects either of scorn or of sexual desire. In the latter sense, they belonged in the singular, as in such compound nouns as *Teufelsweib* ('she-devil'), *Klasseweib* ('smasher'), *Rasseweib* ('classy piece'), and so on.

The women's choice of name for their group was a way of mocking male scorn and suggesting that where possible they intended to seek sexual fulfilment with one another. The Frankfurt *Weiberrat* delivered its first shock to an avid or disgusted public through a cartoon known as the 'lop-them-off-leaflet'. Under the heading 'Liberate the socialist stars from their bourgeois phalluses' and a picture of a huge pair of scissors, were sketches of a number of castrated members; figures referring to footnotes indicated the possibility of identifying contemporary SDS celebrities as the owners of the phalluses. It was also in the Frankfurt *Weiberrat* that the first lesbian group was formed.

I was a member of the Berlin Action Committee, which was affiliated to the Republican Club – a last effort to give central coherence to the extra-parliamentary left. Initially we planned and organized activities in two fields. The first idea was that children should be given an alternative education – we had vague notions of buildings modelled on Israeli kibbutzes, which we intended to finance through the expropriation of comrades with a high income. We spent many nights writing to all the infant teachers in West Berlin, trying to gain their support for a demonstration against their working conditions; in connection with this, the first play-groups were started. Every Wednesday there was a meeting of the full assembly, and on these occasions we devised outrageous campaigns against the degradation of women into sexual objects for men, and the functional utilization of their bodies in advertising to increase sales.

Leaflets were drafted against the wearing of bras, and corsetry firms exposed as profiteers from female degradation; a public bra-burning was staged on the *Kurfürstendamm* at Christmas. An Action Committee uniform of jeans and padded 'Mao jackets' would prevent men from singling us out according to criteria of fashion and thereby bringing us into competition with one another. I still remember clearly the occasion when Helke Sanders, dark-haired and elegant, suggested stealing yellow scarves for everyone from department stores to complete the outfit (shoplifting was a standard way of demonstrating personal and political courage among the left at that time) and a plump blond woman indignantly retorted: 'Yellow doesn't suit me, and anyway in a padded jacket the difference between us stands out even more clearly than in normal clothes.'

The calculated shock-value of individual actions also shocked many members themselves, and there was growing unease at the possibility of making ourselves politically ridiculous. Operations like tying up the particularly oppressive husband of a woman in the campaign, and parading him down the *Kurfürstendamm* past tourists devouring mountains of cake, prompted misgivings that our grasp of the connection between oppression by men and oppression by capitalism was perhaps not yet sufficiently sound for us to be advancing to such public actions. A proposal of mine that we should first try to get to the root of our problems in political seminars caused dissension. Faced with the decision whether to throw all our energy into the foundation of play-groups – for which a fairly elaborate programme of education had been prepared – or to familiarize ourselves with Marxism so as to equip us to study the bases of women's oppression, the majority opted for political instruction. Today I find it strange that I wanted to impose a theoretical study of Marxist classes on such an actively inclined, agitated group of women from such different backgrounds, and I am even more surprised that I succeeded in doing so. There were always about forty at our meetings, of which roughly half were students; book-sellers and social workers formed another strong component from the start. The majority of women present had no children, so that the play-group scheme, which stressed active concern, was no direct concern of theirs at all and in all its concreteness was more abstract than the study of Marx's *Capital*. In fact, a criss-crossing of concerns designed to thwart conventional representative politics was thereafter characteristic of every major campaign of the women's movement. For example, lesbians were particularly active against the abortion law, while students committed themselves to the cause of full-time housewives.

For more than five years each group tried to surpass the others in the number of 'real proletarians' in its ranks, or else harboured a guilty conscience which it sought to relieve through proclamations against piecework and cheap labour.

In 1970, the West Berlin Action Committee split – or more accurately seven women, including Helke Sanders, withdrew to found a new group called 'Bread and Roses'. This highly active core of women from the media world launched a multitude of projects, products and campaigns which gave direction to the fast-growing women's movement in a number of cities. Their first publication was a book opposing the abuse of women in advertising; an abortion advisory service was organized in 1972; the journal *Frauen und Film* was founded in 1972; a health-care manual came out in 1974.

What remained of the Action Committee rapidly swelled to more than a hundred women, organized in study groups. Until a few years ago it consistently maintained this number, for while it steadily lost members, mainly to the regrouping forces of the left, it also managed to attract a flow of new women to replace them. The group adopted a complex charter which was principally designed to reconcile the problems of obligation and rank-and-file democracy, and which was supposed to combine theoretical instruction with action, and the wishes of individual women with extensive analysis of society in general. A number of working groups were formed to consider education, health, theatre, the history of the women's movement, sexuality, family, the state, bringing up girls, and so on. The Action Committee founded its own journal, *Pelagea*, with a circulation of 2000, and after a heated discussion renamed itself the West Berlin Socialist Women's League (SFB). The choice of name marked both a departure from hyperactivism and the adoption of a more radical position than that of the women's organization on the periphery of the West Berlin Communist Party, the 'Democratic Women's League'. The epithet 'socialist' was intended to express the principle of proximity to the labour movement.

Paragraph 218

In 1971 Alice Schwarzer was looking for women's groups in West Germany to launch a campaign against Paragraph 218 of the abortion laws that would be as successful as the one in France. In the Socialist Women's League she found a well-organized unit ready to carry out such a project in a spectacular and therefore media-effective style. The magazine *Stern* printed a voluntary declaration, mainly by women from the SFB, proclaiming: 'I have had an abortion.' In a tough debate we had also managed to reach agreement that the statement should include the theme of 'class-related discrimination against poorer women' and raise the demand for 'the payment of abortion to be covered by public health insurance'. The country-wide response was such that the event may be described as the second beginning of the new women's movement. While all organized women's groups in established parties and trade unions baulked at any action which smacked of 'illegality', thousands of individual women replied – women from little towns and villages, of every age and from all social and occupational strata.

Everywhere women united in small action groups. The Frankfurt *Weiberrat* took the initiative of summoning a great joint meeting. This first Women's Congress, held in Frankfurt in 1972, was a risky venture to which we went only after hesitation but as a party of thirty-five delegates. To our surprise the rooms were as full as in the heyday of the student movement, now itself diminutive. More than 400 delegates had come, from over 48 groups opposed to Paragraph 218, and the press, radio and television decided that the event was suitable media material and thereby contributed to the growth of the movement. The press came predominantly in the shape of men; but for the first time, in a very militant spirit, we tried having exclusively female attendance. The various groups in the hall engaged in embittered fights about political line and direction, and afterwards delivered compromises to the outside world in press releases. Some phrases of mine found their way into the resolution which was finally read in front of the television cameras: 'At the congress we reached agreement to organize ourselves separately for as long as women are oppressed more specifically and to a greater extent than men.... We call upon all women to organize themselves for the satisfaction of their rightful interests.' These propositions were enshrined in the SFB statutes and later gave us the reputation of now being truly autonomous, because we perceived the woman question as transitory.

The main point of contention at the congress was whether to aim for the straightforward deletion of Paragraph 218 or for a law allowing termination of pregnancy within the first three months. At the same time we all felt that we were changed people. So many women had come from so many places in such a short time that we really felt like a movement. We sang our first women's song – hesitantly because of the presumption of claiming to have one, and hence by implication our own culture, and also because of its awkward lines. For example, I remember how we stumbled over such lines as 'An end to being an object in bed!' or 'Women, stop competing and march together!' before entering loudly and with relief into the refrain 'Together we are strong'. (As a result, the SFB concluded that songs must be written professionally in order really to move one, and we wrote to famous women authors, including Christa Wolf, who had in some way been involved in the liberation movement, asking them to write a song for women. None replied.) At the end of the congress we held a women's celebration.

Nowadays such things are standard in the movement, but I did recently hear a unionist from a chocolate factory express the same feelings which moved us back then, and, as in our case, a harmless social event unleashed a new dimension of political action in her firm. In this firm, as in every business with a female workforce, all the menial jobs were done by unqualified women and a small amount of specialist work was assigned to men (naturally the management was also male). This woman had suggested holding a Christmas party for women only; it was her last attempt to achieve anything as a unionist in her firm, where not even 5 per cent of the female staff was organized. The idea of a single-sex party met with opposition. Her colleagues dismissed it with comments like: 'It's no fun without men', 'That's not my idea of a party', 'We won't be able to dance', 'There's no excitement involved'. The next day the women discovered that the male members of the firm had arranged with the management to cancel the Christmas party that year 'owing to the poor economic situation' and instead were planning a stag night of beer and cards. The women were united in their indignation. Suddenly it seemed to them as if the men were trying to steal 'their' Christmas party, to which they had been looking forward for a long time. Feverishly they set to – now wanting to achieve a 'women's Christmas' at all costs. The result was an exuberant and invigorating celebration. The entire female staff joined together and did so from

then on in all matters. By means of practice they had learnt a very difficult theoretical lesson: that a common culture is necessary to overcome
the isolation which prevents political action. Furthermore, they learned
that the straightest paths in politics are not the shortest, indeed in
certain circumstances are barely passable.

In the period that followed, more and more groups opposed to
Paragraph 218 sprang into action all over West Germany. These soon
extended the fight against this particular legislation to general questions of sexuality – from heterosexuality and violence against women in
marriage to questions of the body and health. Meanwhile we in the
SFB, with ever-diminishing enthusiasm, strove to link the abortion
issue with the overall problem of men's interest in oppressing women,
and finally with the reproduction of the social system as a whole. The
very assertion of individuality, which found expression in the popular
slogan: 'My womb belongs to me', seemed to us no whit more
advanced than ordinary civil liberties. In short, we could no longer find
a socialist dimension or perspective in this fight over Paragraph 218.
Today we realize that we were looking at the issues from the standpoint
of an abstract kind of socialism and a model of politics derived from it.
We thereby overlooked the abundant political dimensions of the
struggle against Paragraph 218, which would have led us to a veritable
cross-roads of power and exploitation: not only church and state, but
also the medical profession, the pharmaceutical industry, health insurance and the inadequate protection of lives born in our society – all
these were potentially condensed as targets in the contestation of the
abortion law.

While we were still organizing large demonstrations, together with
women's groups and trade unions, numerous cells of the women's
movement grew into a force which turned itself emphatically and
vehemently against every other organization and thereby against all
women with other involvements. With the word 'autonomous' there
had come on to the agenda something like a rejection of the organizations of the labour movement and of the women who had any connection with it. The SFB and women in parties and unions were culturally
ostracized.

Polarization

This ostracism must be pictured as a material act. We were not given any space in the women's centres which were founded after 1972. The name and address of our group did not appear in the women's calendar. We were no longer invited to conventions. Attempts to participate in 'autonomously planned' campaigns came to nothing. This polarization of the women's movement was probably a phenomenon peculiar to West Germany and can only be explained in terms of the virulent all-purpose anti-communism in our country. A revealing expression of the situation can be found in an autobiographical 'Story from the Women's Movement' by Julia Bähr – (*Klatschmohn*, 1984). There we read of 'Jutta Menschik of the SFB, which had now moved nearer the West Berlin Socialist Union Party (SEW)' or 'the groups close to the German Communist Party (DKP)', which shied away from the demand for unconditional deletion of Paragraph 218 because of their illusory hope in a united front with the SPD and the unions. At that time the author perceived herself as a 'socialist feminist' and I assume that, like many, she simply went along with the policy of ostracism that brought with it such inaccurate labels, and did not invent it herself. For neither the SEW nor the recently founded DKP played any part in the 218 campaign, and the SFB had no connection with either party.

Our activities initially resembled those of the rest of the movement: disruptions of medical conventions were attempted everywhere; we went into parliament and distributed leaflets in churches; we appeared on television and gave interviews in magazines like *Stern*. But although we were in this respect a part of the movement, I believe that we made considerable theoretical and political mistakes. Our socialist traditions, inherited from the student movement, had equipped us with a theoretical tool-kit which ensured commitment, continuity and stamina but, at the same time, inhibited our progress as if our feet were fettered. In all our feminist radicalism we adhered so strongly to the socialist perspective that one of our chief activities was to prevent women's issues from continually slipping down the agenda to a position of subsidiary importance – where we saw them heading. We enjoyed marching in the streets on May Day much more than on the 8th of March, International Women's Day, or on the 30th of April, Walpurgis night.

Women 'reclaimed the night' in crazy war-paint, while we organized a conference on unemployment. Others (the Bread and Roses group) denounced Berlin doctors for tax-evasion, negligence, bodily harm and sexual offences with dependants, while we pondered over leaflets on the situation of training for women. In short, the women of the new movement were first and foremost *conspicuous* and thus transgressed the boundaries of the image of women on which we had been brought up: a reserved, modest, inconspicuous, demure social being.

Issues of the Third World and of war and peace always seemed to us of greater importance and hence politically necessary alternatives to questions of women's right to work, nursery schools and the fight against wage discrimination. Today we can perhaps summarize this by saying that the way in which we understood and appropriated Marxism hindered us from adopting a really radical approach to women's issues. Conversely, women from the 'autonomous' women's movement had no difficult in recognizing peace protests as a women's cause, albeit via a theoretically dubious equation of the military with masculinity, war with patriarchy. Hence right from the start the women's movement constituted an important wing of the peace movement in the Federal Republic.

2. The Autonomous Women's Movement

Free from any socialist shackles, the new autonomous women's movement sped nimbly through the country. There was no town, indeed almost no village, without a women's group, no district that was not affected. It was like a bush fire.

Sexuality

Out of the action groups against the abortion law were formed groups fighting violence (first of all violence against women in general, later specifically violence within marriage). The first women's refuge was founded in 1973. Heated discussions about heterosexuality broke out. The question of the female orgasm became a focal point of a multitude of problems, theories and practices. The 'myth of the vaginal orgasm' was destroyed; the proclamation of women's right to their own desires meant that the nameless lack of desire of so many women could be brought into the open. The knowledge that women were not only capable of orgasm but also that the limits of this capacity were set much higher than in men gave women a sexually mediated sense of identity that enhanced their self-confidence. Not least under the influence of Kate Miller's *Sexual Politics*, the area of sexuality seemed to be the central terrain of women's oppression – at any rate a great deal more central than the economy.

The lesbian sector became a kind of vanguard of the women's movement. In the mid seventies several lesbian magazines started to appear – the best known are probably *74* (1974), *Hexenpresse* (1975) and *Clio* (1976). In Berlin a lesbian cinema was opened. Every Whitsun a lesbian reunion took place. Lesbian discussions were the focal point at the Women's Summer University which started in Berlin in 1976 and until 1984 was attended every year by as many as 10,000 women from the Federal Republic or abroad, who came to spend a week there. 'Original lesbians' disputed with 'movement lesbians' which were the more radical.

Health and lifestyle

In the abortion campaign, clashes multiplied with the medical profession. Disruptions of medical conventions were followed by analyses of the additional incomes which gynaecologists earned from the illegality of abortion. Plays were performed denouncing the roles of church, state and the medical profession and their highly materialistic interests. The political imagination of women proved almost inexhaustible. One poster depicted Minister of Justice Jahn (who had jurisdiction over Paragraph 218) in an advanced state of pregnancy. Another had a naked woman in the centre, whose abdomen was being grasped by male figures representing the authorities of church, state and law – the caption underneath was a quotation from the Federal law: 'The dignity of women is inviolable.' (For a while every feminist had this poster in her room.) In Cologne there was an advertisement for a football match for 'pregnant' women (with cushions) versus state and church. Not only was this imagination applied to diverse forms of political language; it also uncovered new territories where domination was located and liberation attempted.

The conflict with the medical profession had drawn women's attention to the power exercised over them by reason of their lack of juridical competence over their own body. 'My womb belongs to me' was only one of many slogans. There logically followed self-examination groups, intended to help women lose their shyness about themselves. Mirror and speculum became tangible symbols of a movement which eventually was expressed in institutional form through women's health centres. These centres still survive, and in them a statutory minimum of approved female doctors work together with women psychotherapists for a kind of total medicine. In October 1984 an international convention of feminist medicine took place in Switzerland.

Where self-transformation and physical discovery overlapped, 'body groups' were formed ('fat groups' with the motto: 'I'll stick with my fat') which provided direct counselling for many. The propagation and preparation of the most natural foods (muesli, grains like millet, which were forgotten elements of the diet of the poor) has long been a standard item on the agenda at feminist conventions. The dream of 'Womenstown' where it would be possible, even today, to live naturally and free from domination remains in the minds of women all over the world.

There were drastic changes of lifestyle for women in the movement. In addition to the communal evenings in the pub, women started travelling together, in pairs or groups – an adventure that we had until then not dared to undertake. It was not only culturally out of the question, it was also dangerous – after all, a woman needed male protection in public. One or even two women travelling alone were seen as willing victims, nothing short of provocation for sexual assaults. In this respect it becomes particularly clear how restricted women still are, without there necessarily being any tangible restrictions – their cultural status as 'not public beings' is sufficient. Equally shocking for middle-class neighbourhoods were the first women's housing associations. They too are now a common feature of cities.

Writing, publishing, bookshops

The discovery of a 'female sexuality' which went beyond the sort usual in marriage, like the general discovery of our own bodies, brought a wave of new books on to the market, which were seized upon by the movement like so many cult texts and discussed in small groups. Born from the movement, the books themselves contributed to its further development. One of these was Verena Stefan's *Häutungen (Shedding)* in 1975, and later Svende Merian's *Der Tod des Märchenprinzen* ('The Death of Prince Charming', 1980). From France the female representatives of Lacan's psychoanalysis (Irigaray, Cixous, Kristeva) gained an influence which has lasted to the present day. Their books were published by bourgeois publishers in Germany and, despite their difficulty, achieved large circulations. Alice Schwarzer's *The 'Little' Difference and its Large Consequences* came out in 1975 and was another book adopted by the movement. In the same year a small group in Munich founded the first women's press (*Verlag Frauenoffensive*) which, after the success of Verena Stefan, also published titles from abroad, among them Barbara Ehrenreich and Deidre English's *Witches, Midwives and Nurses.* This firm, in view of the crisis in the publishing industry as a whole, still has a successful record. In 1976 the 'assembly of women writers' was convened, which today still holds annual conferences and produces its own journal, *Lesen und Schreiben.*

Right from the beginning, the new women's movement discovered a mass response in the media. The journals of the left, like *Alternative* and *Kursbuch* and *Ästhetik und Kommunikation,* seized upon the subject and to a certain extent cultivated the ground for its rapid expansion. After the failure of the joint publication of a periodical for the movement in 1973, two great nationwide magazines came into existence in the mid seventies. In 1976 *Courage* with (according to its own figures) 20,000 readers initially, rising to as many as 80,000. In 1984 publication was discontinued, owing to disputes among the sisters and a growing lack of interest in political matters in the face of a counter-tendency to politicization of the magazine. *Courage* had also tried to re-establish a link with the old feminist movement, but after fascism and war in West Germany hardly anything had remained. The conservative *Frauenrat* ('Women's Advice') had a huge readership of several hundred thousand. In 1977, at great expense, came the launching of *Emma,* Alice Schwarzer's magazine, with an initial circulation of 200,000. This rival far surpassed *Courage* in popularity and is considered *the* journal of the women's movement in virtually every small town. In every major town there were soon women's bookshops, which do not admit men – West Berlin even has three. Together with the women's cafés and pubs that opened in the mid seventies, they form a cultural network through which news and information can be quickly communicated. In this way women's own subcultures came into being.

Language and feminist studies

Studies of sexism in language, pursued with enthusiastic detective work (the studies of Senta Trömel-Plötz and Luise Pusch were particularly popular), met with a large response in innumerable groups of the women's movement. After all, reports dealing with everyday speech were concerned with a practice to which all women were exposed. Women in the movement could almost be identified by their linguistic modifications alone. The most famous example was the suppression of the indefinite personal pronoun '*man*' (= English 'one'), which because of its similarity to '*Mann*' was replaced with the word '*frau*' (literally: 'woman').

In addition, the speech habits of women – their frequent use of adverbs and their tentative manner of talking, manifested in the extensive use of conjunctions – became a subject of research and a branch of the women's studies which emerged in almost all West German universities in the late seventies. After women students had won their battle to hold women's seminars in different subjects, these turned out to be very exotic occasions; they were crowded and there were always alternative teaching methods and discussions. Practical experiences were included; there was a great deal of work done and much time spent on the problematic of teaching structures. And the women did their knitting.

The insignificance of these seminars in the eyes of the academic staff (which was 90 per cent male) was in inverse proportion to the intensity with which they were conducted and the effort put into them. The teachers were mostly unpaid, the students received no certificate or proof of achievement. Today, despite strong opposition in the teaching body, almost all universities have succeeded in integrating at least one women's seminar into the regular teaching programme. Nearly every term in the larger universities, there is a cycle of lectures by different women speakers. Even a women's student union has become accepted. Like the seminars, the women's studies lectures cover all subjects – from science to philosophy. Women studying social sciences have been the most committed. They formed their own professional association in sociology, from which emerged in 1978 the first theoretical journal by women: *Feministische Beiträge*. Four years later, in 1982, an ordinary publishing firm decided to bring out a second one: *Feministische Studien*. Alongside these attempts to spread feminism through the universities, semi-commercial women's research centres were founded – in Berlin in 1980, in Hamburg a little later. Like adult education institutes, they offer a course of meetings.

Most important, however, have been the 'alternative universities' – the West Berlin Summer University and its successors, decentralized women's weeks at various other campuses (which, to name but a few, have been taking place in Hamburg for four years, in Bremen for three years, and have recently been started in Bielefeld and Hildesheim). They are always attended by over a thousand women, with an agenda that has little in common with ordinary academic courses. Organized entirely by women from the movement, self-discovery groups and suggestions for alternative lifestyles are predominant. A colourful craft fair offers produce ranging from home-baking to home-made jewellery and wool. On the other hand, there are hardly any bookstalls.

Alternative feminist studies also organize major public events – annual meetings of women historians, philosophers or engineers, and conferences on themes like the future of women's work, feminist science, feminist culture. By allowing the programme of events published by the (now officially financed) women's research centre at the Free University of Berlin, one can attend an important convention of feminist learning about twice a month. This result is encouraging.

Economics

Feminists have also made a number of significant intellectual advances in the field of economic analysis, with political consequences. In fierce contention within and against Marxism, women called into question orthodox theories of value, interpretations of 'primitive accumulation' and accounts of the relations between profit and industrial output. Their object was to show that women's labour was a 'blind spot' in the Marxist critique of political economy; to establish the significance of housework as a permanent form of primitive accumulation; and to reveal the absence of reproductive labour in Marx's theory of surplus-value as symptomatic of a general neglect of women in his thought. In practical terms these analyses helped to spark off a campaign of 'wages for housework' – which, however, like the myth of a 'new motherhood', was quickly taken over by conservative political forces (in south Germany a housewives' wage was even partially granted by the CDU in the form of money for education), hence generating no great enthusiasm in the women's movement itself.

Critique of standard theory was extended to analyses of the Third World. The relationship between the First and Third Worlds seemed to mirror the relationship between men and women on a global scale: exploitation of subsistence production. In addition, the immense volume of domestic labour performed on a world scale seemed to contradict the image of the proletarianization of the world – hence there was talk of a tendency to universalize the 'housewife' format of labour. The best-known studies have been those of Claudia von Werlhof, Maria Mies and Veronika Bennholdt-Thomsen. Sigrid Pohl's dissertation attempted to prove, on the basis of a thorough survey of the evidence, that discrimination in women's pay is perfectly reasonable from a capitalist perspective, since, because of their reproductive labour, women are indeed 'worth less' as employees.

Economic issues provoked tensions in a third area, where the movement itself underwent commercialization. The fact that women work for nothing in many areas of life, and that many are not involved in fixed employment structures, was perhaps among the reasons for the rapid growth of the movement and its broad basis. The endless projects, the multiple women's centres, the innumerable campaigns – these could only work if everyone committed themselves enthusiastically, without thought of remuneration for their labour. The women's movement has no official organization and no professional politicians.

Yet such a large movement is also a market for selling products at a profit. It was the bourgeois publishers who first realized this and one after the other set up a women's list. But inside the movement too there were 'career women' who used feminist issues for their own advancement. The biggest scandals developed round Alice Schwarzer, who with great business acumen not only made use of the laws of the media market, but also abused the voluntary labour of movement women. The controversy thus aroused, settled partly in the courts, in no way impaired the popularity of *Emma*. But the question of paying women who work for liberation is now constantly raised in the movement. In fact, practically every job for which a group of women fights poses a moral problem, because normally only one woman will benefit from it. This mechanism weakened the movement in universities during Social Democratic rule, splitting it into women with jobs and those who had fought only in order that other women should have a job.

Literature

I know of no other movement (except perhaps the gay movement) where literature has had such power to organize people. A few books established what amounts to a reading cult. New groups were formed with the sole aim of community reading and discussing some recently published book, using it to articulate their own experiences. It was as if women's lack of voice in public life took possession of the experiences of other women, mediated through language, and so developed a movement. In such cases, what made a book a success was often neither literary quality as such nor a cultural exclusion of socialist content (*de rigueur* in the 'autonomous' movements) nor even necessarily substantive intention itself. One such cult book for the movement was Verena Stefan's *Häutungen*, a novel whose aesthetic merits are much disputed. Its subject was sexual liberation. Svende Merian's *Tod des Märchenprinzen* is similar in theme, but a totally inadequate literary treatment of it makes the book little more than pornography.

The wide circulation of works like these reflected a felt need for self-expression in sexual matters, where they communicated female experiences from a women's viewpoint to which many readers could relate. At a more serious artistic level, two authors from East Germany became figures with whom the women's movement particularly identified: Christa Wolf and Irmtraud Morgner. Surprisingly, the socialist commitment of both writers in no way hindered their reception in the 'autonomous' movement – their radically feminist outlook apparently made their socialist convictions acceptable. In each case, novels and short stories of great distinction explore subjects that are anything but popular. Christa Wolf writes of her own story, then rewrites that of historical characters like Günderode and Cassandra. Through the history and daily life of East Germany Irmtraud Morgner brings to life a female character, forced to split into two beings, terrestrial and bewitched. These two authors challenged and changed women in the West German women's movement, affecting even their expression of feelings through language.

No general report on the acts and effects of the women's movement in West Germany can do justice to the manifold awakening it has brought, whose life cannot be reduced to a list. I have concentrated here on those areas that have immediately affected large numbers of women. But there are others, of great significance, where feminists have major and radical achievements to their credit, but which because of their more specialized nature could not be so directly appropriated or translated into activities for everyone. Among these have been painting, music, photography and film. In the cinema, thanks to relatively favourable starting conditions, a whole series of West German directors have succeeded in producing internationally acclaimed women's films – Helke Sanders, Helma Sander, Jutta Brückner and Margarethe von Trotta.

Since I have concentrated on the majority of women in the movement and the ways in which they were active, I should like to conclude this section with a remark on some aspects of the new culture which arouse my reservations rather than my support.

Self-discovery, therapy, magic

It is not quite fair to move from self-discovery groups (an international phenomenon) to feminist therapy, but the groups developed a dynamic which almost inevitably led to mutual therapeutic counselling among group members. The domain of psychotherapy is in general not a very reliable or clear-cut one. The reintegration of patients into existing social structures virtually of necessity implies some coming to terms with oppression. This is particularly true when male therapists try to diagnose and cure female ailments. It is therefore understandable that feminists devoted much energy to entering this field. In the Federal Republic a series of feminist psychotherapeutic advice centres were founded. I have yet to hear what practical successes or theoretical insights they have yielded.

On the periphery of such activities there evolved a series of groups which sought to recover 'femininity' as something latent in us, our own power of liberation and healing. This is another international phenomenon. In the late seventies, cults of the mcon and menstruation, magic, astrology and fortune-telling were combined with speculation about goddesses and maternal power, and led to the worship of childbearing and female nature. I do not know how strong such trends are, or whether their renown is largely due to their exotic appeal to the media. However, it is clear enough that a recourse to the transcendental powers of a quite different kind of female nature fits perfectly well, as one piece among others, into the mosaic of current conservative politics.

Socialist feminists

The radical spirit in which the autonomous women's movement took up the most diverse problems, regardless of preconceptions as to which were more or less important, shook a whole series of ideas till then taken as self-evident, and showed up major gaps in our own thinking as socialists. During the upsurge of the movement we had continued our work. In 1972 we had organized a spectacular women's election campaign in opposition to the CDU. In 1977 we co-ordinated a convention against female unemployment and every year we worked out an extensive programme for the 8th of March. In each case 300–400 women came to our events. This was by no means as exalting as the concurrent meetings of the autonomous women's movement which, in a place like Berlin, easily attracted a thousand women. But for us it was a lot. We successfully resisted the efforts of various left-wing student groups to incorporate us. Women's year in 1975 had for the first time brought us into a league of action with two Communist, two Social Democratic and trade union women's groups. This committee stayed together for a while longer until we left it – more out of boredom than for political reasons. On May Day there were political conflicts. The Communist Party representatives on the joint committee did not want to publish our contribution in the May Day newspaper, because it disparaged their attitude to women. We had chosen the scandal of the numbers of women alcoholics to draw attention to the appalling situation of – among others – housewives. Later in the demonstration they tried to take away our defiant banner 'Everyone Must Know Everything', claiming it was inappropriate and pernicious. At the time we had just decided that our women's organization should be primarily dedicated to instruction. A good general knowledge still seems to us to be a necessary factor for the capacity to act. Heated arguments with male Communist officials considerably strengthened our self-confidence.

We resolved to write a study book for women. The difficulties of this undertaking were, I believe, the cause of our second shift in the direction of feminism, for we were beginning to realize that what we had dealt with was learning not women. Broad analyses of the transition from animal to human were followed by descriptions of the capitalist obstacles to human learning, but the living women, who had studied with burning enthusiasm, did not appear anywhere. The political and intellectual reorientation we now underwent was in every respect momentous.

We began to write and adapt stories from our everyday life, from our memories. In this way we developed a method of investigating female socialization which we called 'memory-work', which allowed us to work empirically, drawing in large numbers of women and making theoretically novel findings. The first lecture I myself gave in this context was at the first West Berlin *Volksuniversität* (People's University) in 1980 under the title 'Women – Victims or Culprits?' (see this volume, pp. 3–12). In it I suggested we look at the ways women continually reproduce their own oppression and thereby stabilize prevailing social relations. Intended as a rejoinder to the feminist movement, contesting its usual presentation of women simply as victims, my talk instead exploded like a bombshell in the ranks of politically organized women (the unions, the SPD, DKP). In the next two years almost every newspaper in these organizations repeatedly discussed the theory. It annoyed women's groups because of the negative (but also positive) activity suddenly attributed to them – if they were contributing to their own oppression, they could also contribute to their emancipation. By 1984 this debate had virtually resulted in my ostracism as a Marxist by the DKP. On the other hand, groups of women writing stories were started in many towns. We had to improve our concept of the theorization of memory, in order to avoid the fate of self-discovery groups.

We wrote textbooks for a basic course in women's studies which were centred on the working through of personal experience and were designed to bypass the problem of the institutionalization of the women's movement. Our first two volumes, *Frauenformen* – 'stories of everyday life and a plan for a theory of female socialization' – and *Sexualisierung der Körper* (*Female Sexualization*, Verso 1987), were both successes. But now it was time to clarify our tense relationship with the labour movement – one which a socialist perspective had earlier seemed to make quite straightforward.

The new autonomous women's movement and the various organizations of the labour movement either had a negative relationship with each other or none at all. Feminist causes were not the same as those of labour, and we socialist women, who had a stake in both movements, were continually confronted with the problem of establishing the priorities and connections between them. Our commitment to women's research had slightly shifted our position. While writing about female socialization and the numerous mechanisms that had kept women in a subordinate position, we could not always allow labour issues to take precedence over our own.

Basically, until now we had approached women's causes in the way they were presented inside the system – as issues relevant to women, such as nursery schools, cheap labour, unemployment, and so on. From the point of view of wage-labour and its reproduction in relation to capital, these are the relevant women's issues, where discrimination against the female sex is unequivocal. We were not sufficiently experienced to trust our own experiences, and were too theoretically minded to appreciate the strengths of spontaneous practice. But the various campaigns of the autonomous women's movement against directly experienced forms of domination – whatever their worth in an overall strategy – greatly increased our awareness of the range of women's oppression, bringing home to us that the supremacy of capital over labour is not exhausted by profit and exploitation, which represent only one dimension of a complex structure of power and inequality. Practice taught us the simple but hard lesson that experience is not to be derived from any preconceived theory, but itself forms the point of departure for theoretical work (albeit in a determinate categorical framework). Only thus did we come to reject the 'question of women' as it is posed within the system, and to understand that the real issue at stake is the relationship between the sexes, which itself forms part of prevailing relations of production. In this social order, different lines of power criss-cross in a pattern which typically strengthens each one, although on occasion they are also mutually obstructive. Thus, patriarchal and capitalist powers normally build on each other – but it can happen that the quest for profit may improve the situation and rights of women. This often makes single-fronted battles difficult and autonomous organizations of oppressed women necessary.

3. Politics and Society in the Eighties

The diverse campaigns of the autonomous women's movement loosened the knots of domination in many places but could not avoid their tightening in others. Spontaneous actions against every kind of oppression produced no strategy for attacking the network of social power structures taken as a whole. To see this, it is necessary to look at the larger national background against which the feminism of the seventies unfolded.

For what was happening, meanwhile, in the established institutions of the West German socio-political order? There, the degree to which women were organized was very low. Symptomatically, the percentage of female members of the DGB – the West German trade union federation – was not more than a mere 20 per cent in the seventies. The rapidly dwindling number of women representatives on elected bodies, including the *Land* (regional) assemblies and the *Bundestag* (Federal Parliament), was as discouraging as the bureaucratic and hierarchical structure of these entities themselves. The percentage of women delegates to DGB conferences was rarely even half that of women members. On party lists women contested unwinnable seats, and were represented in the Federal Parliament at best decoratively – by one or two 'token women' per party.

This situation started to change under the influence of the women's movement, and its echoes in the bourgeois media. 'Women's councils' or 'women's committees' were set up by all the principal parties and trade unions. The women's sections connected to the labour movement in this period devoted their energies to trying to remedy female disadvantages by better education, executive opportunities and political preparation, and to securing protective legislation for women on the basis of their biological difference – raising demands for job protection, nursery schools and day-centres, equal pay, and training schemes. Formally speaking, the trade unions accepted these demands as legitimate and included them in their programmes. But they were never made the focus of any campaign and had little impact on traditional union concerns. The first wave of female unemployment in the mid-seventies passed almost unnoticed because of prevailing concentration on male skilled labour and the male breadwinner. Women returned to the family. 'Double wage-earning' entered the vocabulary.

It may seem surprising that the women's sections of the labour movement were so ineffective in the seventies, when one considers how large they were. The ASF, for instance – the women's committee of the Social Democratic Party, set up by the SPD in 1974, with 200,000 members – today numbers 226,000. It is a mistake, however, to think of this organization as a women's front, let alone a feminist one. Female members of the SPD automatically join the ASF on entry. Their number provides a simple tally for the percentage of women in the party as a whole – a percentage which (as in all the organizations of the labour movement) is now growing faster than that of men, rising from 20 per cent in the early 1970s to some 25 per cent today. The concentration of associations like the ASF on remedial action for the 'social' deficits in job protection and equal pay meant that 'political' deficits in party organizational structures themselves were subjected to scant analysis. The result was to widen the distance between the women's sections of the labour movement and the projects of the autonomous women's movement which, on its side, insisted all the more vehemently on the innate strength of women, the higher meaning of housework, feminine virtues, and so on, whilst simultaneously rejecting politics in the associations and assemblies altogether as a male diversion.

The relationship of the autonomous women's movement to the women in the labour organizations was not always quite so strained, however, at an individual level. In the second half of the seventies some groups in the labour sector started to take up 'more or less related' and even 'personal' issues, as was standard in the women's movement at large. Consciousness-raising groups sprang up in the trade unions. At the *Volksuniversität* in 1981 female members of works committees discussed the patriarchal obstacles they faced in their daily lives as unionists. To the left of the ASF, in the Democratic Women's Initiative (DFI) – allied to the Communist Party – questions of sexuality, group dynamics and personal relationships were much more freely discussed and political demands more straightforwardly linked to problems of capitalist exploitation. The DFI now has 140 groups throughout the country.

Meanwhile, the SPD in office was presiding over a number of welfare reforms which, however limited, did materially improve the position of women. 'The right to work' (understood as remunerated work) was on the whole applied in these years. Paragraph 218 was amended. Family and marriage law was revised, on the premiss that women had something like minds of their own, and financial survival (as in divorce) was made no longer dependent on good conduct (by substituting the principle of marital breakdown for that of guilt). Social services for young children, the old, the sick and the disabled were extended, and in part the training of women was specially promoted – for example, in trial attempts at training girls in men's jobs. In fact the educational behaviour of women changed considerably in the seventies, as we shall see. In many towns equal-opportunity offices were set up. For their part, the bourgeois media were often loudly echoing the autonomous women's movement, so that it was often not entirely clear if its campaigns owed everything to the media or if they appeared so prominently in the news only because they sold well. Many journalists themselves belonged to the movement or saw themselves in that light, so that business and liberation blended just as inseparably in them. Television, too, went so far as to plan political programmes on women's issues (something which continues), while interest in general political debate fell. Women's films were regularly broadcast on it.

Most of these changes were quite modest. It was not until the early eighties that a really major alteration in the atmosphere and direction of West German politics occurred. Its precipitate was the twofold transformation of the national scene in 1982–83 – first the return to power of the CDU/CSU, relegating the SPD to opposition for the first time in sixteen years, and then the entry of the Greens into the *Bundestag* – not to speak of *Land* assemblies and the European Parliament itself. It was the second of these developments that marked the more important watershed. For the Greens were the first political organization to achieve a breakthrough at national level which expressly gave prominence to goals of women's liberation in their programme. Soon after they took their seats in the *Bundestag*, moreover, the Greens elected an all-women parliamentary leadership – a small but in its own way sensational step. Green women, both inside and outside parliament, developed a kind of feminist populism, whose influence was soon to be seen in other parties as well. When the Greens argued that men should be able to combine jobs with housework, the SPD now hastened to 'question not only motherhood but also fatherhood, not only maternal but also paternal qualities'. While government spokesmen intoned official rhetoric about female unemployment, Green deputies gave lively illustrations of the connections between patriarchal daily life and women's unemployment. When these were greeted with defensive yawns of 'Here we go again' from the rows of Christian Democrats, G. Potthast (the Greens) shouted back: 'You had better all keep quiet! We have been talking to your secretaries and learnt that women are sacked if they do not sleep with their bosses – and that women are also sacked if they do sleep with their bosses, because then the wives come down on them.' The Green women's disclosure of sexual harassment by male members of their own parliamentary group provoked ambiguous responses from the public at large. Should such 'dirty linen' not be washed in private, for the sake of party unity?

The record and role of Green women in relation to the autonomous women's movement is hard to judge. Although the parliamentary leadership is called a 'women's panel', this female collective does not claim to belong to the women's movement or to be involved in feminist politics. At the same time, however, a great number of women from the movement have joined the Green Party or, at the very least, work in an electoral alliance with it – though the majority of projects still in existence continue to reject out of hand any form of organization, above all any party or parliamentary politics, as suitable for women's emancipation. On the other hand, the appearance of the Green women in parliament has undoubtedly had the effect of radicalizing women in the SPD. The call for equal treatment now gave way to the demand for positive discrimination to achieve equality. At the beginning of August 1985, the ASF members working in parliament passed a motion declaring that they 'could occupy all current *Land* ministries and fill at least half of the Federal cabinet'. Their initial demand was for 25 per cent of such positions. Even CDU women now started to press for proportional representation in their party hierarchy, and for mayoral office.

The ASF has recently raised the stakes so far as women's representation in the Bundestag is concerned by declaring that unless the SPD
nominates women for 40 per cent of winnable seats, it will not be able
to advise its members to vote for their own party in the next election.
The ASF leadership's ability to deliver on this threat may be doubted.
But the existence of the Green alternative, with its greater representation of women, does give it an extra edge; and for their part, the
Greens will be looking for every possible vote to keep themselves about
the 5 per cent threshold. In taking up broader women's issues, the ASF
has been able to draw on the ideas and experience of the pioneer
socialist-feminist groups, thus somewhat alleviating the latter's isolation within the women's movement. The stance of the ASF has also
gained strength from the example of neighbouring countries, and in
particular from Denmark, where the People's Socialist Party has
accepted the principle that there should be a minimum quota of
women's candidates for the next election. In June 1991, the European
Forum of socialist feminists met for the sixth time. The next conference
will be held in Brussels in 1992.

Against this political background, the Christian Democrats have
proceeded to draw up a new policy on the family and women.
Ingratiatingly worded in feminist language, it was greeted by parts of
the women's movement as 'exceptionally progressive'. It talks of a
feminization of society – about feminine strengths and virtues, about
revaluing housework and reinstating the ethos of family life. 'The
ability to see the world from a woman's viewpoint is what enables one
to forgo advantages, to make do with scarcer means, to develop soft
technology and new forms of economy, caring for people's needs.' The
fortes of the new women's movement – at any rate of its radical
feminist autonomous wing – are here converted into tropes of a right-
wing policy aiming to legitimate cutbacks in welfare ('The future must
be shaped by motherly virtues'). The women's movement has proved
ill-prepared to contend with such cashing-in. 'A mother's work retains
more of the original creative quality of labour than all the humanizing
efforts put together can restore to paid work.' Whoever hears and
protests at such association of the revaluation of femininity with the
reprivatization of social care for people to the detriment of women is
nevertheless practically forced to recoil from any emancipatory
demands and return to traditional household duties. For the actual

cuts in welfare imposed by the Kohl regime – the reduction of resources and jobs in the welfare sector – have worsened public provision for children, old people, the sick and the disabled in such a way that the individual conscience pulls strongly back to home and hearth. The CDU no longer needs to propagandize a conservative model of women. Instead it offers a dynamically remodelled hybrid: the caring housewife and mother with part-time work. Just how much, according to this scheme of things, the household chores are shared between the 'marriage partners' is a matter of individual choice. Meanwhile, on the popular cultural front, the founding of the newspaper *Bild der Frau* by the Springer group can be seen both as a bid to ride the tide of the women's movement and, simultaneously, as a blow levelled against it. Unlike its older brother *Bild*, the mass tabloid, *Bild der Frau* is more mildly coloured, with beauty tips in place of football. Chancellor Kohl has addressed the women of West Germany in its pages.

The wording of the CDU policy on women makes it clear that Christian Democracy has learnt from the women's movement. Conversely, the women's movement needs to learn that the study of everyday oppression must be combined with societal analysis if it is to survive as a revolutionary force for liberation, capable of resistance to this society and aspiration towards an emancipated future.

The balance-sheet

What objective balance-sheet, then, can be made of the results so far achieved – in either respect – by the new women's movement in West Germany? There is no doubt that significant transformations have occurred in at least two years. First, the structure of women's participation in the workforce has undergone something of a revolution. Although female paid employment rose by only 4 per cent between 1966 and 1983 (from 34.4 per cent to 38.9 per cent), its distribution changed fundamentally. Whereas as late as 1950 approximately a third of all gainfully employed women were 'assistants in family-run concerns' (especially in agriculture), by 1981 this category accounted for only 7.5 per cent. Over half gainfully employed women are now white-collar workers (in 1950 it was 19 per cent). Women have thus become wage-dependent. Second, a more radical change can be seen in their educational pattern. In part because of the Social Democratic educational reforms, 60 per cent of today's twenty to thirty year olds have vocational training and 50 per cent a middle-school or sixth-form diploma (roughly equivalent to GCSE and 'A' levels). The percentage of women at universities rose from barely 24 per cent in 1960 to nearly 38 per cent in 1981 (though admittedly they concentrate considerably in teacher training courses – 56 per cent – whilst the percentage in engineering remains under 10 per cent). The percentage of women also thins out rapidly the 'higher' one goes: in 1981 they filled only 4.8 per cent of teaching posts at universities, and female professors have not yet exceeded the 3 per cent mark.

Despite the higher qualifications, however, employed women are still concentrated in seven main occupations: clerical work (female percentage 77 per cent), assembly work (53 per cent), mail order (72 per cent), cleaning (77.9 per cent), education and welfare (70 per cent), retail (72.5 per cent), and textile and clothing (86.8 per cent). Since these branches are particularly affected by rationalization, female unemployment is rising quickly (in 1983 at 43 per cent it was far higher than the percentage in paid employment). Needless to say, the old argument that women are not qualified is invalid. More than half of unemployed women have completed a vocational training.

A situation where paid employment is taken for granted, better education is available, and a social environment exists in which the women's issue can be publicly aired ought to make it possible for mass resistance to be mounted to the CDU's policies, which are promoting a rapid feminization of poverty – itself, of course, currently a worldwide phenomenon. In West Germany today more and more women are doing part-time work (in 1981 they already accounted for 31 per cent of all employed women). At the same time the proportion not liable for national insurance is growing – in 1981 this applied to a third of all part-time jobs. Funding for vocational further education has been cut by 25 per cent. Rehabilitation provision for the unemployed is conditional on the length of compulsory contributions, so that it is predominantly the women who have been housewives who remain excluded. The cutbacks in the welfare sector affect women doubly: as potential employees – nurses, social workers, teachers – their jobs are being dispensed with, whilst the work is shifted back on to them in their families as private individuals. Women's pay remains on average still 30 per cent below that of men (in the low-pay sector women constitute 90 per cent of employees); accordingly, women's pensions are considerably smaller than men's. Owing to a complicated system of calculation women must on average reckon with a 70 per cent loss of income when they retire (men with 30 per cent). Since their income even before retirement is generally small, this means that a large proportion of female pensioners live below the social security line. In 1983, 39 per cent of women were receiving a monthly pension of less than DM 500, 30 per cent a pension of between DM 500 and DM 1000, and 8 per cent a pension of between DM 1000 and DM 1500. The largest groups receiving welfare benefits are old women and single women with children.

Where then, after these depressing insights, does the success of the women's movement ultimately lie, and where its defeat? Undoubtedly, the new women's movement has succeeded in making the position of women in society a public issue in the fullest sense – rescuing it from the mere individual bedroom, the family kitchen, the personal quarrel. Social Democracy nationalized a part of the women's cause. It financed women's houses and women's projects, and established at great bureaucratic expense co-ordinating centres for women's research, indeed even the odd women's professorship. The autonomous women's movement had some historical reason to cling to the import- ance of the personal and the private domain, as against intervention in the 'masculine' domain of politics. It did reveal some of the virtues – not merely failings – of what society deemed feminine. Yet it is these qualities which the CDU, reprivatizing women's issues after the Social Democrats nationalized them, is now seductively exploiting: myths of motherhood and magic, as opposed to the less effective columns of figures from the SPD's humanization programme. Women's insistence on the sphere of personal experience between man and woman is now gallantly conceded: the family is to be the amphitheatre of women's emancipation.

Feminism has infiltrated all levels of bourgeois culture. It has dissected its language, profaned its literature, ridiculed its sciences. But it has become stuck in the pores it has penetrated. Retreat from mascu- line politics and production now takes its toll as self-defeating modesty. To prevent the reconsolidation in new forms of the network of social oppressions, the movement needs to combine feminist insubordi- nation, utopian fantasy and socialist perspective. Feminists must enter politics, and in them they must make control of social production their own concern too. Even today it remains equally unclear how far the oppression of women is crucial to this society's survival and, conversely, whether women's liberation would necessarily revolutionise the structure of society as a whole – and how that can be done.

ELEVEN

Rosa Luxemburg and Women's Politics

Rosa Luxemburg was born in Poland in 1871, the fifth child of a Jewish timber merchant. She studied at a girls' grammar school in Warsaw and, while still at school, began working for the illegal Polish labour movement. Before she was eighteen she had to flee to Switzerland as a political refugee. There she studied science, mathematics, politics and economics, obtaining her doctorate in 1897 at the age of twenty-six with a dissertation on the industrial development of Poland. A year later she moved to Berlin to work in the German Social Democratic Party. While still in exile she collaborated with Leo Jogiches, Julian Marchlewski and Adolf Wartski to produce the first Polish Social Democratic paper – at the age of twenty-two. Her first intervention of note in the German social democratic movement was *Social Reform and Revolution*, the pamphlet she wrote against Bernstein at the age of twenty-seven.

For ten years she represented the interests of the Polish and Lithuanian Social Democrats at the office of International Socialism in Brussels. For seven years she taught at the party school in Berlin. In 1919 she was arrested in Berlin by government troops and murdered with what Lelio Basso called the benevolent support, if not at the behest of the Social Democratic Party.[1] She was forty-eight. The murderer was acquitted.

If we do not liberate ourselves, liberation remains without consequences for us.
(Peter Weiss)

What can we learn from Rosa Luxemburg about our own problem of an effective politics for women? In 1902 she wrote in the *Leipziger Volks-zeitung*:

> The political emancipation of women would bring a vigorous, fresh breeze into the political and intellectual life of Social Democracy too. It would dispel the stifling atmosphere of our present philistine family life which has coloured the lives of our party members, both workers and leaders, so indelibly.
>
> vol. 1/2, p. 185

At that time the issue was votes for women. Today we are quarrelling about quotas.[2] But we are still trying to dispel the same stuffy atmosphere which surrounds the male party representatives, bureaucratizes the political system and veils it in a fog of personal advantages which threatens to dissipate every combative impulse. Once women fill the parliaments and supply the parties and the unions with leaders, as well as filling all other public offices, this must lead to a different kind of politics – at least we hope so, for all our critical awareness of the many defects of our sex.

This politics would be closer to people's needs, less technocratic, less cold-hearted, extravagant and militaristic. Such hopes are not based on the idea that women are 'naturally' warm-hearted, gentle, friendly and peaceable people – in contrast to the other sex. Our hopes derive from our analysis of the sexual division of labour. This is based on separating out from the labour of society as a whole a set of activities devoted to profit-making. This includes wage or salaried labour and is assigned predominantly to men. All other activities, chief among them the tasks of caring for people themselves, are assigned to women, to be performed for nothing, but under the protection of men who earn their living. A third sphere which has been carved out is concerned with the control of this primary division of labour by professional politicians. Since this work too is carried out for money, it has been assigned to men. In this connection we are convinced that women could introduce into the world of politics the experience they have gained from their own work and thereby bring the world of politics down from the lofty heights of legal clauses and resolutions inimical to life. But they would go beyond that; their intrusion into this masculine domain would also create chaos in the whole division of labour to the point where the general reproduction of domination and oppression would be disrupted. In order to fill such general ideas with concrete vitality we decided to study Rosa Luxemburg,[3] among others, and evaluate her particular interventions in politics.

Until a few years ago her name was barely mentioned in the women's movement. She was relegated to the category of masculine women, that is to say, one of those women who had to deny their femininity and conform to the masculine world in order to achieve success. Historically, whenever women get anywhere they are dismissed in this way. Women in the movement looked for women's strength in their characteristic weakness and inferiority, not in their ability to achieve parity with successful men.[4] Such a view is comprehensible, but despite it our conception of politics made by women also contains the assumption that every woman who goes into politics and is not just a front for the existing structures will break through the traditional sexual division of labour in such a way as to make us re-define it. This redefinition may force us to modify our view of the world, and perhaps her view of the world may turn out to include women's areas. It was in this spirit that we wished to read Rosa Luxemburg.

Needless to say, our choice of subject was no accident. We wished to appropriate Rosa Luxemburg as a theoretician and fighter for the liberation of humankind and not simply abandon her to the annals of a male labour movement. We also wanted to see if we could discover in her a relevance for contemporary feminist politics.

Reception

Rosa Luxemburg had played absolutely no part in my own political education in the years before the student movement. We had barely begun to discover the Marxist classics. As women we had not gone beyond Bebel. As the women's movement rapidly developed, the recoil from our newly discovered Marxism was so violent that we could only cling to the Marxist classics we already knew. Had anyone asked us whether a woman like Rosa Luxemburg had any contribution to make to a socialist feminism we would have been embarrassed for an answer. As socialists we 'knew' that she had contributed little by way of theory, that she 'overestimated' the masses and 'underestimated' the party. Her reputation was poor, and anyway we had too much to read and learn. So we bypassed the eleven volumes of her collected writings, speeches and letters.

The rediscovery of Gramsci by the left at the start of the eighties and the publication of Peter Weiss's great work, the *Aesthetics of Resistance*, were accompanied by a certain awareness of Rosa Luxemburg. All over the world – even in China and Japan – there were conferences and initiatives, all of which culminated in the establishment of an international committee for the study of Rosa Luxemburg in Zurich in 1980. Its themes – imperialism, peace and reformism – demonstrated her contemporary relevance, but there was still no mention of women and no echo from the women's movement.[5]

Furthermore, the discussions about *perestroika* in which a number of Luxemburg's ideas have become reality seem to have provoked a new, negative response to her. The 1988 book by Giselher Schmidt,[6] which is full of 'free-floating platitudes' was favourably reviewed in the *Frankfurter Allegemeine Zeitung* on 8 August 1988, in a notice which amounted to an exercise in all the old weapons of patriarchy. According to the reviewer Luxemburg was 'of a happy girlish disposition', 'physically handicapped', became a 'youthful star' in the SPD, uttered 'fine-sounding' phrases and indeed 'free-floating platitudes'. She allegedly ended up 'succumbing to temptation' and finding 'intellectual fulfilment' in Marx. Thanks to that her 'inner world' became increasingly unbalanced.

In 1982 Raya Dunayevskaya published her book *Rosa Luxemburg, Women's Liberation and Marx's Philosophy of Revolution.*[7] It appeared in the USA, but, to the best of my knowledge, it has scarcely been noticed in Germany. She recommends feminists above all to study Luxemburg's ideas on organization and to conceive of revolution as she does, namely as a process with several stages which means not just overcoming the old, but also constructing the new. This calls for political activity at every level by women who, given their personal stake in the politics of their emancipation, are alone in a position to bring that emancipation about. But even more important in her eyes is Rosa Luxemburg herself as the possible ideal of an emancipated woman. Precisely because she refused to restrict herself to the women's question and instead in her public speaking and her writings transgressed the customary limits of the feminine, Luxemburg appeared to her as a model for women's liberation. She thinks it wonderful that Rosa Luxemburg could become a passionate public speaker at the age of twenty-six and that she broke with her lover because of a political difference of opinions, that is to say, she was capable of independent judgement and of going her own way. She rejects the views of the usual masculine biographies (such as Nettl, 1966), according to whom the years following the separation from Jogiches were 'wasted'. She shows instead that it was precisely during this period that Luxemburg conducted her most important political debates, wrote her most important works and moreover was the only woman teacher in the party school. In Dunayevskaya's view, women's liberation begins when women stand up and speak in public, thus overcoming twice over the traditional limits of the feminine.

The idea of political role models was alien to us initially, since we had all grown up in a society in which the public sphere was so exclusively dominated by men that the absence of women was no more noticeable than the absence of boys in a girls' school. However, the study of the role of, and response to, Rosa Luxemburg in the labour movement made us aware that the invisibility of women as political role models was and is a cultural absence – an active exclusion – which confronted us with a task that we would have to face up to. Reading Rosa Luxemburg became an increasingly exciting undertaking.

In her film on Rosa Luxemburg Margarethe von Trotta seems to have had a similar end in view. She convincingly dramatizes Luxemburg's *attitude* and the audience leaves the cinema in an optimistic mood, composed equally of the will to bring about a change and an almost breathless sadness. She presents her as a revolutionary who is affected by life in all its manifestations. It is this that gives her both the passion to live and the inexorable resolve which is necessary to bring about change. The peculiar feature of this film is that it constantly shows us Luxemburg speaking in public, without ever really presenting her ideas, theories or political views. From this angle it could just as well have been a silent film.

In this age of the progressive destruction of nature it was refreshing to read Luxemburg's letters. The pleasure she took in every flower, her tender descriptions of the birds in her garden, the affection she felt for her cat – all these things were a constant invitation to transform the revolutionary fighter into a woman who had wonderful feminine feelings, for all her cold rationality. We were not unimpressed by this. But we felt uneasy when we saw how the great humanity which was generally agreed to characterize her writings (and especially her letters), scarcely differed from what centuries of women's oppression had defined as peculiar to women: love of nature, a rich emotional life, and a capacity for love to the point of the ability to express it in letters. Our mistrust of such an interpretation determined our selection of her works, in other words, we did not concede any central importance to her letters.

Nor did we escape the influence of the view current in the labour movement that Rosa Luxemburg had 'made but little contribution to theory', although in a negative way.[8] Our aim was to find out about a woman who had spent almost her entire life with the day-to-day business of politics, in speeches and assemblies, and writing newspaper articles. These were to be the object of our study. We resolved therefore not to concentrate on her main theoretical work, *The Accumulation of Capital*, but instead on her numerous smaller writings, speeches and articles, the influential Junius pamphlet and the articles on the mass strike.

Rosa Luxemburg as a Woman:
First Results of Our Reading – Language

We were taken aback by her language. She used many words we found unacceptable. Military words, for example. The Party stands *at the very front, in formation, one after the other* [*Mann für Mann*] – even though Rosa Luxemburg was down in our book as a passionate fighter for peace. A 'fighter'? It is true, we need such warlike words too – but not as frequently and not so bluntly, it seems to me. In the age of the women's movement, when we have become more sensitive about obviously masculine linguistic usages, we are still unsure about how to replace the master–servant metaphor. If, like Rosa Luxemburg, we make no bones about applying it to the proletariat, which thereby becomes the 'master of its own fate', women are just as effectively removed from the scene as they are in Marx's *Communist Manifesto.*[9] But even worse follows. According to her, 'The future of culture and mankind ... depends on whether the proletariat will hurl its manly sword on to the scales with manly resolution' (vol. 4, p. 62). Should we lay the blame for this at the door of the labour movement, in which Rosa Luxemburg and Clara Zetkin once described themselves as 'the only men'?

In other respects her language is full of telling images and a sharp wit. It often relies for its popular appeal on the way in which theories or political and economic facts are described in words and scenes drawn from household or other feminine activities. She refers to the politicans' 'household remedies' (vol. 4, p. 98). Or again we learn that 'legislation and revolution are not alternative methods of historical progress that you can select from the buffet of history, like hot sausages or cold sausages ...' (vol. 1/1, p. 428). She works with proverbs which she uses in their simple meaning whilst unmasking their use by the ruling classes. Take, for example, the saying, 'When the house is burning, should you not first douse the flames and only then look for the man who set it alight?' In her opinion this was used to give a common-sense credibility to the idea of using workers as 'cannon-fodder'. Austrian imperialism makes an appearance as the 'twin' of German imperialism, and the latter is eager to make use of 'the archducal corpses while they were still fresh' (vol. 4, p. 105). Imperialism is also described as a system in which:

> thread by thread is knitted together with the necessity of a law of nature until the tightly woven net of imperialist world politics has ensnared all five continents – a vast complex of historical phenomena whose roots reach down into the infernal depths of economic activity while its highest branches beckon to the emerging new world whose vague outlines can be barely discerned.
>
> vol. 4, p. 137

She shows a partiality for metaphors from the realm of sexuality and reproduction. In her critique of Bernstein, social democracy appears 'not as the legitimate offspring of capitalist society, but as the bastard of reaction' (vol. 1/1, p. 437). 'The reservists are no longer accompanied by the loud rejoicing of the maidens pursuing them'. Instead, there are 'marriage agencies for the widows of those who have fallen in battle' (vol. 4, p. 52). The economic struggle is 'wedded' to the social one (vol. 4, p. 54); and 'The South Russian businessmen, the darlings of the government, know how to win its favours for further increases in custom duties and all sorts of other little charitable gifts [*Liebesgaben*]' (vol. 1/1, p. 281).

Such metaphorical expressions, which are used to make statistics or other theoretical material clearer, have the great merit of bringing the complex problems of world politics down to the level of the reasoning that operates in individual households. This makes reading her enjoyable and comprehension easy. On the other hand, this deployment of images from the world of women has the disadvantage that this world is otherwise not discussed at all, and is assumed to be known and self-evident. Consider, for example the tacit acceptance of the condemnation of the victim implied in that monstrous metaphor written in her despair after the First World War:

> Defiled, dishonoured, knee-deep in blood, dripping with filth – thus bourgeois society appears before us, and thus it is. It stands revealed naked, in its true form, not when it is all spruced up and on its best behaviour, miming the values of culture, philosophy and ethics, order, peace and legality – but as a raging beast, an anarchic witches' sabbath and a miasma polluting culture and humanity in equal measure.
>
> vol. 4, p. 53.

Disconcerted by her language, we set about searching for texts that raise feminist issues or address women directly. It has since then become generally known that the women's movement was of no political interest to her and that she left such matters largely to her comrade, Clara Zetkin. According to one scholar not one of Rosa Luxemburg's interventions in parliamentary debates was concerned with women's problems.[10] But what is the position with her writings? Altogether we found four brief pieces – on International Women's Day, on women's franchise and class struggle, and on women's and children's labour. In a total *oeuvre* of almost 4000 pages they run to no more than 12 pages.[11] Rosa Luxemburg's lack of interest in women's problems cannot be doubted. Moreover, at first glance she uses the approach which had become traditional in the labour movement. She focuses on women's work and, quite unlike the refreshing description of 'the stifling atmosphere' and the spiritual impoverishment and pettiness of housework, which I quoted above (p. 220), she joins in the usual complaints about the decline of the family:

In the course of a year over 50,000 women and children were swept out of their homes by the iron broom of proletarianization and forced on to the labour market, the market for living wares. More than 50,000 women and children of the working class, who a year before had been able to live on the earnings of their husbands and fathers, are now dependent on the labour of their own hands.... Family life, health, a secure existence have now become empty phrases.

vol. 3, p. 164.

This is followed by the usual arguments that women's work reduces men's wages, that skilled labour is replaced by unskilled (women's) labour, and on to the call to join the class struggle (vol. 1/1, pp. 291ff).

A particularly instructive and contradictory challenge was provided by our reading of the brief essay 'The Proletarian Woman' (vol. 3, pp. 410ff).[12] The text appeared old-fashioned, and despite its pathos we were unable to identify with it emotionally. Indeed we found her language and imagery ultimately hostile to women. Here is the passage that upset us most.

For the bourgeois woman of property her house is her world. For the proletarian woman the whole world is her house, the world with its suffering and joy, with all its cruelty and its harsh grandeur. The proletarian woman wanders with a tunnel worker from Italy to Switzerland; she camps in sheds and sings while she dries her baby's clothes alongside rocks that are being dynamited. In the spring, as a seasonal labourer in the fields, she sits on her modest bundle amidst the din of the railway stations, a scarf over her hair with its simple parting, and waits patiently to be transported from East to West. Between decks on an ocean-going steamer she wanders around with the motley crowd of starving proletarians, buffeted by every wave that washes up the flotsam of the poor from Europe to America. And when the opposite wave of an American crisis gathers itself, she is swept back to the familiar poverty of

Europe, to new hopes and disappointments, to a renewed hunt for work and bread.

We first read this text in the hope of discovering a new model for women. What we found angered us. We were unable to respond to this proletarian 'ideal' of women with 'scarves over their hair with its simple parting', 'singing' and 'patient', that is to say, coming to terms with their wretched conditions and trying to be as decent, unaffected and inoffensive as possible. We missed any sign of insolence, of women willing to protest and defend themselves; we missed the troublemakers and saboteurs who were prepared to throw a spanner in the works and to put the dynamite to better use. We detected no sign of women's politics as we understood it. Instead the very thing that an insight into the women's movement shows as reproducing the oppression of women seemed to be celebrated as a virtue: women's patience is men's power.

Our irritation suffered an initial setback when we discovered that qualities ascribed to women and which she seemed to accept without question – patience, modesty and a willingness to hope for better days – are qualities that she also attributes with equal frequency to proletarian men. That is to say, she makes no distinction between the sexes. The virtues she praises are those of the oppressed in general. We decided to try to turn our uncertain irritation to productive use and asked one of the group to rewrite the scene described above, incorporating the actions and attitudes we had expected. The result was instructive. The description of the world turned out to be very bleak; the world was now uninhabitable for our proletarian woman whose strengthened powers of resistance appeared correspondingly ineffectual. We could see no way of bridging the gap between the powerful women we now imagined and the evils of the world. In short, what we had been looking for in Rosa Luxemburg was a radical but unpractical rhetoric. It now became clear that for all our criticism we had not really understood precisely what she had presented as women's strength, and how she had done so.

A further reading made clear that Luxemburg does not describe the proletarian woman. Instead she depicts three situations, showing how she moves through large-scale, international and even inter-continental spaces. These places have no particular functions. Instead the prolet-

arian woman encounters in each of them and with the same prob-
ability and naturalness, the same 'suffering and joy', 'hopes and
disappointments'. Home and family, which we usually think of as
places of refuge, do not appear as such. Conversely, foreign countries
and the public sphere do not appear alien and hostile. For the proletarian woman is equally at home and equally alien wherever she may
be. So we came to the – for us – surprising conclusion that in these few
sentences Luxemburg had overcome the separation of the public and
the private and that she had undermined the competence of the usual
authority of the family as the source of warmth, comfort and well-
being. In their place she confronts us with the need to be humane in all
our actions wherever we may be. The patience she had described also
contains the demand not to wait for this or that solution in a different
place, but to have our wits about us and to make the most of life here
and now – in stations, ocean-going steamers and dynamite charges.

The impatience we had felt at our first reading now turned against
us, since we had spontaneously converted something into its opposite,
sensing weakness, where she was depicting strength. We declared
ourselves satisfied with our second reading. We went on to ask what
use her words would have in political agitation. We decided that her
speech did contain optimistic elements and that it would probably
encourage and fortify women listeners even though it did not directly
address questions of women's work, politics or the family.

For practical purposes the family is dealt with in the second paragraph of her speech with her statement that capitalism has torn women
out of it. She repeats her statement about the separation of the public
and private spheres, and in this context 'domestic privation' is as unacceptable as the 'yoke of social production' (p. 410). In her further
comments the family is superseded completely and the proletarian
woman is defined exclusively in terms of her place in the social process,
'in which alone a woman becomes a human being' (p. 411). Like proletarian men she appears here as a potential subject of the emancipation
of society as a whole.

Politics are mentioned at the end of the text when women are
exhorted 'to obtain a foothold in political life through their activities in
all its aspects' (p. 412). Luxemburg invites women to become active in
the interests of their own emancipation – and not that of their
husbands or children. And by apostrophizing the proletarian woman

as 'the poorest of the poor' (p. 413), she also sees her, logically enough, as 'the champion of the working class and of the whole female sex' (p. 410).

We are accustomed to speeches to working women which expound their double oppression, their oppression both as workers and as women, in order to provoke their indignation and, if possible, their actual resistance and will to fight. There is nothing of all this in Rosa Luxemburg. In her sketch of the situation of working women there is both criticism and a view of their prospects. The proletarian woman has no home of her own, but the world is her home. She has no family, but only women like herself. She has no mother-tongue, but moves among the Babel of the entire world. The prosperity of bourgeois women is at the same time the straitjacket that ties them down. The proletarian woman has neither the one nor the other. The fact that she is unconfined means that she is able to reach the distant shore. In this Luxemburg's agitation differs radically from the common run which regards the vivid evocation of poverty as an effective liberating force. But nor does she write as if the oppressed can only be motivated by strength and a positive, optimistic enthusiasm. Instead she shows that it is what we usually think of as poverty that contains the seeds of hope and liberation. To that extent her speeches also present us with a challenge because they compel us to rethink our attitude to poverty and to the kind of happiness we think worth striving for. Her form of negation looks towards the public realm and the future, and implicitly criticizes our spontaneous point of view as one which has not yet crossed the threshold of the private house and ventured into the world outside. In that sense her writing is not populist, either, as we had at first assumed from her employment of homely images which would invite easy identification. Her writing is directed against empathy with the immediate conditions that have given rise to complaint. Instead of empathy, she seeks the germs of the future in the defects of the present. This approach is disconcerting because it is alien, familiar only in the form of hope. But by presenting hope as sadness about being torn free and dispossessed, her criticism becomes truly radical. She depicts progress not as a peaceable children's dance, but as what it is – being violently torn away from the present. The energy that this injects into her speeches also enables her to ignore the injustices of the day, unless they contain a future dimension. Because of this the extent to which the relations between the sexes are a component of the relations of production is something that necessarily eludes her.

Both excited and depressed by Rosa Luxemburg's approach to women's questions we were now able to understand why she was largely ignored until recently in the annals of feminist historiography. She was no feminist. But who was she as a woman among socialists? Why was she scarcely any more prominent in the ancestral line of socialist classics than among the recent feminists? And we still had to explain what we as socialist feminists should learn from her.

Words in Movement: Second Reading

Her masculine, military vocabulary, her frequently idiosyncratic use of female imagery, are not the only linguistic impediments she imposes on us. Without any self-consciousness or even hesitation she uses words like 'the masses' or 'the leaders', which we find unacceptable and which make us react defensively. Behind the word 'masses' lie layers of ideology which go back for decades, as well as the practices of the many and our own attitudes and feelings. 'The masses' – the term always refers to other people, aimless activity, a great noise. We know that we are part of the masses, but we can always set ourselves apart by using the word. However, talking of the masses conceals a double movement. By distancing ourselves we also become aware of our involvement in the masses in a rather anxious-making way. We are forced to perceive ourselves as belonging to the throng.

In reaction to the mass movements of the early twentieth century a new discipline emerged to explore the potential of the masses. This was mass psychology. It, too, taught contempt for the masses as a way for the individual to distance him- or herself from them at will. Hence a taboo on the use of the concept may be viewed as an act of compensation.

Rosa Luxemburg's writing comes into conflict with our linguistic habits, and exposes their ossified nature. We may not wish to utter the word 'masses', but we still have the thought. The masses – that means those down there with their mass culture which we have learned to criticize as an instrument of mass stultification and which we ourselves enjoy only with a bad conscience. And then there is mass consumption which depoliticizes, and mass tourism which converts the beautiful holiday dreams into mass experiences. Our ways of speaking channel our thoughts. What else do we suppress when we refuse to speak of the masses?

Overriding our initial hesitation, we take note of Luxemburg's enthusiasm for the masses. The masses, they are the people in movement, when it gathers itself and advances towards change. Intellectuals are also part of the masses; they help the movement to express itself. The masses need no leaders because they are the people in a state of political consciousness. The very word has become mobile. These references to the people as something active and in movement give rise to images of people at political meetings, demonstrations, on strike. And we catch ourselves hoping that there will be many of them and that they will grow more numerous from one moment to the next. The images are augmented by music, songs – instead of just noise. Our scepticism towards 'the masses' as the term for a crowd to which we do not wish to belong and who are responsible for spoiling pleasures that used to be sublime, has somehow changed. We suddenly feel ourselves as part of the masses, active, hopeful and in movement.

The lessons about stultifying silence are not the only ones we can learn from Luxemburg's way of talking. There are other words which have been swathed in reverence and hence protected from criticism. These too start to become mobile. Peace, for example, can mean imperialism and war. And this is not just a simple example of bourgeois manipulation of language. Even socialist peace conferences can degenerate into talking-shops which help to prepare a devastating attack on peace. Words lose their solidity. But they have a fixed meaning in the hopes of whole peoples, in a socialist perspective. But until then they are malleable and have different meanings in each context. Morality, honour, wealth, conscience, workers' protection, defence – it scarcely matters where the words originate – they all join in a wild dance and it is the task of socialist intellectuals to decode their configurations.

Looked at in this way, Rosa Luxemburg's works are a kind of 'language school', or perhaps a proposal about the use of language. She writes in accordance with Brecht's later suggestion. Her words are like snowballs – firm, but they can be made to melt at any time; they are in motion, they can be dropped; they are malleable, which makes them more useful. If we fall in line with this way of dealing with words, we shall find ourselves drawn from the firm ground of unconsidered certainties into the maelstrom of conflicting interests. The breathless movement whirls around in our heads. Thus when we read approvingly of 'the peace formula of the workers' and soldiers' councils', 'no annexations and no compensation, a peace on the basis of national self-determination' (vol. 4, p. 275), we quickly find ourselves moving in an unexpected direction. The formula does not remain constant, but turns out 'to serve the interests of *entente* imperialism ... by virtue of the objective situation and its logic' (vol. 4, pp. 276ff). And 'when the Russian proletariat fights for this goal of universal peace, it is really just tying a noose round its own neck' (vol. 4, p. 281). The language teaches political lessons. Because the words refuse to remain fixed they tell us something about the frames of reference which guide our normal speaking habits. In other words, they inspire us to look more carefully at our own use of words.

But Rosa Luxemburg goes even further. She shows us that in almost every problematic situation it is essential to go beyond the given frame of reference and not to go on struggling inside it unless we are prepared to accept a tragic role as the playthings of the old dominant relations; for nothing remains what it was. 'Since the outbreak of the World War international socialism has actually played the part of the reliable guardian of bourgeois class rule' (vol. 4, p. 289). And in this context she uses words like 'loyal' 'understanding' and 'peace', all of which pave the way for imperialism and become a shroud for the Russian Revolution.

And in moments of crisis her words become compressed into metaphors of overwhelming power. Crisis puts an end to unprincipled shifts and elisions of meaning. Society shows itself for what it is. 'The policeman on the corner becomes the sole representative of human dignity' and 'The cannon fodder that had been loaded on to trains amidst patriotic cheers in August and September is now rotting in Belgium, the Vosges and in Masuria, in graveyards from which profits are sprouting up luxuriantly' (vol. 4, p. 52).

Her words just sweep you along, her arguments move you just as the concepts are all in motion. It is this passion, this political commitment, which extends into the theoretical plane, that has recently induced women to reread her from a feminist standpoint.[13]

The Living and the Dead

Irene Dölling describes Rosa Luxemburg's stance and style as 'a political and cultural programme' for humanity. She writes:

> She possessed the rare ability to see and judge the world with a sharp analytical intelligence and yet at the same time to approach it with her sense and her feelings. It was this *joie de vivre*, the capacity to enjoy the small things in life, to be at one with nature and other living creatures, which gave her the strength to be 'firm and clear and cheerful' even when times were difficult, such as during the internal party feuds and her disappointment over the failure of social democracy.[14]

She suggests that we should think of Rosa Luxemburg's love of nature, her ability to feel compassion for her fellow creatures as one of the sources of her political attitudes and her qualities of resistance.

Christel Neusüss goes much further.[15] In the light of the threats posed by nuclear energy, the destruction of the environment and genetic engineering she attempts to reconstruct the replacement of all life by the dead hand of patriarchy in Western thought. As the inventor of the model of the 'master-builder with head and hand', Marx is re-interpreted as a figure who emphasized the importance of dead things which had been first designed in people's, that is, men's, heads and were then put into practice by human hands. These were given the role of historical dominance over everything female and living, over nature and belly. Hence he overlooked the essentials, and in his wake the workers' movement continued this labour of a patriarchal denaturing of the world. This framework enables Neusüss to arrive at a new view of Rosa Luxemburg. She concludes, 'She looks at society with a woman's eyes' (p. 282). Wherever she looks she sees violence. She situates Rosa Luxemburg on the side of the 'natural'.

> Natural – artificial. This binary pair can be found in the earliest writings.... The process of social development is no machine that has been constructed in advance according to a precise plan. Nor can it be controlled like a machine, switched on or off or constructed purely according to the intentions and plan of any so-called subject.
>
> p. 331

A little further on she defines her political model more concretely:

> Without learning from experience nothing works. This is a burden the
> party cannot relieve the masses of.... Learning from experience is what
> distinguishes human beings from animals. This is why they come
> naked, ignorant and helpless from their mothers' wombs. And this is
> why it is essential for adults to look after them for so long, and by adults
> we normally mean: the mothers.
>
> p. 337

It is Christel Neusüss's achievement to have stressed the importance
of learning and experience, the emphasis on living people in Rosa
Luxemburg's works, and to have drawn it to the attention of feminists.
Luxemburg's ridicule of party leaders, who set out to control revolutions or call a halt to class conflict, dictate forms of struggle and
pervert Marxism into a dogmatic doctrine – instead of using it as a
guide, like Ariadne's thread – is something that informs her writings
and speeches throughout her life. For example, '... great popular
movements cannot be conjured up by technical formulae from the
pockets of party functionaries' (vol. 4, p. 148). And:

> The 'best prepared' mass strike can, in certain circumstances, collapse
> in ruins just when the party leadership gives 'the signal' for it to begin,
> or it can fall flat after a promising start. Whether great popular
> demonstrations or mass actions really take place, in whatever form, is
> decided by a whole host of economic, political and psychological factors
> which reflect the actual state of class tensions, the degree of enlighten-
> ment, the maturity of the fighting will of the masses. These factors are
> incalculable and cannot be artificially created by any party.
>
> vol. 4, p. 149

But I felt confused by Christel Neusüss's talk of the caring mothers
who look after ignorant, helpless children. In Luxemburg's writings
the masses, the movement, the class and the party all learn. She only
talks about children in connection with child labour. For example, we
can read in the programme she wrote for the newly founded German
Communist Party in 1918/19 the simple statement, 'Elimination of
factory labour for children in its present form. Combining of education
with material production, and so on' (vol. 4, p. 488). We are familiar

with these ideas from Marx and the early discussions of polytechnical education. To shift Rosa Luxemburg on to the side of mother and child, nature, tradition and conservation is made possible, in my view, by the claim that the development of the productive forces was anathema to her, over and above a certain modest degree (Neusüss, p. 282). 'Enthusiastic noises' about the function of the world market in the 'development of the total global society ... never pass her lips' (p. 315). Neusüss shows the passion with which Luxemburg exposes and denounces the violent and destructive aspects of capitalism, and goes on to assert: 'She completely lacks the ability to express enthusiasm about all the works of the master-builders to be sighted in the countryside. Man-made wonders of the world do not induce the relevant feelings in her' (p. 287). The opposite is the case. It is true that she does display enthusiasm for the living, for people, learning, experience and culture, but it is no less true that she is similarly enthusiastic about master-builder activities and technical progress. And if it is no less true for all that that she excoriates the violence and destructiveness that capitalism and imperialism have brought upon the world, this only means that this either/or logic – artificial or natural, for or against – does not apply to her way of thinking.

In what follows I wish to demonstrate her enthusiasm for the development of productive forces and hence a link to Marx which, given her particular emphasis and urgency, I regard as a feminine way of working from which we could usefully profit for our own approach. I call it the logic of crises and ruptures.[16]

Productive Forces and Crisis

To start with, here are two out of a whole series of enthusiastic statements on the development of productive forces. I am quite consciously taking concrete examples from technological products which we would find more problematic today, even if in general we had high hopes of the development of the forces of production: the creation of waterways and railway lines.

For the moment both of these giant undertakings [canal-building in North America] are the offspring of quite straightforward commercial and military interests. But they will outlast their creator – the capitalist economy. They prove once again what colossal forces of production lie slumbering in the womb of our society and how progress and culture will thrive once they have cast off the fetters of capitalist interests.

vol. 1/1, p. 283

Like everything else the bourgeoisie creates, the great transport systems [i.e., railways] can ultimately only have a destructive effect on the bourgeois world. But for the general advancement of culture they are of enormous and lasting value.

vol. 1/1, pp. 287ff

These statements are unambiguous. Technological advance appears as progress and in the context of a culture which is worth preserving, it is evidently of value in a different social system. Rosa Luxemburg obviously takes seriously the contradiction Marx had worked out between the forces and the relations of production. The productive forces ripen in the womb of bourgeois society, Marx had claimed; they will burst asunder the mould in which they were produced. What separates Luxemburg from other theoreticians of the labour movement is not her rejection of technological progress. On the contrary, it is the radical application of Marx's dialectical thinking to the condition of bourgeois society. The productive forces the latter develops are destructive of that society, and are in it. Their incompatibility with the existing forms of society manifests itself directly. They reveal themselves most immediately to those living in it, above all to the workers and to peoples who have been colonized. Thus Luxemburg regards violence and destruction as the companions of forces which have cultural value in a different, higher form of society. And she sees very clearly that such contradictions have a contradictory effect on the workers themselves.

It is evident that as far as production techniques are concerned, the interests of the (individual) capitalist coincide perfectly with the development and the progress of the capitalist economy as such. It is his own need that drives him to introduce technical innovations. The situation of the individual worker, on the other hand, is the opposite. Every technical improvement conflicts with the interests of the workers directly affected by it and worsens their immediate situation because it devalues their labour power. Hence when the trade unions intervene in the technical side of production, they can only act on behalf of the latter, that is, on behalf of the group of workers directly affected. That is to say, they will oppose innovation. But in so doing they do not act in the interests of the working class or its emancipation as a whole. For the latter is in harmony with technological progress, that is to say, with the interests of the individual capitalist. Consequently their intervention coincides with the interests of the reaction.

vol. 1/1, p. 390

In this situation, in which the capitalists are initially at least on the progressive side, and the workers on the side of a conservative mode of production, she develops her complex but also inspiring agitation and socialist politics. She has to go on the attack against capitalism, and at the same time she has to join forces with it and oppose the spontaneous interests of the workers whom she passionately supports. But her method is not to start from her analysis of the false interests of the workers so as to dictate the true ones from above. Instead she appeals to the people as if they were already in power. These appeals are directed concretely against the state and aim at the long-term takeover of the government by the people. Every step of everyday politics leads in this direction.

Her sharp awareness of the contradictions in our society leads her to take up one of the fundamental figures in Marx's writings, one which to my knowledge has never been adopted with such vigour by others. For example, Marx describes the terrible conditions in the factories. This has been readily taken up and has become more or less canonical in industrial sociology. He describes the workers in the most negative terms: they are brutalized, stunted, overworked, one-sided, morally degraded, and so on. He then makes an intellectual leap and builds all his hopes for change – all his hopes for revolution and socialism – on these very creatures. The link between the deprivation and the hope is a rupture, a crisis. In this crisis our feelings spontaneously take the side of the old, of the obstacles to the new society. Consider, for example, this celebrated passage from the *Communist Manifesto*:

All fixed, fast-frozen relations, with their train of ancient and venerable prejudices and opinions, are swept away, all new-formed ones become antiquated before they can ossify. All that is solid melts into air, all that is holy is profaned, and man is at last compelled to face with sober senses his real conditions of life, and his relations with his kind.[17]

Despite the indisputably negative context, we are clearly expected to celebrate the demise of venerable, firm, solid and holy institutions. In capitalism it is evidently the skills, the secrets, the specialized knowledge that stand on the side of decline. In this confusion our feelings stand unmistakably on the side of the old, and scientific understanding is essential before we can come to terms with our feelings. In this process we have to rely on our experience to help us to perceive that what is holy is also an ideological phenomenon.

This whole complex of thought is taken further by Rosa Luxemburg. Again and again she uses these linguistic tropes to give a vivid picture of the catastrophe of war and the movement of crisis. In the little essay 'Ruins' (1914), for example, she writes:

But every war destroys not only physical property, not only material values. It is also no respecter of traditional concepts. Ancient relics, revered institutions, formulae faithfully repeated, are all swept away by the same iron broom and deposited on the same rubbish heap which contains the remnants of used cannon, rifles, back-packs and other refuse of war.

vol. 4, pp. 52ff

And in the vehement introductory section of *The Crisis of Social Democracy* she expands the words from the *Communist Manifesto* to create an image of bourgeois society as a whole.

Business thrives on the ruins, cities become heaps of rubble, villages cemeteries, whole countries are laid waste and whole peoples are turned into mobs of beggars and churches into stables. International law, state treaties, alliances, sacred words, the highest authorities are all torn up. Every sovereign by the grace of God describes his cousin on the opposing side as an idiot and a treacherous scoundrel; every diplomat dismisses his opposite number as a wily rogue, every government criticizes every other government as the enemy of its own people. And famine ... and disease ... and misery and despair are everywhere.

vol. 4, pp. 52ff

But the 'world-historical catastrophe' (*ibid.*) is not this 'witches' sabbath', but 'the capitulation of international social democracy' to anarchy.

> And what happened in Germany when the great historical test presented itself? The greatest fall, the worst possible collapse. Nowhere was the organization of the proletariat so completely in the service of imperialism; nowhere was the state of siege endured with such little resistance; nowhere was the press so muzzled, public opinion so stifled and the economic and political class struggle so totally abandoned as in Germany. But German social democracy was not merely the most powerful vanguard of the International, it was also its brain.
>
> vol. 4, p. 55

Her despairing indignation about the role of social democracy in the approval of war credits is grounded in the view that no orientation of the masses is possible unless they are constantly being brought together and their movements given shape and direction. When social democracy called a halt to the class struggle for the duration of the war, it robbed the labour movement of any meaningful strategy. Left without guidance the masses could be catapulted into the arms of the imperialist war.

The fact that the thrust of her political agitation is directed against existing ideas means that she begins by opposing everything we spontaneously approve of. She rejects the home in favour of the world. Since everything is in flux and hence available, she makes a virtue of patience, endurance and gaity. She advises us to find pleasure in the existing situation. This foothold in the present is also an attitude, a stance. She combines pleasure with an indignation about the wretched conditions in society. This enables her to bypass a criticism which views women (or people in general) as victims. She shows who is going where, and what power she or he possesses. Her route goes out into the world, not back into the home. This is why it is vital to form a clear picture of the world; it concerns us, it is our home, here is where we have to establish our point of view. In contrast, our own social criticism always leads us to contemplate flight. In the present state of society we can find no safe haven (consider the right-wing backlash, Chernobyl, genetic engineering, and so on). In contrast, Rosa Luxemburg shows that socialist elements in capitalism are not experienced as socialist. Otherwise they would render superfluous a struggle for socialism which fights with and for individuals. In a whole host of speeches, articles and examples she shows that the reforms which are introduced to improve the condition of the workers always serve the interests of the ruling class too (consider workers' protection; see her discussion in 'Bourgeois Workers' Protection Acts and Social Democracy', vol. 1/1, p. 791). She describes measures to protect workers as the regulation of exploitation (in vol. 1/1, p. 394 for example).

This coincidence of interests reaches a climax when capitalists turn against society. She illustrates this with reference to tariff policy and militarism. She can even manage to discover a progressive element in militarism: 'Tariff policy and militarism have both played an indispensable and hence too a progressive, revolutionary role in capitalism' (vol. 1/1, p. 396). She makes a distinction between the *development* of capitalism and its standpoint in the contradictions of the historical process, on the one hand, and the activities of the capitalist *class*, on the other. While the former drives society on by means of war, murder and theft, the latter has an even more devastating effect because its impact outlasts its own time. Opposing groups of capitalists fight each other making use of now obsolete weapons such as tariff policy and the military. The state now becomes a class state because it neglects the interests of society as a whole in favour of those of the capitalists of each nation. The contradictions within the state are intensified. This complex situation is the arena of political intervention. Rosa Luxemburg's anti-state policy appeals to the interests of society as a whole against the political expression of capitalist class interests. Such political analyses lead her in the opposite direction to any schematic base–superstructure model. She even makes fun of these, for example, in a letter to Robert Seidel:

There are plenty of materialists who assert that economic development rushes like a self-confident train down the tracks of history, and that politics, ideology, and so on, just trot helplessly and passively in its wake, like lifeless freight cars. But you will certainly be unable to find such views even in the remotest Russian district (and in Russia, as you know, they are very well informed on such matters. But within five minutes they will prepare you such an omelette out of all possible old and new materialists that you won't know whether you are standing on your heads or your feet). But if you ever do manage to find such a materialist as I have described, you can put him on show in a panopticon.[18]

Instead she shows how politics and the legal system act as bulwarks for a society which is full of self-contradictions.

> The relations of production in a capitalist society increasingly approach those of socialism, but their political and legal institutions erect higher and higher barriers between capitalist and socialist societies. These barriers are not penetrated by social reforms or increased democracy. On the contrary, such changes just make them stronger. The only way to break them down is with the hammer blows of revolution, that is to say, through the proletariat's conquest of power.
>
> vol. 1/1, p. 400

This brings us back to the proletariat and its historical role. But far from conceiving of that role as a law, as a mechanical historical process, Luxemburg believes in the necessity of proletarian action to preserve society from collapse. This remains a historical possibility.

> Socialism has become a necessity, not simply because the proletariat is no longer prepared to live under the conditions which the capitalist class makes available for it, but because unless the proletariat fulfils its duty as a class and makes socialism a reality, we are all doomed to destruction.
>
> vol. 4, p. 494

The politics which is made against the spontaneous involvement of individuals, but which is implemented together with them and for them, is self-contradictory, and hence necessarily a scientific politics. That is to say, analysis accompanies it at every step.

The specific pathos of Luxemburg's approach is defined by her use of Marx's logic of crises and ruptures, the resulting involvement in the contradictory experiences of individuals and the search for hope in the midst of deprivation. This politicization of experience, the political articulation of everyday experience, the transformation of the wish to endure into the will to change – these things are indispensable for women's politics. But the scientific analyses which would convert their daily oppressions into strategic solutions have scarcely begun.

Experience and the Subject

The attempt to develop a politics of crisis, a strategy which hopes to construct the bases for a different society by destroying existing traditions, cultures and forms, had few successors in the labour movement. It led Rosa Luxemburg to the violent rejection of a trade union policy which she found reactionary because of its preservation of property rights. Curiously, it was not this which provoked any conflict worth mentioning in the tradition of the labour movement. The main criticism of her was that she 'overestimated the masses'. This accusation was even taken over by Christel Neusüss and it was repeated by the feminist writer Bonacchi.[19] Her theoretical approach might have led us to expect her to demote the spontaneous hopes and wishes of the masses in the name of a perspective which does not appear to them immediately. The reverse is the case. Her insight into the crisis-ridden nature of historical development makes it essential for individuals to act even against their own immediate spontaneous interests. They can only do this if they wish to do so, if they grasp the nature of the historical trend, in short, if they become intellectuals. In this context she enthusiastically refers to Marx's *Critique of Hegel's Philosophy of Right* and quotes the following passage from it on the question of how it can be possible for the oppressed and maltreated members of society to act as its liberators.

In the formation of a class with *radical chains*, a class of civil society which is not a class of civil society, a class [*Stand*] which is the dissolution of all classes, a sphere which has a universal character because of its universal suffering ... and finally a sphere which cannot emancipate itself without emancipating itself from – and thereby emancipating – all other spheres of society, which is, in a word, the *total loss* of humanity and which can therefore redeem itself only through the *total redemption of humanity*. This dissolution of society as a particular class is the *proletariat*.... Just as philosophy finds its *material* weapons in the proletariat, so the proletariat finds its *intellectual* weapons in philosophy; and once the lightning of thought has struck deeply into this virgin soil of the people, emancipation will transform the *Germans* into *human beings*.[20]

Thus for Luxemburg *education* is a great source of hope, one which will enable the oppressed and the exploited to act strategically in their own interests. But education is not simply indoctrination from above, it is not just enlightenment or instruction. She does indeed speak of education and enlightenment (see, for example, vol. 4, p. 482), but her general line is clear enough. By enlightenment she understands not the unmasking of hidden misdeeds, but rather a call for more knowledge according to the motto: the knowledge we need is still lacking.[21] If we look at her newspaper articles from this point of view we find that they contain a great fund of knowledge for the people. Education is primarily the self-activation of the masses. This is another way in which we as women can benefit politically from Rosa Luxemburg. After all, we have to resolve the paradox that women are largely excluded from participation in public life and politics but that it cannot be our aim simply to infiltrate the existing structures. Instead, as women emancipate themselves they must simultaneously overthrow the institutions that oppress them. What is at stake therefore is not a compensatory education of the sort traditionally conceded to women in the labour movement, that is to say, not simply an education that helps them catch up. On this point Rosa Luxemburg writes:

> I believe that history does not make it as easy for us as it was in the bourgeois revolutions, where it was sufficient to overthrow the official violence at the centre and replace it with a few new men. We have to work from the bottom up, ... we have to achieve the conquest of political power not from above, but from below.

> vol. 4, p. 510

The education she has in mind is acquired through action. She takes up the famous but, at least as far as practical socialist politics are concerned, neglected Marx quotation from the Feuerbach theses. 'The coincidence of the changing of circumstances and of human activity or self-changing can be conceived and rationally understood only as *revolutionary practice*' (The Pelican Marx: *Early Writings*, Harmondsworth 1977, p. 422 [Third Thesis]). She constantly turns to this thesis and works out its implications. A collection of her statements on this point would fill a small book in themselves. I shall confine myself to a few of them.

Her basic idea is that a socialist revolution can only come about as the work of the masses, but for this they have to be educated.

> Today, the working class must educate itself, gather itself together and provide its own leadership in the course of revolutionary struggle itself.
>
> vol. 2, p. 148.

Or:

> Neither a revolution nor a mass strike can be brought into being with the psychology of a union leader who refuses to take part in May Day celebrations until he has been guaranteed a specified level of assistance in case he is disciplined for doing so. But in the hurricane of revolution this same proletarian is transformed from a paterfamilias anxious for financial aid into a 'revolutionary romantic' in whose eyes even the highest good, life itself, to say nothing of mere material well-being, is of little value in comparison with the ideals he is fighting for.
>
> vol. 2, p. 133

The word she uses to describe this process, or rather result, is *maturity*. It was prevalent in the discourse of the working-class movement of the time where it referred to a condition which had to be waited for. But she conceives of it as a kind of 'self-development' which takes place in the movement by fits and starts and which can be supported by the party. In her view this process of education is primarily an action of the masses in movement. 'The masses must learn to exercise power by exercising it. They cannot learn it any other way' (vol. 4, p. 509). Here she puts her hopes in the experiment of the workers' and soldiers' councils (see her discussion of the *Founding Party Congress*. vol. 4, p. 484), for which she did not think that the masses were 'mature' enough, but assumed that they could learn to exercise 'state' power by trial and error. The experiment failed. But this does not refute the important idea that learning from experience is an essential component of self-determination.

Did she overestimate the masses? The assumption that she did is so widespread that it merits a brief examination. To anticipate our findings: this criticism is rooted in a static understanding of the word masses which is alien to Luxemburgian thinking.

Let us begin by taking the criticism at its face value. If we consider her statements about the working masses or the people in general, we find them sharply criticized. To start with the question of 'immaturity', we discover in the article on the *Founding Party Congress*, 'We are aware of the conditions that prevail among the people and how immature they are' (vol. 4, p. 482). During the crisis of social democracy she does not mince her words when she describes the masses' war fever, their 'patriotic intoxication' (vol. 4, p. 64), their participation in the 'mass slaughter' which had become a 'wearisome daily chore' (vol. 4, p. 51). Here is her climactic overview:

> Gone is the excitement. Gone is the patriotic shouting in the streets, the hunt for golden automobiles ... the excesses of the public on the lookout for spies, the surging crowds in the cafés where ear-splitting music and patriotic songs drowned out everything else. Whole cities were transformed into mobs, ready to denounce their neighbours, assault women, shout hurrah and be made delirious by wild rumours. There was an atmosphere of ritual murder ... in which the policeman on the corner was the only representative of human dignity left.
>
> The play is at an end. German scholars, those 'tottering lemurs', have long since been driven from the stage by whistles and cat-calls. The trains of reservists are no longer accompanied by the loud cheers of young women running after them along the platform; nor do they wave joyously to the people from the carriage windows. Nowadays they trot along through the streets in silence, their cardboard boxes in their hands while the population goes about its business with morose expressions.
>
> vol. 4, p. 51

There can be no question of overestimation here. On the contrary, the masses are the drunken, undignified, murderous mob of the kind produced by bourgeois society, acting in the only way open to it in this society. 'Only the slavish obedience of the German proletariat' enabled German imperialism to exploit the Russian Revolution for its own purposes (vol. 4, p. 378) and the forces of reaction could only venture on such a bold experiment because it could 'have absolute confidence in the unshakeable stupidity of the German masses' (vol. 4, p. 375).

Indeed, even the working class acted as the 'willing executioner of the freedom of others' (vol. 4, p. 381).

Thus Luxemburg does not tread the customary path of putting her trust only in the class-conscious worker. On the contrary, in her speech on the Founding Party Congress in which she calls upon the KPD to take part in the elections she dismisses that attitude as a facile solution, characteristic of the faction led by Otto Rühle (see vol. 4, pp. 481ff). But at the same time, 'the masses' is not a fixed concept for her, it is no static agglomeration. The masses are always in motion. As human beings they are in a position – although not necessarily today – to take their fate in their own hands. For Luxemburg this is the epitome of socialism and the reason why it is worth fighting for. At the same time it expresses her view of humanity:

> Human culture in its entirety is the product of the combined efforts of many, it is the work of the masses ... This history [of mankind] is full of heroic sagas, of the great deeds of individuals; it echoes with the fame of wise monarchs, valiant generals, daring explorers, brilliant inventors, heroic liberators. But all this admirable and varied activity is, as it were, no more than the outer, ornamental cloak of human history. At first glance all good and evil, both the golden ages and the tragedies of the nations are the work of individual rulers or great men. In reality it is the people themselves, the anonymous masses who create their own destinies, their glory and their misfortunes.
>
> vol. 4, p. 206

These words remind us of Brecht's poem 'Fragen eines lesenden Arbeiters' about Thebes with its seven gates – an idea which Peter Weiss, commenting on Luxemburg, elaborates in the *Ästhetik des Widerstands* (The Aesthetics of Resistance): 'No, the pyramids are in reality the work of thousands and thousands of patient slaves who were compelled to erect the stone monuments of their own slavery amidst sighs and groans in cruel forced labour.' The masses – they are humankind itself, the creators and victims of their own history. 'It is not possible to have a war for which the masses of the people are not responsible, thanks to their warlike enthusiasm or their subservient docility' (*Ibid.*). And Luxemburg:

Men do not make their history according to their own will. But they make it themselves. In its actions the proletariat is dependent on the state of maturity of the society of the day, but social development does not advance independently of the proletariat. The proletariat acts as both its cause and driving force, just as it is both the product and consequence of society. Its action is a determining factor in history.

vol. 4, p. 61

But precisely because the masses are entangled in existing circumstances, in their immature state, the realization of socialism and revolution depends on their carrying out their own process of maturation. The medium by which they achieve this is experience. We recollect that experience was also a barrier to progress because it advises patience and endurance. To overcome this attitude calls for a scientific approach to experience and thereby determines the transitory function of intellectuals in the labour movement and the necessity for workers to become intellectuals themselves. Her particular way of speaking to the people and of causing them to speak is what gives rise, on a superficial reading, to the impression of overestimation. People are addressed as the people of the future, as those whom they could be and would like to be.

I come now to my conclusion that it was not actually the overestimation of the masses which gave Luxemburg the reputation of romanticizing the masses, but its apparent reverse, the wish to adjust the relation between the party and the leadership. Here her beliefs and utterances are unambiguous. The leadership provides the masses with 'political expression, its slogan and direction', but it serves the masses and not the other way round. Assuming the leadership means 'that in every phase and at every moment the entire sum of the available and already released, activated might of the proletariat should be made real ... it should never be less powerful than the actual balance of power warrants' (vol. 4, pp. 149ff). This requirement again alters the meaning of words. Let us take 'discipline', for example. 'Social-democratic discipline can never mean that the 800,000 organized party members should have to bow to the decisions of a central authority, a party committee, but that on the contrary, all the central organs of the party should carry out the will of the 800,000 organized members' (vol. 3,

p. 39). This process, too, is in constant flux. The party leadership becomes bureaucratic when the masses fall asleep. Luxemburg comes to the conclusion that 'the proletarian masses require no "leaders" in the bourgeois sense. They are their own leaders' (vol. 3, p. 42.). Even though this sentence may seem to confirm the view that she over-estimated the masses to the point of illusion, it really only confirms the simple fact that the liberation of the masses must be its own work. If that is not the case, then it will be no true liberation, but just another form of subordination.

> We must speak quite frankly. Only when the present abnormal relationship has been reversed would the life of the party become normal. The emancipation of the working class can only come as the work of the working class itself, according to the *Communist Manifesto*, and by working class it does not mean a party leadership seven or twelve strong. It means the educated *mass* of the proletariat acting on its own behalf. Every step forwards in the struggle of the working class for its own emancipation must also mean the growing intellectual indepen-dence of the masses, their growing self-activation, self-determination and initiative.
>
> vol. 3, p. 38

This holds good for people in general, but it has a special relevance for women. The sexual division of labour and the separation of the political and the private realms, the public and the domestic, position women in such a way that their social disenfranchisement becomes simultaneously a prison and a comfort. In the history of the labour movement, too, women do not emancipate themselves; they are emancipated by others. This leads to the noteworthy situation that women's issues have been on the agenda for a century, but they figure there as the last item in perpetuity, the item that is never discussed because time has run out. The political agenda is one in which all sorts of changes are possible for the male members of the movement, and it gives them the opportunity to intervene, to participate as human beings. But this is not the case with women. If their situation is to improve – and despite the enormous growth in national wealth in the last twenty years it has scarcely improved at all socially – they must take up their own cause. We have not even reached the point where their status as human beings can be taken for granted. So on this point, too, Rosa Luxemburg is of relevance for the women's movement: women must act, or else they will always be acted upon. This is not merely, or not only, the usual call for women to do something. The modest division of labour between those who care and those who are cared for, a division which has once again become fashionable politically, also points to something much deeper: our stabilized acceptance of our inferiority. Only when it is thought possible for great numbers of other, for example, female human beings to live in tutelage, can man bring himself to accept his own inferiority. In this sense women, or rather their place in society, is a coin which helps to stabilize the exchange rate.

I have drawn attention to the characteristics which made it so hard for the labour movement to digest Rosa Luxemburg's contribution. Her lack of respect for the leadership, her absolute reliance on the masses as the heart of Marxism, the logic of crises and ruptures which enabled her both to do justice to the enormous suffering and destruction and also to envisage the formation of a different society, different people and a humane humanity. Her viewpoint is the seizure of power by the people. All these features seem to me to be indispensable for a women's politics. They are both universal and abstract, and yet they are capable of being filled with concrete content and are historically new. For such mundane activity Rosa Luxemburg coined the term: revolutionary *realpolitik*.

The search for useful ideas for a women's politics led us to Rosa Luxemburg. She led us unexpectedly to a project for revolutionizing politics in general. Wherever we were able to find something useful or important for women's politics it turned out to imply a critique of views which think of politics as something coming from above, of the party as a form which those lower down have to serve, as a bureaucratically sclerotic structure, a tool for ensuring the passivity of the masses. Rosa Luxemburg's teachings make plain that where fixed images are built into dominant forms of oppression, political struggles must be conducted at every level. It includes the use of language, the experiences of the many in social relations where spontaneous feelings attach themselves to the very bonds from which people must liberate themselves. This 'must' is conceived as a necessity which determines whether humanity is to survive. The ability to bring about change grows out of people's own activity. This leads us to conclude that socialist politics hitherto has not found it necessary to include the emancipation of women, but that conversely a radical politics of women's liberation can only be formulated and carried out as a universal project for liberating humankind.

Notes

1. Lelio Basso, *Rosa Luxemburgs Dialektik der Revolution*. Frankfurt am Main 1969, p. 8.

2. After long debate the SPD recently decided that 40 per cent of the places on all SPD committees should be filled by women. – *translator's note*.

3. In a Women's Seminar at the University of Hamburg in 1987/8.

4. See for example Bettina Heinz, Claudia Honegger, *Listen der Ohnmacht*, Frankfurt am Main/New York n.d.

5. In *Leviathan* (4/1976) Eva Senghaas-Knobloch published an article on Rosa Luxemburg, in which she examined Rosa Luxemburg's idea that capital requires the constant exploitation and destruction of non-capitalist societies for its own reproduction and attempted to extend it to housework. This idea was later taken up and developed by Claudia von Werlhof and Veronika Bernholdt-Thommsen. Housework and subsistence work on a worldwide scale was defined as the non-capitalized part of the economy which capitalism requires for its survival and expansion.

6. Giselher Schmidt, *Rosa Luxemburg. Sozialistin zwischen Ost und West. Persönlichkeit und Geschichte*, Göttingen 1988, pp. 132–3.

7. Raya Dunayevskaya was born in Russia in 1910 and died in 1987 in the USA. She is regarded as the founder of a Marxist humanism. Her essential contribution was to incorporate existing freedom movements into Marxist theory so as to provide them with theoretical guidelines. In this context the important revolutionary forces were blacks, young people and women.

8. Robert A. Gorman's article on Rosa Luxemburg in the new *Dictionary of Socialism* is of exemplary importance here. He provides a detailed biography which reports on her physical disabilities as thoroughly as on her 'outstanding intelligence', courage and influence. After reading him we learnt that she had married a Mr Luebeck 'out of political opportunism'. On theoretical issues she is described as feeble and second-rate because Lenin rejected her (p. 202). Her agitation against the First World War is highlighted, as are her qualities as a strategist and a fighter. Despite this there is a brief account of her book on accumulation. Contradicting the assertion that she was no theorist, the book's emphasis on the self-destructive forces within capitalism is said to confirm and to shed further light on Marx's economic theories. Moreover, she is said to be deeply indebted to Engels and Kautsky in her orthodox condemnation of reformism and nationalism. Furthermore, an outline is given of her stress on the spontaneity of proletarian revolutionary mass consciousness. It is asserted that in her view a revolutionary party is incapable of either producing or preventing a revolution on the grounds that it could not control the human spirit. The bureaucratic Leninist party would fall on deaf ears. This is followed by a reference to her ideas about the mass strike as a useful form of revolutionary action. Finally, she is cited as the star witness on

the subject of the failure of Bolshevism. In this context it is claimed that she remained orthodox right to the end, while simultaneously repudiating the only organization which made a reality of orthodoxy – the Leninist party. She was, it seemed, a living contradiction. It is further alleged that she was a firm believer both in historical determinism and in the spontaneity of the masses. In an implicitly Hegelian move she is said to have recognized the absence of subjectivity in Bolshevism. To that extent she anticipated the more subtle discoveries of Lukács, Korsch and Gramsci. In the history of the workers' movement she was described by Lenin initially as an 'eagle' and was said to be of use 'in the education of many generations of communists the world over' (Lenin's *Werke*, vol. 33, p. 195). For Karl Radek she was 'the greatest and most profound theoretician of world communism' (Karl Radek, *Rosa Luxemburg, Karl Liebknecht, Leo Jogiches,* Hamburg 1921, p. 25). And Franz Mehring praised her some fifteen years earlier as 'the most brilliant mind among the heirs of Marx and Engels' (Franz Mehring, *Historisch-materialistishe Literatur,* in *Neue Zeit* XXV (1906–7), no. 41, p. 507). In *History and Class Consciousness* Georg Lukács described her as the only disciple of Marx to have really continued his work (Berlin 1923, p. 56). But almost before a year had passed since Lenin's death her name was veiled in silence (as Lelio Basso points out, see note 1). Social democracy shifted to the right and only reprinted those few writings which were critical of the Russian Revolution. Under Stalin the enlarged executive of the Communist International condemned a series of her theses. A reprint of her works now became out of the question. Her name became a term of abuse. Ruth Fischer, for example, referred to her as the 'syphilis of the party'. Not until forty years after her death did communists (in Poland) initiate a reprint of her works. The GDR edition was launched in 1972. It was with this interpretative baggage that we began our reading.

9. One well-known example is the following: 'But not only has the bourgeoisie forged the weapons that bring death to itself; it has also called into existence the men who are to wield those weapons – the modern working class – the proletarians.' (Karl Marx, *The Revolutions of 1848,* The Pelican Marx Library, Harmondsworth 1973, p. 73) [The German verb *zengen* (here, to call into existence) has the basic meaning 'to beget', 'to father'. It is, in other words, an exclusively masculine verb with strong sexual connotations.]

10. See Heinz Niggermann, *Emanzipation zwischen Sozialismus und Feminismus. Die sozialdemokratische Bewegung im Kaiserreich,* Wuppertal 1981, p. 234.

11. 'Women's and children's labour' (one page) in *Wirtschaftliche und Sozialpolitishe Rundschau,* 1898, vol. 1/1, pp. 291ff; 'The International Conference of Socialist Women on 17 and 19 August 1907 in Stuttgart' (one page), vol. 2, pp. 233ff; 'Votes for Women and Class Struggle', 1912 (seven pages), vol. 3, pp. 159ff; 'The Proletarian Woman' of 1914 (three pages), vol. 3, pp. 410ff.

12. This account of our work is based on a seminar paper given by Anja Weberling.

13. See also the recent biography by Elzbieta Ettinger, *Rosa Luxemburg. A Life,* London 1988, which examines her life in its relationship to family, home and sexuality whilst stressing its exceptional nature in its freedom from the usual woman's ties.

14. Irene Dölling, 'Zum Luxemburgfilm der Margarethe von Trotta', in *Weimarer Beiträge* 4, 1987, p. 633.

15. Christel Neusüss, *Die Kopfgeburten der Arbeiterbewegung oder die Genossin Luxemburg bringt alles durcheinander,* Hamburg 1985.

16. See my contribution to the centenary of Karl Marx's death, 'Verelendungsdiskurs

oder Logik der Krisen und Brüche. Marx neu gelesen vom Standpunkt heutiger Arbeitsforschung', in *Aktualisierung Marx*. Argument-Sonderband 100, West Berlin 1983.

17. Karl Marx, *The Revolutions of 1848*, *The Pelican Marx Library*, Harmondsworth 1973, pp. 70–1.

18. *Briefe*, vol. 1, p. 9.

19. Gabriella Bonacchi, 'Autoritarisme et anti-autoritarisme dans la pensée de Rosa Luxemburg', in Weill and Badia, eds, *Rosa Luxemburg aujourd'hui*, 1986, pp. 101–7.

20. Karl Marx, *Early Writings*, Harmondsworth 1977, pp. 256–7.

21. See the article by Regina Gruszka and Anja Weberling, 'Was sich von Rosa Luxemburg zur Frage der Volkszählung lernen lässt', *Das Argument* 162, 1987.

TWELVE

The End of Socialism in Europe: A New Challenge for Socialist Feminism?

Women's Issues as Paradoxes

Rethinking the breakdown of the socialist countries and especially the unification of the two Germanies as a socialist feminist from the West, I am first of all confronted with the experience that a number of the left's convictions have become problematic. Concepts such as market, plan and property have to be rethought by all branches of the left. Are there also new uncertainties for socialist feminists? Thinking about women's issues in these times of rapid historical change, in which one entire world system is in collapse and the other winning a surprising victory, the first thing I noticed is a series of paradoxes.

The political paradox

The former socialist model did not eliminate women's oppression; in fact, the situation of women was not even relevant to the dominant theory, which saw feminism as a bourgeois deviation. Nevertheless, it is above all women in movements in the former socialist countries who appear to be ready to think about an improved model of socialism. The Independent Women's Union founded in December 1989 in East Germany was one of the groups which fought for a different socialism, rather than for incorporation by capitalism.

A paradox in theory

Socialist feminists all over the world have long sought to work out the correlation between capitalism and patriarchy (see, for example, Hartmann, 1981). The question was not whether it was only capitalism which oppressed women or whether women's oppression would altogether disappear with the elimination of the capitalist mode of production. Rather, it was necessary to understand the specific useful-ness or even the fundamental role that women's oppression plays in the capitalist mode of production. I have tried to outline this correlation as follows: the production of use-values in accordance with the profit motive is only possible given the precondition that a whole series of use-values – as well as the production of life itself and its direct nurture and preservation – operate beyond the laws of profit. Women provide this necessary pillar in capitalist relations of production, owing to their ability to give life to children, and as the outcome of struggles lasting throughout a long period of history. The rest is the work of culture and ideology. This system we understand as 'capitalist patriarchy'. But this confronts us with a theoretical paradox: as much as this analysis might satisfy those of us who live under capitalism, there remains the amazing discovery that women's emancipation made hardly any progress in those countries which did not function according to the profit motive. Indeed, in the various conferences of East and West German women in Berlin and elsewhere after the opening of the Wall, the one point of dispute was whether Western women were more liber-ated than those in the East who needed to be taught feminism by their *apparently* more advanced Western sisters. Hope for a strengthening of the women's movement by uniting forces with Eastern 'feminism' was soon overthrown by a sort of Western despair that the unification would not only fail to strengthen the movement but indeed weaken it, because of a gap in feminist consciousness in the East.[1]

The cultural paradox

When we study the attitudes and behaviour of women in East and West, we find other paradoxical results. After forty years of socialism, many women from the East are much more self-confident than most women in the West. Their stride seems more extended, they habitually walk erect, and above all they lack what I will provisionally term a passive sexism. By this I mean that they do not act as if they were constantly balancing the effort to please men in a provocative or even exciting way while at the same time maintaining the necessary distance and inaccessibility. The recent victory in East Germany of Beate Uhse (who owns the biggest chain of sex shops in the West), the invasion of Western peepshows by Eastern men, and the new 'freedom' to obtain pornography all indicate that my impression of East German women is valid, and that East German men 'suffered' from the freedom of their women. This relative absence of pornography, while the oppression of women continued, also serves to contradict recent feminist ideas about pornography being the original source and the basis of women's oppression. This desexualization of the bodies of East German women coexists with a lack of awareness, even an indifference, concerning quite obvious instances of discrimination against the female sex. Among other things, there has been no feminist revolution in language. Without any hesitation, women in the East refer to themselves in the masculine form (for example, as businessmen or craftsmen). This is a particular problem in German, for many occupational labels, including doctor, economist or historian, assume maleness; to refer to a woman the ending '-in' must be added. It was one of the victories of feminism in the West to bring this into public consciousness, but this has not taken place in East Germany. To speak a male language prevents any clear perception of existing masculinist culture, which among other things determines access to specific jobs.

I summarize these different observations as a paradox, because they point to a great self-confidence on the part of women in the former GDR combined with female support for a traditional division of labour. The self-confidence stemming from their being needed in society went along obviously with an acceptance of the very structures which we are accustomed to think of as especially oppressive for women.

The paradox of reproduction

We come to a further paradox – or more precisely to two – in regard to the intense struggle over the abortion law that has accompanied the new union of the two Germanies. On the one hand, a fight over reproduction technologies is taking place in the West which poses the question of whether experiments with human embryos should be allowed. On the other hand there is renewed strength in the effort to tighten the abortion law based upon a 'right to life'. This struggle is given new impetus by the East German demand to keep abortion legal. We hear male members of parliament in the West, whose bodies are affected neither by the law nor by the experience, showing endless bigotry as they debate which principle should govern abortion availability, place of residence or site of operation, and whether the more liberal East German law should remain in force for another two years as a compromise.

But at the same time, this battle is fought with the female population in East Germany in the background, for they have obviously viewed having children as an essential dimension of their lives. Almost all East German women are employed, and almost all of them have children when relatively young (in their early twenties), regardless of their occupation and/or marital status. One lesson from East Germany might be that the more liberal the abortion law, the more children women have. The abortion law is therefore not so much a means of regulating birth rates, but serves rather as another means of disciplining women. (I should add that the abortion rate as well as the birth rate was high in East Germany, indicating a rather casual attitude toward questions of contraception and conception.)

The paradox of labour

But the most difficult lesson arises from the paradox of female employment. The right to work is one of the cultural givens in socialist countries, and determines the identities of women – this has been so for more than forty years in East Germany and for more than seventy in the Soviet Union. That female employment is a precondition for their emancipation has been a staple item of progressive politics in the workers' movement (though not in its entirety) since Marx and Engels, Lenin and Rosa Luxemburg. In all socialist countries the right to work was a given (now denounced in the Western media as an effort to hide unemployment), and there was a correspondingly high rate of female employment (over 90 per cent). And yet nowhere did women achieve decision-making positions in numbers that could sway masculinist cultures; socialisms too, besides being authoritarian administrative structures, were above all patriarchies. And where women must return to the home, as Gorbachev recommended in the Soviet Union and as was urged in East Germany in the face of growing unemployment, rumour has it that the women prefer to go back into the privacy of their homes, to escape the stress of overwork and to catch up on unfinished housework. This is probably not true for the majority; the right to work is still one of the privileges that gave East Germany the advantage over the West. (While the politicians have accepted and spoken about an unemployment rate of 50 per cent for the so-called 'new countries' for the summer of 1991 the latest polls suggest that while 25 per cent of the women from the West agree that being a housewife is the job they really want, there are only 3 per cent from the former GDR who think so.)

Some theoretical and practical questions remain open: Did the widespread employment of women in the former socialist countries hasten their emancipation, or are the structures indeed as hermetically patriarchal as the workings of political institutions suggest? And further: In rejecting the former model of socialism, are we dismissing a model of women's emancipation whose fruits we have yet to harvest? Has that model up to now been a burden to socialist feminists rather than wings on their heels only because of its specific form in East Germany? And above all there is the important question: Was it correct to link women's emancipation to labour?

The Concept of Labour and the Emancipation of Humankind

'Our women are the miracle!' This was the title of a propaganda brochure from East Germany in the late seventies. This was at a time when the disadvantages and problems, the bureaucracies and inertias, were already so obvious that to juxtapose women and miracle with regard to the reality of the East communicated the same feeling of derision that Mother's Day does. At the same time it offered that unwelcome glorification of heroines that always turns up when something is going wrong. Then too, this particular adoration can be read as the translation of what we simply, but not very precisely, call the double burden. The term 'double burden', however, is problematic, for it focuses on time, as if someone simply has to carry out two jobs instead of one, which together add up to more than the usual working day in that society – say eight hours. But in reality it means that women are located in two areas with contradictory logics, one of which does not count because it does not bring any money. Is the main problem of women's oppression that they have to work both in the factory and at home, so that their working days are too long?

Although I did not agree with the forms of socialism that have existed to date, I think it is strange to posit the same answer to the question of women's oppression in the two quite different systems. Or, to put it in other words: Has the situation of women nothing to do with the relations of production? Here I presume that the two societies had different relations of production. This is the only explanation for the energy with which West Germany has eradicated root and branch any inkling of forms of production other than the capitalist mode, and this at every level, including its literature.[2]

Critique of the Economy of Time

Pondering further on this problem of work or, more exactly, on the notion that the project of women's liberation is tied to 'work' brings me to the idea that difficulties already arise with the very discovery of the sexual division of labour. Here I believe we can find the solution for our paradoxes as well.

Although this is very unfashionable today, I shall once again return to Marx. He offers a few hints about gender relations in his discussions of work and, above all, we find the sexual division of labour at the most strategic points in the sketches for his complete project. In the *German Ideology* Marx formulates the division of labour as a juncture of oppositions and contradictions. He distinguishes between those divisions of labour in the whole of society: town/country, male/female, head/hand, work and non-work; and those divisions of labour in relation to the total work of a society. In this context we find the following remarkable sentence on family production as opposed to commodity production:

For the study of common, or directly associated labour, we do not have to go back to its natural form, which we find on the threshold of the history of all civilized races. A closer example is the rural patriarchal industry of a peasant's family, that produces grain, cattle, yarn, linen, and clothing etc. These different things confront the family as different products of their family-work, but they do not confront each other as commodities ... the different kinds of labour are in their natural form direct social functions, because they are functions of the family, which possesses its own natural division of labour as well as does a society based on commodity production. ... But the spending of individual labour power, measured by the duration of time, seems to be the social determination of the different works itself, because the individual labour forces only function as organs of the common labour force – the family.

Marx-Engels Werke (MEW), vol. 3, pp. 92ff.

It is astonishing that Marx did not further examine this finding that the various products were not measured and estimated as more or less valuable by the time spent on them, even though it certainly had consequences not only for the sexual division of labour but for our whole model of civilization as well. After all, the calculation of time spent also turns value into a curse from which the products have to be protected. In the end the only things that can stand the social test in capitalism are those which devour as little time as possible – which is the model both of progress and of pauperization. At the same time we get a hint of that yearning which validates the family and guarantees its continued existence, for it is the one place where production is not calculated only in terms of costs and labour. (I am leaving aside the effects that this lack of calculation has for the woman in the household.)

Over all, Marx portrays the division of labour with the following strategic dimensions: the domination of non-workers over workers; the development of labour as a whole at the expense of the stagnation of the individual worker; the development of a socialization of labour without any consciousness or appropriate political actions on the part of the labour-force. The peculiar thing that happened, as it were behind the scenes of this categorization, is that the sexual division of labour only appeared at the outset as a division of labour. Later on the role of women has vanished, at least as labour. They are named at the same time that they become nameless. From that point on, the terms 'division of labour' and 'total social labour' refer only to the partial labour of industrial and agricultural production for the market. There is no analysis of the problem which arises from the subordination of all activities that do not fit the waged-labour model, and therefore the logic of a cost-benefit analysis. This is a problem crucial both for the development of humankind and its needs and for the judgements humans make concerning social meaning and value, thereby determining both culture and identities.

However, the consistently blank spaces, occurring where the activities of women should have been analysed, appear only after Marx has already made elementary statements concerning gender relations and labour. To begin with, a sentence occurs in the *German Ideology* in a discussion of the relationship between property and the division of labour: 'This latent slavery in the family, though still very crude, is the first property, but even at this early stage it corresponds perfectly to the definition of modern economists, who call it the power to dispose of the labour-power of others' (*MEW*, vol. 3, p. 44). Engels viewed gender relations as 'the cells of civilized society' and 'the first class oppression of the female sex by the male' (*MEW*, vol. 21, p. 68). Domination therefore is inscribed in the division of labour between the sexes.

In his extensive analyses of labour in capitalism, the sexual division of labour no longer appears. Here Marx more or less assumes that women, usually referred to together with children, should not be included in the capitalist labour process in its current state (although he is ambiguous at this point). He describes their appearance in the factory as a particular misery, and also takes it for granted that the male worker should work and be paid both for his own and for his family's reproduction. In this connection he seems to see the sexual division of labour chiefly as natural, a division occurring on a 'mere physiological basis', which through exchange leads to areas based on mutual dependence (*MEW*, vol. 23, p. 372). But he does not go so far as to analyse the constellation of these areas, which is central for the capitalist model of civilization.

After all, it is upon this basis that a social formation has developed, in which more or less only those things are produced that bring profit; so that all work which cannot follow this logic, which can neither be rationalized, nor automated, nor accelerated – like cherishing and nurturing both humankind and nature – are neglected or left to women's unpaid care. Today we can proceed on the assumption that the crises concerning both the unrestrained and uncontrollable development of the productive forces and the ruinous exhaustion of nature are related to the logic and domain of profit, which rests upon women's oppression. Current discussions regarding an extended concept of labour, which would include reproductive and learning activities, and provide a minimal income to guarantee the survival of those who are not 'normally' incorporated in the employment process, show the convulsions occurring in an area where the sexual division of labour was taken for granted.

Here I want to take a further step by looking back from today's standpoint to the development of humankind in relation to those activities and needs which could pass the test of the market and upon which it therefore seemed worthwhile to spend time. All those products and activities which demanded an extensive amount of time, without resulting in a sufficiently grand product, fell by the wayside. Most agricultural activities as well as the conservation of nature, and even the rearing of children, were incompatible with the logic of continuous time reduction. (The efforts to industrialize agriculture have produced those horrible products which Brecht predicted: 'You will no longer recognize the fruits by their taste'.) Although the products attained are indispensable for the survival of humankind in the short term, this development has accelerated the division of humanity into one group which can pass the test of the market and another group of partial people who live and work on a lower level than is usual in the industrial world. Here we find the countries of the Third World, with their continuous immiseration.

In the countries of the First World developments are more complex. On the one hand, women are kept economically dependent; at least most of them cannot survive on their own even when employed in a low-paid female job. They are supported economically by a husband, the same breadwinner Marx and Engels discussed. Were it not for them, the majority of those time-consuming activities would simply remain undone. Here humankind has not developed. Thus, as the productive forces develop industrially, creating ever-new human needs in the Western capitalist countries, a monstrous brutalization of humankind appears. Crimes, drugs and alcohol are merely the visible signs of a model of civilization in which human development is subordinated to utter rationalization, and to the products and needs established under its rule. The progress of the material productive forces is far from setting people free to take into their own hands their development as human beings. On the contrary, such human development remains a by-product of general industrial development and of the work of women. In this context it is logical that Gorbachev hopes to cure the demoralization of the youth by sending women back into their families. We also get a hint of this problematic when we recognize our feelings of longing when we come into contact with simpler civilizations and can enjoy their unselfconscious hospitality and the many delights coming from labour-intensive domestic production. In this sense the statement that the degree of human liberation can be measured from the degree of women's liberation is completely realistic today. It affects people's interactions with one another, as well as their needs and their relationship to sensuality, to surrounding nature, to the work of hands and heads, and to themselves as individuals.

Rethinking again the puzzle concerning the passion with which men in government regulate the production of the species by law, we can decipher it as an effort to use the law to enforce those activities which cannot be regulated by profit and which therefore appear worthless. If women started to think about their desire for children from the perspective of their standard of living or of the most economic way to get by – that is, according to the predominating sense of time – they would repudiate such activities as a waste of time and energy. Thus there are legal safeguards to prevent women from yielding to the temptation of the predominant social logic of time. With moral concepts like 'love' and 'right of life', they are forced into a logic of life-consuming time which contradicts the logic of profit and of speed which they experience as members of capitalist societies. We shall probably find that wherever the predominant cost-benefit analysis is not sufficient for survival, the law creates some compensation, which is imposed on women through appeals to morality, such as caring for the elderly or disabled. At the same time it is less of a puzzle why politics, which is after all the codification of human relations and the business of regulating society, had to remain a male domain through all the decades of the women's movement and the fight for equality. Women could make themselves rulers in a social structure that makes them subordinate beings on the basis of sex only at the cost of their very identities.

The answer to the question posed above, concerning whether it was appropriate to link the liberation of both women and humanity to work, has to be 'no' as long as work is conceived of only as waged labour, which has been and still is the tradition of the workers' movement. Here it is necessary to base our analysis on a concept of *self-determined social activity* instead of work. Or we could on the contrary expand the usual concept of work to include those activities necessary for the development of humankind, and adhere to it. It is a pragmatic question.

Economy of Time in the Former GDR

With these considerations in mind let us return to developments in the former socialist countries. To begin with, there was little readiness to take up the task of overcoming the divisions of labour and their effects throughout society. Following Lenin, some effort was made to reduce the cultural gap between city and countryside, but the question of gender relations fell into oblivion. Or more correctly, there was a general assumption that including women in the social labour process was sufficient to overcome their oppression. Our Western media never grow tired of pointing out to us that things have been the same in East and West, as in both societies women bore responsibility for household and childcare and were therefore totally overworked, carrying the entire burden of labour-force participation. However, their mocking contempt of the socialist economy and its management points to inroads into the logic of profit-making that at least deserve mention.

East Germany was obviously more advanced in those very areas now blamed for being non-productive and described as industrial scrap-yards. The fringe benefits offered by Eastern companies included some which contributed to women's liberation. They involved a partial suspension of the profit motive as the general basis of production. This made the companies appear particularly unproductive from the standpoint of the logic of profit. Childcare centres, meals, portions of health insurance were paid for by the companies, as were holiday centres. In regions of exceptional beauty, by the seashore, where we would expect grand hotels for the moneyed élites, we still find a variety of holiday camps run by different companies (these camps by the way offer a somewhat vulgar obstacle to proper capitalization).

It is true that the more 'society' appropriates the work of women free of charge, the richer it gets, so long as only healthy male workers are considered to be temporarily used while they exert their labour power to the utmost solely for the advantage of the company. As one might expect, the numbers of women and youth among the East German unemployed were already remarkably higher than those for adult men just four months after the introduction of West German currency.

Although our conservative press does not report on the brutality of the West, but only on its freedom, wealth, and so forth, we can decipher out of the very details it does give just how great the dehumanization exported by West Germany really is. I shall give one small example; a few months ago there was a short report on the unparalleled lack of productivity at an East German chemical company. As a result, 700 employees, all of whom were well over sixty-five years old, were to be dismissed. Women as old as eighty-four regularly came to the factory and were paid, because they were lonely at home. The company will now switch its policy and dismiss all persons over fifty-seven. It will also get rid of eighty Vietnamese workers and send them back to Vietnam. The company had also had a health centre staffed by thirty doctors that cared for the health of adults and children in the entire region. These institutions are to be separated from the company and only after all these improvements have been made will a Western chemical factory be so kind as to appropriate this factory.

Let us assume that women's oppression is grounded in the division of society into an area that is 'productive' and one that is 'non-productive' and therefore superfluous in terms of the logic of profit. Their interrelation in the realm of political administration, which necessarily remains a male domain, decrees that women are responsible for the unproductive segment and ensures their non-development culturally and bureaucratically. In this respect we see in the former socialist countries a deliberate effort to establish a cost-benefit analysis that takes a segment of those unproductive tasks over into the productive account balance. On this basis female waged employment became ordinary and was culturally and politically realized.

The question remains of why this shift and rearrangement did not lead to a greater liberation and inclusion of women in the regulative structures of society. At present it appears as a problem of patriarchal bureaucracy. A burden was lifted for women so that they could enter the 'productive' area; but the division between these two areas, and the fact that social progress only related to one of them, was not recognized as the problem. Those at the top decided which products, which free spaces, which activities were to be exempted from the general cost-benefit analysis. Freedom planned from above cannot be perceived as freedom. Agreement to a certain way of life can only be productive and creative if those concerned take the satisfaction and development of their needs into their own hands. But to carry out the planned economy and the subsidizing of particular areas in the East, the eternal patriarchy was once again required, emerging from past circumstances both morally and mentally (as Marx put it in his *Critique of the Gotha Programme*). And this patriarchy believed it knew how best to foster human development and enacted laws, duties and regulations to accomplish it.

What could the 'miracle women' do but agree? A women's movement aiming at liberation could hardly grow under these circumstances. But, on the other hand, it becomes clearer why women from the former East German state are less inclined to turn their backs on a socialist project. The so-called return to a market economy definitely hits them the hardest.

The development of one area was not simply accomplished at the cost of the other, men did not develop solely at the cost of women, but by the centuries-old neglect of human development, except as a by-product of profit and utilitarianism. Time for human development would have required the direct subjective participation of all concerned in order to achieve liberation, rather than planning, commands and administration. Such a step would have also shown that time is not only a dimension that is measured as productive in the sense of growth and competition in the world market, or unproductive in the sense of giving more scope to humanity and generally improving the standard of living, but that time is also a dimension that permits the development of human lives, and that it is necessary if people are to participate in the political regulation of the community as a civil society. Thus the women's question is a question of democracy and, concomitantly, there will be no democracy and no socialism without a solution to the women's question.

As far as the new reunified Germany is concerned there is a social commitment to the currently existing freedom and democracy of the West. Any violation will be prosecuted. As long as this democracy and this freedom are understood in the old patriarchal way, women will remain outlaws and will be forced to fight for a new order.

Notes

1. This supports the conclusions of a recent comparative study on gender inequality in socialist and capitalist countries, which found that a strong women's movement is necessary for any form of women's emancipation. Hence the absence of any women's movement; and the concomitant lack of any feminist consciousness explains the almost total absence of women in decision-making positions in socialist countries (see Vianello and Siemienska, 1990).

2. See the fight against socialist literature in the Western media, especially against Christa Wolf.

References

Hartmann, Heidi 'The Unhappy Marriage of Marxism and Feminism: Towards a More Progressive Union', in Sargent (1981).

Marx, Karl and Engels, Frederick *Marx-Engels Werke.*

Sargent, Lydia, ed., *Women and Revolution: The Unhappy Marriage of Marxism and Feminism*, Pluto, London 1981.

Vianello, Mino and Siemienska, Renata *et al.*, eds, *Gender Inequality: A Comparative Study of Discrimination and Participation*, Sage, London 1990.